MW00790748

ARE YOU READY?

THIN LIZZY: ALBUM BY ALBUM

First published in Great Britain in 2015 by Soundcheck Books LLP,
88 Northchurch Road, London, N1 3NY.

Copyright © Alan Byrne 2015
ISBN: 978-0-9929480-8-5

All rights reserved. No part of this book may be reproduced or transmitted in any
form or by any means, electronic or mechanical, including photocopying, recording,
or any information storage and retrieval system without permission in writing from
the publisher.

This book is sold subject to the condition that it shall not, by way of trade or
otherwise, be lent, resold, hired out or otherwise circulated without the publisher's
prior consent in any form of binding or cover other than that in which it is published
and without a similar condition being imposed on the subsequent purchaser.

Every effort has been made to contact copyright holders of photographic and other
resource material used in this book. Some were unreachable. If they contact the
publishers we will endeavour to credit them in reprints and future editions.

This title has not been prepared, approved or licenced by the management,
or past or present members of Thin Lizzy.

A CIP record for this book is available from the British Library

Cover images courtesy of: Mark Hurley, Jan Koch,
Dave Manwering, Magnus Rouden
Book design: Benn Linfield (www.bennlinfield.com)
Printed by: Bell and Bain Ltd, Glasgow

ARE YOU READY?

THIN LIZZY: ALBUM BY ALBUM

ALAN BYRNE

soundcheck books
the stories behind the sounds

ARE YOU READY?
THIN LIZZY: ALBUM BY ALBUM

ALAN BYRNE

CONTENTS

CONTENTS

ACKNOWLEDGEMENTS

Assembling *Are You Ready?* was a welcome and unexpected chance for me to revisit the adventures of Thin Lizzy. In late summer 2014, this adventure began and with it the challenge to locate and interview those that were willing to re-trace their steps in the Thin Lizzy story.

Without the industry of the people that were directly connected to the Thin Lizzy adventures this book would have been impossible to put together. The Thin Lizzy personality, the spirit in which band members presented the music continues to bring warm memories to the surface. I'm also very grateful to Phil and Sue Godsell for considering and accepting that *Are You Ready?* was an appropriate addition to the ever growing canon of Soundcheck Books. I feel very privileged to be able to share board with the writers that have already had Soundcheck Books house their efforts.

Are You Ready? was based on a very simple concept: to document the creative life of Thin Lizzy in the studio. Aside of providing links to the inspirations behind many of the songs, recollections are also provided by the folks who manned the recording consoles, capturing the magic of the band as they slogged through recording 12 studio albums and two live albums in their career.

It's been a savage journey to the heart of the matter and this book concludes a trilogy of my efforts which I hope you enjoy and embrace. So for fuck's sake, make sure you're ready! Especially you Frank Healy.

Without whom, it just wouldn't be ... Roll Call:

John Alcock, Peter Antony, Laurence Archer, Louis Austin, Dez Bailey, Mick Bailey, , Jimmy Bain, Eric Bell, Tim Booth, Ted Carroll, Neil Carter, Philip Chevron (RIP), Ian Cooper, Roger Cooper, Chalkie Davies, Robbie Dennis, Lawrie Dipple, Brian Downey, Andy Duncan, Bob Elsdale, Patrick Fenning, Fish, Jim Fitzpatrick, Dave

Flett, Robin George, Junior Giscombe, Scott Gorham, Nigel Grainge, Kirby Gregory, Dave Grinsted, Paul Hardcastle, John Helliwell, Tim Hinkley, Pete Holidai, Bill Hughes, Gus Isidore, David Jensen, David Knopfler, Sören Lindberg, Chris Ludwinski, Dave Manwering, David Mallet, Jeff Marvel, Rodney Matthews, Jeanette Melbourne, Tina McLoughlin, Conor McAnally, Charlie Morgan, Ken Morris, Maurice Mulligan, Jeremy Nagle, Sean O'Connor, Michael O'Flanagan, Terry O'Neill, Graham Parker, Tony Platt, Andrew Prewett, Suzi Quatro, Tex Read, Will Reid Dick, Leo Rickard, Jerome Rimson, Brian Robertson, Frank Rodgers, Jean Roussel, Peter Rynston, Jalle Savquist, Chris Sheldon, John Slater, Bill Smith, Mark Stanway, Ed Stone, Linda Sutton, Nick Tauber, Fiachra Trench, Chris Tsangarides, Brian Tuite, Derek Varnals, Simon Vinestock, Darren Wharton, Daire Winston, Snowy White, Kit Woolven.

For the continued friendship and support throughout this mania: Phil Osborne and Nick Sharp. One wonders what the wonders of the Lizzy world would do without these two kind folks. Also, very special mention to those that lent photos for this project: Wolfgang Gúrster, Jan Koch, Kieron Loy, Dave Manwering, Will Reid Dick, Magnus Rouden, Jalle Savquist.

Salute to: Adriano Di Ruscio, Peter Neilsen, *Classic Rock* magazine, Howard Massey and Dick Weindling (Author of Decca Studios and Klooks Kleek), Roddie Cleere, Terry Brown and Irish Jack for their assistance. Also thanks go to the music magazines for use of quotations. To Philomena Lynott who helped me enormously at the start of this trek into Lizzy land. Huge thanks to Will Reid Dick for his foreword.

Also, special thanks and appreciation to: Dr Tommy Keane, Bone Digger Willie Arnold, Christine "handbags" Looney, The Famous Séamus Burke, Gunita Graube & Gunter Grasmanis - miss ye neighbours, All the Jennings at Rathdene and the impossible to ignore Amber Jennings. The wonder of Noinín Toibín. To Phil and Gill, Nick and Jane, Hell's Bell's Fieldy, Ca Hughes for animated vibes, the much missed LP- I think of you often, I among many. Dave Manwering, Kieron Loy, Mark Killen (artist at large) Sharon, Vicky, Cian, Claire and that crowd of layabouts in CIL. Andrew "photos"

Acknowledgements

Oliver and particularly to Sinéad "Tantrums" Toibín for obscure background noises. Also Per "The Baker" Olsson.

A congratulations to my aging friends Shane Murphy and Michael Keating and their new broods! You too, Pernod!!

City Lodgings and decompression chamber facilities: Sarah Byrne and Christian Carley. To Kevin (my favourite Uncle) and Christine Byrne. Ray and Pauline Cahill – much love as always.

Tip of the hat as always to Bill Hicks, George Carlin, Mitch Hedberg and Hunter S Thompson for the laughter, words and those cleansing moral spears.

This book is especially for Biff and Gino.X.

FOREWORD
BY WILL REID DICK

Thursday 8th January 1976

What a day that was; one that I shall never forget. How could I? It was the day that I first met Thin Lizzy. An event that, without doubt, changed the course of my life. I look back on it now with a sense of pride but I remember the feelings of fear and trepidation as I stood in the studio waiting for the band to arrive. I was entering an unknown world. I was about to record an entire album for the first time in my career and with an established band who had something to prove to the world.

It was make or break time for them. Their previous two albums had received acclaim but had not propelled them to the heights that their record company had expected. Personally, I really liked their previous effort *Fighting*; good songs and very well put together. But it didn't have that all important single to introduce them to a wider audience.

The reality of the situation was that I'm not sure who was more nervous at that point, them or me. As a firm believer that fate and luck play as big a part in one's direction in life, as opposed to talent alone, I had somehow found myself about to record what was to become Thin Lizzy's *Jailbreak* album.

Having decided five years or so beforehand that audio engineering was where I wanted to go in life, I was lucky enough to be offered the position of tape op at Ramport Studios in October 1973. At the time I couldn't believe my luck. Talk about all your Christmases coming at once; I'd not only managed to get myself the position I'd been looking for but it was in a studio owned by The Who, one of my favourite bands.

Looking back on it, Ramport was a gem of a studio. Not to everybody's taste, but if it worked for an artist they generally came back for more. Such a studio couldn't exist now; it was too bizarre! With The Who's backing, we had the cream of equipment and lots of it and there was a fine crew of backroom staff (mostly lunatics) to go with it.

Thin Lizzy seemed to like it. So there we were, John Alcock producing, myself engineering and Neil Hornby as my assistant about to set off and record their new album.

It's impossible to overestimate John's contribution to the making of *Jailbreak* and *Johnny The Fox*. He had the unenviable task of pulling together any loose ends in the band and getting the best out of the material. His association with The Who probably helped in many ways as the internal politics of The Who were somewhat similar to Lizzy's; plenty of talent but sometimes needing guidance. The recordings went well in general and John's air of confidence that everything was going in the right direction was very reassuring. Phil and John worked well together and it felt like a team effort with everyone pulling in the same direction most of the time. Phil used to say "That would be all right if I were a reasonable man but I'm not, so let's do it again". A saying that cropped up many times during the recording. He knew where he was going.

Brian Downey took a back seat after the initial tracks went down leaving Robbo and Scott to finish their guitar overdubs and Phil to do the vocals. We had our rough moments: Robbo refusing to listen to his guitar solos after falling out with Phil over some issue, and various other niggles but we got through it. A tight deadline at the end of mixing resulted in a session that went on for over 36 hours, but we got there. I've always been critical of my work, but those Lizzy albums from 1976 seem to have stood the test of time and have their place in rock history, so I can be thankful. I was lucky enough to be involved with the band for a few years after that and did a number of live and studio recordings with them around the world.

I'm in no doubt that Thin Lizzy would have been at the top of the Premiership of bands for many years here and around the world had it not been for their misfortunes with illness and accidents. Their

1976 line up had everything required for it: great songs, intriguing personalities, a magnificent live show and that extra undefinable ingredient necessary for the very top.

Great credit must go to Alan Byrne for his continuing work in prolonging the memory of Thin Lizzy with his books. His knowledge and love of the band is admirable and I applaud him for that and for giving me the opportunity to relive some fond memories.

Phil once sent me a postcard from Florida where he was on holiday with a girl we both knew. It read "Having a ball! Phil" So did I in 1976. Thanks guys!

Will

RIP The Butchers Arms, Thessaly Road, Battersea.

PREFACE

My earliest recollection of Thin Lizzy relates to one of our weekly road trips with my dad, visiting his parents. His dad, Tommy, came from farming people in the midlands of Ireland. They kept a donkey who had teeth that reflected a 200 a day cigarette habit. A wonderful ass with bad breath.

On one of our adventures, I was ensconced between both front seats, elbows wedged for leverage; speaking in a high-pitched voice. I was 7 years old. My dad mentioned that we had a major problem to resolve: that being to name my recently-born sister (the soon-to-be prospective stealer of all my thunder). Her godparents to be couldn't pronounce her possible name correctly; Naomi became Wyoming. We're talking summer of 1984 – Naomi might well have been the Britney of today back then. Not that I was aware! It just seemed, and still seems, a wrong name.

Black Rose (A Rock Legend) was a mainstay cassette in our Ford Capri and it blared all the time alongside AC/DC, The Dubliners and Otis Redding. As me and my Dad were both losing ground with each other, the Lizzy song "Sarah" started blaring from the tape player.

Dad's been claiming credit for suggesting the name ever since. Out went Wyoming, in came Sarah. My sister, Sarah, has largely been receiving misinformation about how she was named for 31 years and counting. So now, I'm glad to be able to clear it up finally, with slivers of truth, splinters of honesty and a very one-sided recollection: it was Thin Lizzy that did it, for good or ill. This remains my clearest memory of how Thin Lizzy took root, even though they had ceased to be a recording unit, thinking back. With Philo at the helm, they were a wonderful band. There is without doubt an enduring simpatico between Thin Lizzy and their fans.

Are You Ready? is the final part of a trilogy of research that has been ongoing since 1999. In January 2012, a press release indicated to the public that a trove of unreleased Lizzy/Lynott related recordings had been discovered. In some cases, the find was reported to be as many as 700 unreleased songs. To distinguish: this exaggerated number was largely reflective of Lizzy demos, outtakes, unreleased live material and an unknown quantity of Lynott solo material. Lynott died while constructing a number of songs for a planned solo album which was to be released by Polydor Records. His death in January 1986, whilst in the stages of plotting the course of this album, resulted in its shelving. The demos survive and the directional course he etched with the songs remain intact, untouched since his last additions and awaiting a final destination.

The announcement of such a large quantity of material was the result of a party coming forward that had largely protected the legacy of Thin Lizzy by storing the tapes which Phil Lynott had personally catalogued. Philo kept everything ever recorded, filed it privately and this legacy was under the protection of a friend since his death. Without such protection, the recent years which resulted in the release of deluxe editions of the Lizzy back catalogue simply wouldn't have happened.

In my time researching the Lizzy story, and also that of Lynott's solo adventures, I've been fortunate to have been able to review the dates and details of the band's and Lynott's times in the recording studio. I've also been able to document the recollections of the engineers involved who, in many cases, kept copies of their work.

In the light of the announcement that an archive of Thin Lizzy and Phil Lynott's solo material has been preserved, with this new book I endeavoured to document it and also preserve the recollections of the people that contributed to this wonderful and enduring legacy – particularly those at the control room desk.

Drinking Jamaican Rum …
Al
August 2015

1

ORIGINS

The exhilarating music on the turntable, from two masters of the guitar, opened possibilities in the mind of the young man – who was no slouch on a 6-string either – cosily ensconced on the floor of his tiny flat. On a Monday evening, his only day off, he was imbibing sounds from Jimi Hendrix and Cream which were opening his eyes and his imagination to new vistas. The young man in question was Eric Bell.

Born in East Belfast in 1947, Bell had been in numerous bands by the time of his 20th birthday, and within 12 months was lead guitarist with John Farrell And The Dreams, a Dublin-based showband. Showbands, that peculiarly Irish phenomenon, toured the little country from the 1950s until their gradual decline from the late 1970s onwards. They specialised in good time dance music, but there was little room for artistic interpretation, which frustrated the blues-influenced youngster.

Bell's band gigged the showband circuit playing all the Top 20 hits of the day such as "Simon Says" and "A Chapel On The Hill". By Bell's own admission, he was getting "well paid for it and well looked after but also working very hard for it. It was a very steady job for a musician." Working six nights a week limited his chances to see up and coming bands in the local clubs. On his day off, he would understandably stay indoors to steal some quiet time while "getting well-wrecked and listening to these albums which had nothing to do with showband type music," remembers Bell.

As Bell's frustration with the rigid nature of the showband scene escalated, he found it impossible to ignore the musical inclinations that continued to haunt him. He recalls: "I thought about it for six months, stayed with the showband and didn't say anything to anyone. One night, we were coming back from a gig and I was sitting in the van thinking, right, I gotta lay this out, I can't go on like this. Will I?

Won't I? I gotta make a decision. And I made the decision to split. So I went to the manager in our office and I told him. He said I was making a big mistake, saying, 'You have a job for life here Eric, why do you want to ruin it?'

"So he asked me what I was gonna do and I replied that I was going to form a group," says Bell. "'Who've ya got?' he asked, and the funny thing was I had to reply, 'No one'. 'Have you got a PA?' 'No'. 'Have you got any transport?' 'Well no'. No manager, no equipment. So I'm sat there thinking, 'Oh my God, I haven't got anything, not even my own amp'. So he says, 'I'll put ya on two weeks' notice, work the two weeks and make up your mind'. I said, 'I have made up my mind' and he says, 'OK, there's a guitar player I know from Belfast that we can get to replace you. I'm sorry to see you go – and you can take the amp with you as a going away present', which I thought was really nice of him.

"So, I left the band and the next morning you kind of realise, 'I'm not in the band anymore'. It's like, 'What do I do now Yogi, ya know?' This went on for about a week. You sort of hang about for a while, at least I did anyway. So I started going out to pubs and clubs that I had never gone to before."

It was a strange time for Bell, looking out for musicians to try to form a new group. He was sailing into uncharted waters, the kind of pubs and clubs that showband members never entered for their own safety. Having just left the showband he had short hair and still looked very straight. "Back then all the groups drank in pubs that the showbands wouldn't go in to. It was like two different armies," he recalls.

Bell made his way into the Bailey Pub, just off Grafton Street in Dublin's city centre, one late November night, and, though full of people, he struggled to identify any musicians. Weeks had gone by and his dwindling funds were fast becoming a source of worry. "What have I done?" was the mantra racing around Bell's brain.

"I thought I'd probably have to go back to Belfast and work in a shirt factory," reasons Bell "but then a keyboard player named Eric Wrixon (who sadly died in July 2015) walked in. He had done the same as me, as he too had left a showband called Terry And The Trixons. We knew each other but really only to see. He suggested we move on to a nearby club because some of the owners knew us and we'd be able to get in for free. We made our way to the Countdown Club, which was then run by Ollie Byrne – who we both knew. So, we got in and went to the bar and got a couple of plastic cups of paint stripper; they called it sherry. We took a half tab of acid each and sat on the floor watching the band playing."

The band gracing the stage that night was called Orphanage. Their drummer and lead singer were named Brian Downey and Philip Lynott respectively. After a backstage encounter, during a break in the set, Bell convinced the pair to wrap up their obligations in Orphanage and form a new band with him and Wrixon, which they promptly did.

An aside in the story behind how this new band emerged, was that it wasn't the frontman Phil Lynott that stood out that night at the Countdown Club for guitarist Eric Bell, it was drummer Brian Downey. Bell remembers: "He came across, for his age, as a very mature player, very natural. He got a beautiful sound off the kit, fabulous blues drummer, really had it off to a tee. I just sat there and I didn't even see Philip. He was up front with this Indian kaftan on, throwing all these exotic shapes. But I just saw Downey and I remember thinking, 'Man I really gotta get that guy for my band'. But I didn't know if the guy might have been interested or not, that was neither here nor there."

Thin Lizzy were formed in December 1969, just as the new decade was beckoning. It was, inevitably, a distillation of the individual experiences of the members who had played in: Skid Row, Sugar Shack, Shades Of Blue, Van Morrison's Them and, latterly, John Farrell And The Dreams, Orphanage and more. It took a little time before the outfit was christened Thin Lizzy, though it was hardly any time at all before they were taking Dublin, and soon, wider Ireland by storm.

The band name derived its inspiration from a mechanical maid called Tin Lizzie who featured in the *Dandy* comic in the 1950s. The character of Tin Lizzie was later featured in the *Beano* comic, which is where guitarist Eric Bell found the name. The John Mayall *Bluesbreakers* album sleeve features Eric Clapton reading a copy of the popular comic. That album itself is now commonly referred to as *The Beano Album.*

Desperate to come up with a name for the band, Bell began leafing through copies of comics and found Tin Lizzie. With a little patience and editing he was responsible for the amendments which gave the band their name: Thin Lizzy.

Brian Downey was born in the Harold's Cross area of Dublin in 1951. His friendship with Lynott dated back to their schooldays and was later cemented when he auditioned for the drummer's stool in The Black Eagles, whose lead vocalist was one Philip Lynott.

Downey recalls the audition for this group vividly: "We played maybe eight songs at the audition, 'You Really Got Me' by The Kinks, 'I Saw Her Standing There' by The Beatles and I got through them well. Then I asked how they thought I was doing and they started saying it was good and that there was a gig coming up on Saturday night. I was looking at them a bit shocked as this was the Monday or Tuesday before. So the audition turned into a rehearsal for the Saturday night gig."

Downey was a set of tom-toms short of a full drum kit (literally, not metaphorically!), so for the audition had borrowed a set from outgoing drummer Mick Higgins who was about to join the army. As Downey explains, "After about three weeks of playing with the band I was talking to my dad. Well, it was me pestering him about getting some tom-toms. So he went down to a shop called Cavendish's and put some money down on a small tom-tom. He took the bass drum down to Cavendish's and they moulded the tom-toms to the bass drum." Downey and Lynott flitted in and out of a series of bands once The Black Eagles reached its natural end but reconvened during the Orphanage period.

Phil Lynott was born 20 August 1949 in West Bromwich, England, but was raised in the Crumlin area of Dublin by his granny from around the age of five. The impact of Ireland on his young imagination was immeasurable, with references to it on every Thin Lizzy album ever released, even down to the artwork used. Born to an Irish mother and British Guyanan father, his unique background would play out across his published and unpublished writings over the next 15 years.

In an interview with Niall Stokes of *Hot Press* magazine, Lynott provided some background information on Orphanage:

> I thought of the name Orphanage partly because I could have ended up in one. For a woman in Ireland in the fifties, having a kid when she wasn't married and a black kid in particular... keeping it was hard. But there were other reasons. The pad where I first met Tim Booth, Orphan Annie, Tim Goulding and Ivan Pawle and that lot, that was called The Orphanage. Also it just seemed like a good moody name. (*Hot Press*, 16 Sept 1977 by Niall Stokes)

The last founding member of the original Thin Lizzy line up was Eric Wrixon. Born in 1947, he was the oldest member of the band. Like Bell, he hailed from Belfast but had slightly more experience than the rest of the group. Each band member brought with them valuable contacts from when they had played in bands prior to Lizzy. Shay Walsh managed Sugar Shack, a blues band that Downey had drummed with, and he knew Roy Esmonde, a local photographer in Dublin, who was soon to play a part in the early Thin Lizzy story.

Another important link was made when local poet Peter Fallon introduced Lynott to Jim Fitzpatrick, an artist then best known for his 1968 Che Guevara poster which adorned the walls of thousands of student and hippie flat shares and bedsits. Fitzpatrick's first official introduction to Lynott was in Neary's Pub just off Grafton Street, of which he says "I recall seeing him before [Neary's] as we were both getting photos done by Roy Esmonde at his studio. We only passed each other on the staircase and exchanged 'How are ya's' but there you go".

Lynott's introduction to Fitzpatrick was a pivotal moment as the pair would soon develop a wide range of graphic ideas suitable for promoting Thin Lizzy. It took time though, as Fitzpatrick would only come into the fray towards the tail-end of the band's stopover on Decca Records. Also during this early period while the band were rehearsing their set and attempting to co-ordinate the inclusion of original material, they featured on the radar of local businessman Brian Tuite. He owned and managed the Band Centre in Dublin, where a host of local groups sourced equipment for live shows.

"My early recollection that the band had been formed was when Eric Bell and Eric Wrixon came into the shop looking to hire some gear," says Tuite. "I had heard that they had also got Fran Quigley on board as their road manager, who had only recently come back from the UK after doing some work for a prominent Irish band called Granny's Intentions. The problem with the two Erics was that they didn't have much money and so they were looking for some kind of deal. In the end we did a deal with them for some equipment, and that was how my first involvement with the band started."

Once the issue of hiring low cost equipment was resolved, another point of concern was lead vocalist Lynott. He was still learning bass guitar, having been given rudimentary instruction by Skid Row frontman Brush Shiels [Skid Row was the band that Lynott had been ejected from prior to forming Orphanage]. Soon after Lizzy's inception, Lynott and Bell met regularly at the latter's flat, where Lynott brought some of his first ever recorded songs, put down on an old reel-to-reel tape.

"He said he wanted to do some of his own songs in the band and I wanted to hear them," Bell enthuses. "Also, he wanted to play the bass. I asked him if he could play. I was wondering, as was Brian, just how serious he was about learning to play the bass because when we first met he was just out front singing. He was really excellent as a frontman without playing bass. He used to wear like a white African robe, right down to his ankles.

"So, I was living with the drummer from the showband I had just left along with the guitar player who had replaced me in the showband as well. They were out that night playing, so Phil came up and I had brought a reel-to-reel recorder from this girl I knew. So Phil arrived with this raincoat on and said, 'How 'ya?' and I'm like, 'How 'ya?' He quickly announced, 'I brought the tape but I can't stay long 'cos I'm meeting this chick'. We sat down and played the tape and I thought the songs were fabulous. The songs I remember that were on it were 'Dublin', 'Chatting Today' and 'Saga Of The Ageing Orphan' but there were others that he had written as well. I told him I thought they were great and that I'd be able to fit my guitar style into those kind of songs. Due to playing with the showbands for so long my playing had become very melodic with an Irish lilt to it, and I couldn't drop that style of playing as it had become part of me."

The band grabbed rehearsal space wherever and whenever they could. The first rehearsals took place nearly every day for six weeks in the Countdown Club and, for this use, the band would play a gig for expenses only in lieu of a fee as a thank you. This model was rolled out to other venues. They also used the CMYS on North Frederick Street and the Teachers' Club in Parnell Square. Terry O'Neill, Lizzy's first manager, recalls, "Later I did a deal with Bill Fuller to rehearse in the Town And Country Club, a big underground ballroom in The Ambassador/Gate Theatre building on Parnell Square. In return, we did some Monday nights for a very small fee."

Fran Quigley, whose brother Pat had been the guitarist in Orphanage, was Lizzy's roadie around this period. Another brother, Liam, was also another key player in the early Lizzy story, capturing as he did their progression on camera.

The band was officially unleashed onto an unsuspecting world on 18 February 1970 under the guidance of manager Terry O'Neill, a fellow Dubliner from Phibsboro. Lizzy's first manager was meant to be the late Ollie Byrne who ran an office from the Countdown Club, but, "I started arranging everything including rehearsing in the Countdown Club, so every day they'd come in to talk to Ollie, and Ollie would say talk to Terry," remembers O'Neill. "This went on for weeks. I was also booking out about 20 other acts for Ollie. I was arranging shows, publicity, going to rehearsals and planning world domination for the band. We'd go out to gigs at night, have a few drinks and smoke a bit of dope together."

O'Neill was already friendly with Lynott by this time, as the former had been the first roadie for Skid Row. O'Neill and Lynott frequented The Copper Kettle for Tuesday night poetry readings. Lynott's increasing awareness of lyrics came to the fore at such sessions. By the beginning of 1970, just weeks after the band formed, Lynott asked O'Neill to leave the Ollie Byrne set up and provide the band with his undivided attention.

With about six weeks of rehearsals under their collective belts, a set was constructed to ensure Lynott's debut gig on bass wouldn't overwhelm him. Thin Lizzy's first gig was a low-key affair at Cloghran National School in Swords, Co. Dublin, for which they were paid £27.50. The fee may appear ludicrously small but, back then, a set of drumsticks only cost £1 and a £1 deal would also secure half a dozen joints, so it's easy to see how a band could at least afford life's necessities on such short commons. Little, if anything, survives in terms of media coverage of Lizzy's debut gig but, keen to make a real go of it, the band continued to rehearse before a spate of gigs were booked.

Bell takes up the story: "I'd meet Phil outside a pub on O'Connell Street about 12:30 p.m. on one of those freezing fucking Dublin winter mornings, right. And Phil had this guitar case which looked like a coffin, without a handle on the case. It looked like a monolith. Then Brian Downey would arrive and then Eric Wrixon. We even knew the paperboy on that corner, which is the corner where Abbey Mooney's pub used to be. So we'd all troop down to Abbey Street to get the bus to rehearsals. And Phil would be coming up the stairs [of the bus] with this monolith and people would be coming down the stairs. I swear to God, this is what would be going on.

"So, we'd be on the bus for about half an hour, outside of Dublin, and we ended up walking toward this fucking cricket pavilion which was all locked up, but somehow we got the keys. Now, I was stoned so I can't quite remember how we organised it. It was absolutely freezing. We all brought our own albums and initially I couldn't come to terms with, 'Wow, I can play whatever the fuck I want'. Phil would put on albums by a band called Spirit who I had never heard before, stuff like the Flying Burrito Brothers, Free. We obviously had to play covers when we were starting as well, so these were the bands that Phil wanted to cover some of."

Gigs around Dublin followed in St Anthony's Hall, the Countdown Club, Trinity College and Liberty Hall throughout March, before their national debut at The Astor in Belfast, Northern Ireland. The band were back in Belfast the following month playing The Carousel while being supported by Penny Feather. The Carousel was a new venue, opened the previous January and launched by Joe Dolan And The Drifters. Interestingly the support band Penny Feather, at one time known as the Greenbeats, featured bassist Peter Barden, who would later move into band management and Thin Lizzy's slipstream for a period of time.

The first and only commercial release issued during O'Neill's tenure as manager of the band came about in July when the band released "The Farmer". It was the only officially released Lizzy product to feature a contribution from keyboard player Eric Wrixon. Ted Carroll, who had worked with Lynott during his Skid Row days, confirms that, "It came about over a deal engineered by Terry O Neill with John D'Ardis at Trend Studios. They actually recorded one of his songs for the B-side, a song called 'I Need You'."

Trend Studios was started by John D'Ardis and John Kane in the garage of the D'Ardis family home in Shankill, Co. Dublin. During this period, O'Neill was friendly with Kane who also ran a pirate radio station called Radio Atlantis. O'Neill himself was a drummer, and his then band tested the studio for the pair. About a year later, in 1968, Trend Studios relocated to Lad Lane and O'Neill was the publicist involved.

O'Neill recalls: "We took ads in *Hitsville* and garnered some press for the studio. I got Skid Row in for free and got a four page spread in *Hitsville* in return. Some great photos. Gary Moore had just got a sitar which looked really cool, and we got some other musicians from Granny's Intentions in too, so it looked great and everyone was happy. I think they did 'Saturday Morning Man' and 'Felicity'. Brush [Shiels] may remember. So when I was managing Thin Lizzy I went to John D'Ardis and struck a deal for free in return for putting his song on the B-side.

"The first company I went to was EMI, for whom Tony Hanna was head of A&R in Ireland. We got an OK royalty and they agreed to pay for posters as we were supplying the tapes. It went out on Parlophone DIP 513 and they pressed 500. I got about 250 to give out. All the band got about five each and the rest went to *RTE* and papers and magazines. I was there for some of the recording. There was brass on the B-side. I wasn't there for that – in fact I can't remember if it's on the final mix. I remember when Phil put the talking bit on at the beginning thinking, 'That's it, we've got a hit'. In a way, we did too. Although it didn't sell we got plenty of radio play and press, and I started getting much more money and headlined some ballrooms, where the showband would open and Thin Lizzy would do an hour and the showband would finish the night. We were one of the first to break into those venues." A review in *City Week* dated 10 September was encouraging: "a really first class disc and goes down very well in the clubs."

Keyboard player Wrixon contributed to the single but left shortly afterwards. Posters that were created were clipped to remove his image and subsequent press releases make no mention of him. One of the reasons for his exit was down to his frustration with the slow progress, and Lynott himself:

Eric [Bell] and myself would say, "Have you heard this song by Deep Purple?" We'd spend an hour and a half learning the keyboard and guitar parts. It would then take five days to get the bass player to play it. After six months of this crap somebody said, "There's not enough money to keep four of us", and I said, "I'll leave!". (*Irish Folk, Trad and Blues* by Colin Harper and Trevor Hodgett)

Roughly three years later, in an interview with *Beat Instrumental*, Lynott admitted his shortcomings in the early days whilst also offering further insight:

Yeah, I was really bad, but there were four in the band at that time so I was well covered up, and I just used to play the root notes. I took my example from Brush. He used to practice eight hours a day and sleep with his guitar. It's true I had a lot to catch up on but I'm pleased with my progress as a bass player. (*Beat Instrumental* April 1973)

O'Neill comments on Wrixon's departure: "To be honest you couldn't really hear Eric at the gigs, because of his equipment and the PAs we were hiring at the time. Phil, Eric Bell and Brian knew this too. When everyone was borrowing money to survive I suggested that we become a three-piece, and they immediately agreed but said it was impossible because he was a founding member, so I said I'd do it. I remember walking into rehearsals in the Town And Country Club a few days later and saying that we can't go on because there isn't enough money, and the only thing I could think of was for us not to have a drummer. I immediately said that that wouldn't work. I then suggested not having a guitar in the line-up, but again said no, that wouldn't work. What if we had no bass... no one would notice. Eric Wrixon got it. He just said 'I get it... I'll go'... and he did."

"The Farmer" failed to make a furrow in the charts, but gaining experience of the workings of a recording studio was recompense enough, as the band continued rehearsing and gigging across Ireland over the coming months. So naive were the boys that they brought their own hired PA into the studio for the sessions. On 3 September 1970, the band played the Dublin Music Festival in Richmond Park alongside the likes of Granny's Intentions, White Magic, Teddie Palmer and others before holidaying in London the following month, where the band visited Skid Row – now domiciled in East Ham. At some point during late October or early November there was a managerial shift, mainly due to financial problems. To try to alleviate the financial burden, O'Neill had visited all the big showband managers trying to do a deal for part of the Lizzy management in return for money which the band desperately needed.

"They all said it would never work and more or less laughed at the idea," says O'Neill. "I then approached Brian Tuite and he said he'd do it. When we arrived for the meeting in his shop, the Band Centre on Harcourt Row, he said, 'I want to do it with Peter Barden [who was there] and I want you out'. Phil started saying, 'That's not on'. I said, 'Let's go outside'. Phil was saying 'No, fuck them, you're our manager'. So did Brian and Eric. Anyway, I said 'we can't go on without money and I've tried and couldn't get any, so let's just do the deal.' The only real option was to break up. So we went back in and they said they'd pay me 10% commission on all the gigs I had for the next few months and give me £200."

Though the band didn't know it then, of course, there was no point in getting too attached to their managers as this was only the first of many managerial upheavals that the band experienced in their formative years, though as O'Neill contends, "I think the line-up changes were a bigger headache."

Thin Lizzy had been together for just under 12 months before a recording contract came their way via Decca Records. Each band member had slowly built up some experience of recording studios, whether it was for one-off single deals or simply using local studios to demo material. The Decca deal, however, was a quantum leap forward and a somewhat nerve-racking one. The offer was for three albums with £5,000 paid up front, along with the option to release singles, if and when the situation arose. It was an unlikely stroke of luck that saw the band snag the deal in the first place as they weren't the actual band that was initially set up for the showcase gig.

A Decca label manager named Frank Rodgers received a phone call from Brian Tuite, telling him all about this exciting act named Ditch Cassidy. Tuite harangued Rodgers into coming over to Dublin to check him out as he was setting up this showcase gig. Lizzy were backing band for Cassidy that day and Rodgers loved Lizzy and ditched Ditch. Lizzy were eventually signed to Deram, a subsidiary of Decca, which was initially home to prog rockers like The Moody Blues, though it was trying to broaden its appeal by this time.

Rodgers' inclinations to be involved in the music industry were instilled by his father after he moved their family to the UK. However, it was through his brother-in-law that he got the job at Decca. He made his start by plugging The Rolling Stones, Moody Blues, Cat Stevens and others. At an early stage, his interest in A&R was surfacing and, while at Decca, he got to know people like Hugh Mendl and Dick Rowe (the latter being instrumental in signing so many great bands to the label – not least of all The Rolling Stones – though he will be forever known as the man who passed on The Beatles). Operating from an office he shared with Ivor Raymonde overlooking Carnaby Street, Rodgers witnessed the great energy and bustle that the times were revealing. It was here that he took the call from Brian Tuite.

Rodgers recalls: "I had actually been booked to judge a talent contest in Northern Ireland around the same time as the Dublin showcase. So, I brought an engineer named Neil Slaven along, did the talent contest gig and headed for Dublin to see Ditch [Cassidy] in action. By this stage I had got my move to the A&R division, which was probably around the summer of 1970 or thereabouts. I have to admit I was impressed with Ditch and later on he did get a deal with Decca, and we ended up doing one record with him, but what really caught my attention was the band that was backing him, Thin Lizzy. Lizzy were only there after some fallout between Ditch and his own band."

"There were problems with Ditch's band, and so I sort of hijacked the showcase so that Lizzy could be seen," says Tuite giving his perspective on the event. "I was keen to make sure that they were seen but there was also a benefit to all of this. Lizzy had songs ready to go. Decca knew that as the band had a full album's worth of material to record, this would limit the amount of money they'd need to invest in them. All they needed to do was get them over to England and put them to work in the studio. It was an ideal situation for both parties."

Some of the original material that the band was writing was impressive, and ex-manager O'Neill recalls several tracks written during his time with the band: "Most of the songs on the first album were developing or completed like 'Honesty Is No Excuse', 'Look What The Wind Blew In' and 'Remembering'. I think we recorded that in Trend [Studios], and some others too." O'Neill also recalls how the band constructed their live set during this period, which was a slow build: "Well, they were only getting the originals together and they had some amazing covers that they and no one else played and that helped our gigs. Hendrix's 'If 6 Was 9', Free's 'All Right Now' and Martha And The Vandellas' 'Dancing In The Street' come to mind."

The initial showcase was held in early November in Zhivago's, a club in Dublin on Lower Baggot Street, and once Rodgers reported back to his Decca boss, a second showcase was set up for later that month at the Peacock Theatre on Abbey Street Lower, with Dick Rowe and producer Scott English in attendance. Though Tuite's recollection might seem modest in comparison to Rodgers' claim, the fact of the matter is that the deal was sewn up fairly quickly and, delighted to sign onto a label that had history, prestige and possibility, the band quickly became Decca bedfellows.

The next step before recording commenced was to secure lodgings for the band. On the creative side, Lizzy hoped to secure a producer who could help harness the strength of the songs and relay these strengths across the song arrangements. Developing the material that they had written was paramount. The band's limited studio experience ensured that the producer assigned to them, Scott English, had much to say in how the material was presented. Rodgers says: "I had my own ideas of who I wanted to get involved, but having only been in the A&R division a short time I got overridden by Dick Rowe, who insisted that an American named Scott English did the job. I knew right away that he wasn't the right guy for it."

When Lizzy signed to Decca, the label was trying to get into the progressive rock scene, and they had recently done so with the acquisition of Giles, Giles and Fripp, the forerunner of King Crimson. Ex-Crimson roadie Tex Read recalls: "I was aware of the first incarnation of Lizzy with Eric Bell, and got to know them better when they were touring on the back of the 'Whiskey In The Jar' single. By the time they were touring in support of Slade (with Suzi Quatro opening) I again hooked up with the band as I was working with Slade on this particular tour. Those kind of tours were typical of their time, with three acts that could actually headline their own shows."

2
THIN LIZZY

Thin Lizzy sailed to England in early December 1970 to knuckle down at the Decca studios in Broadhurst Gardens, West Hampstead, to record their debut album. The band found there were three Decca studios, imaginatively called Decca 1, 2, and 3 respectively.

Brian Tuite remained behind in Dublin due to a combination of having a young family and business commitments. He remained part of Lizzy's management until July 1972 and assisted in securing the band's first publishing deal.

Rodgers recalls: "[Music] Publishers like bands signed, as they know they have the possibility of making some money from them. In the end, they did a deal with a publishing company called Burlington. From what I recall, there was no other publisher competing for their signature, but the deal signed would have been aligned to the contract they signed with Decca, which was for three years. To my recollection, it was only Phil's name that was on the contract. It was a case of 'after the fact' regarding songwriting royalties but I don't think there was ever any malicious intention on Phil's part to deprive any of the other lads of payments."

The band started to get the feel for the recording studio a few weeks prior to Christmas and completed a fair amount of work before enjoying a short break over the festive period. Acetates of the first album were played for friends during festive downtime as Ted Carroll, who was working for Skid Row, recalls: "I worked as Skid Row's Tour Manager from June 1970 until the end of February the following year, and lived with them in the house in East Ham until December 1970. Skid Row had been on a US tour for the entire month of November and returned to the UK around the start of December. I believe Phil visited us shortly after we got back from the States, so this would have been early December, and I think he was in London recording the Lizzy debut at the time."

A tentative working title for the debut offering was *The Friendly Ranger*, an idea gleaned from a song planned for inclusion on the album. Due to the short gap between the time the band signed the Decca deal and started recording, nothing exists by way of demo material and no recordings appear to have been made of the band in rehearsal prior to laying down the first backing tracks for the album.

But then, that was the deal: their songs were ready to go and, eager to capture the band fresh, Decca put them straight to work with eyes firmly on the bottom line. Tickled by the high of recording at a UK studio for a label keen to expand its progressive repertoire of artists, the band got higher still via goodly quantities of dope throughout the sessions. So much so, that the memories of recording of the album are – how shall we put it? – hazy at best for guitarist Eric Bell: "The whole studio was filled with smoke and I could barely make out where the others were sometimes. We were smiling quite a lot of the time; everyone was. We also knew the songs inside out so we felt free to experiment with them."

Assisting producer Scott English were engineers Peter Rynston and, at a later stage, Derek Varnals. Rynston, like Rodgers, was also of the opinion that "Scott English seemed at the time an odd choice for producer". A New Yorker, English had previously co-written songs such as "Bend Me, Shape Me" and "Hi Ho Silver Lining", the latter of which had given Jeff Beck a Top 20 UK hit. Apart from writing hit songs, he had also become involved in production.

His relationship with the band during the short period of recording was topsy-turvy at best. The group feeling was that he didn't understand what they were trying to do, which resulted in numerous communication breakdowns. Various inconsistencies in what direction the material should go led to frustrations boiling over. Lizzy were an unknown quantity in the UK and, as such, they tended to begin work mid-morning, unlike the later days when this could be the time they would finish up. Of the average working day Rynston recalls "As a new band they would have had to utilise whatever studio time was allocated to them, which could have meant 10 a.m. starts. Late sessions (after midnight) were rare unless you were a name."

It wasn't long into the sessions when Frank Rodgers dropped by to see what progress was being made: "I can remember Brian Downey saying: 'It isn't working, it's rubbish', so it was clear the band were frustrated. At this stage it was really just a case of getting what they could in the can and fixing it up later."

This is exactly what they did after hearing the first mix early in the new year. This in turn led to a delay in the release of the album. Further delays ensued when the artwork came back showing the band's name spelled as "Tin Lizzie"! In a 2013 interview with Paul Leslie, English was keen to deny any culpability for the prevalence of dope in the studio. He commented on his participation on the album briefly and concluded: "I don't know: there was a guy at Decca who wanted me out because he wanted to produce the group and he made the big hits with them, I didn't."

It's still unclear as to who at Decca wanted English out, particularly after he had recorded the complete album in a relatively short space of time, but "out" is exactly what happened. Rynston recalls the sessions as being without any major showdowns but also concludes "any heated discussions may have been made out of my earshot."

Thin Lizzy's eponymous debut contained 10 songs, though curiously omitted most of the early tracks that Lynott had written prior to the four-piece coming together. The only known song to make the grade from Bell's initial meeting with Lynott on Manor Street in Dublin 12 months earlier was "Saga Of The Ageing Orphan". The album opened with the Bell/Lynott penned "The Friendly Ranger At Clontarf Castle" and represents Lynott's softly spoken introduction to the band on Decca vinyl. Its loose groove and trippy guitar noodlings courtesy of Eric Bell make it a curious album opener. Amid the slightly clunky lyrics and fairly basic acoustic backing, the song was a drizzly-eyed nod to the times the band shared a house in Dublin's luxury suburb of Clontarf soon after they first formed. Their tenure there was short-lived as the natives weren't friendly and a petition was raised to force the band's exit. This was an issue later repeated when Lynott himself was forced to leave his flat in London due to his neighbours looking unkindly on his late night practising of the bass guitar.

"Honesty Is No Excuse" followed the experimental and off-centre opener. Ivor Raymonde, the only guest musician on the album, contributed Mellotron, lending a pitch-perfect support to Lynott's ache-edged lead vocal. Once more the backing is largely acoustic and sparse, like much of the rest of the album. The folky element of the band was magically enticing and nowhere was it more evident than on "Honesty Is No Excuse".

As Bell comments, "Well, the first album was the real Thin Lizzy, because we were using acoustic guitars and 12-string guitars as well as electric. So there was a certain Celtic folk element. Also, Philip's style of writing then was more poetic. They were poems put to music, nearly."

"Diddy Levine", an experimental folksy tune, houses a somewhat out of place extended rock 'n' roll instrumental break, a riff perhaps that should have been developed elsewhere and a song built around it. The song itself is, nonetheless, an innovative initiation to Lynott's burgeoning storytelling ability. Delivered with a Gaelic-accented tinge its uncommercial qualities make it both an attractive and difficult-to-access proposition.

Bell earned a sole writing credit on "Ray Gun" with its funky blues and slightly Hendrix-esque appeal. Its soft focus and slightly sci-fi leanings are all wrapped discreetly within Bell's fluid guitar licks. Lynott has yet to find his voice, however, and while his husky un-corralled vocal on the track blends in well, it doesn't quite match the musicianship. It never succeeds quite enough to get the listener to commit to the adventure as it unfolds.

Side 1 closes on the album highlight, "Look What The Wind Just Blew In", a Lynott-penned startler. Carefully weaving a great guitar riff with Lynott's subtle lyric, it unfurls the first of many oblique references to his personal life in song, particularly throughout the Decca years. It really is an early gem from the Lizzy catalogue. DJ David "Kid" Jensen [though he's dropped the Kid nowadays], a champion of the band's first releases on Decca, comments, "His girlfriend at the time was Gale and, of course, she found herself being worked into one of the songs on the first Lizzy album: 'Look What The Wind Just Blew In'. He was very cute with his lyrics."

"Eire" opens Side 2. Penned by Lynott, it was the first of many tributes he wrote in celebration of Ireland's past. Its austere musical arrangement and Lynott's voice collide well, and it arguably allows him to deliver his finest vocal on the album. Clocking in at just over two minutes does the song a disservice, and it may well have benefitted from an extended instrumental solo. Lynott regularly mined the Emerald for inspiration and it's also evident on the Downey/Lynott penned "Return Of The Farmer's Son". It's Downey's provocative and precise percussion which steals all the thunder on this number. Though normally not so much a heavy hitter as some of his contemporaries, the range he displays here is breathtaking, though this approach wasn't to last beyond the Decca years when he settled into a more jazzy style of delivery.

"Clifton Grange Hotel" was written as a salute to his mother's Manchester business. Having spent a great many summer holidays there during his formative years, Lynott had met an alarming array of different characters who would later inspire scenarios for his songs. The hotel was known as The Biz, because it attracted many musicians, comedians and assorted actors. This is the first of many songs where Lynott would acknowledge the continued influence of the folks that peopled his life. David Jensen states: "Phil was a soft-hearted romantic sentimentalist, but, if he needed to be, could be extremely assertive – it just depended on the circumstances he was in. One of the things that's missed as well, or unintentionally ignored, is how likable Phil was and how liked he was by the people that met him. He was a very approachable person and liked meeting people."

"Saga Of The Ageing Orphan", sprinkled as it is with references to family members, also suffers from an ambiguity where Lynott doesn't quite translate the idea from his mind's eye to vinyl with enough clarity. Its mournful motif looms large in the delivery of the lyric, and was identified by Jensen: "I have a big respect for those early compositions and, as I previously mentioned, their approach was very unique. The wistful sense they injected to their music was very appealing to me."

The album closes with "Remembering", another number solely credited to Lynott. The song returns to indulging in the then popular move of including extended guitar solos. Eager to exert their musical muscle as much as possible, Bell's multi-layered guitar playing paves the way for some interesting interplay between Downey and Lynott in the rhythm section. It's by no means a great song but at least adheres to the tone and themes previously established with the album's content. The album represents a band away from home, while their sense of detachment is audible across the record.

According to Frank Rodgers, the album's pressing was just 2,000 copies. While the album was lush and rich with its Celtic overtones, the wistful and eclectic lyrics were sometimes wearisome to interpret, more accessible lyrics from Lynott were a little way in the future yet. However, the album that was eventually released after several delays isn't reflective of producer Scott English's input alone. Unhappy with his final mixes, the band turned to Frank Rodgers and asked for more studio time to re-work the album. Eric Bell maintains that English used the wrong guitar tracks for several songs. Given that the band were recording at Decca No.2, a facility with just eight tracks, engineer Rynston is bewildered by such a claim: "Usually there isn't the room for error when you have so few tracks to work with." The passage of time has made it next to impossible to establish the real reason behind the decision that was soon to be made. A re-mix!

Additional time was allotted by Frank Rodgers, though, again, ascertaining how much work was done during early 1971 is difficult to determine. If alternative guitar tracks were completed, and later dismissed by Bell as being inappropriate, they don't appear to have survived.

Frank Rodgers comments: "In the end I called Nick Tauber and asked him to re-mix it as the band weren't at all happy with Scott English's mix. Now, he wasn't told about this and therefore if Nick was prepared to do the re-mix, he wasn't going to get the credit for it. In fact, Phil went in with him to do it. While all of us weren't 100% satisfied with the outcome, overall we were happy with the results given the environment in which it was recorded. The re-mix job was done in the smaller studio at Decca, out of the way."

Tauber had only recently started work at Decca when Lizzy began recording the album with Scott English. He recalls his participation:

"The band were not happy with the mix done by Scott English. I don't know how he got the job because he was a songwriter and he wrote pop songs, but I think he was a friend of Dick Rowe. I don't think Lizzy were given a choice in who produced the record. Anyway, they weren't happy with the mix. There were some problems about the guitar tracks used even though the album was recorded on an 8-track machine.

"So I went away and did a complete re-mix by myself and the band and Frank were very happy with the work I did. This then led to me being given the job on the 'New Day' EP. One of the main problems with Decca was always getting a decent amount of money to do a record. Frank understood Thin Lizzy, but Decca never really did. They just didn't 'get' rock bands in general, though they did sign a few. They'd sign a rock band and then give them fuck all money to go and make a record."

Aside from Tauber's re-mix of the entire album, more work was completed by engineer Derek Varnals, who confirmed he "remixed at least one track on 3 March 1971". "Remembering" is the track that sprung to Varnals' mind. The art for the cover sleeve was, according to Ted Carroll: "A *fait accompli*. We didn't know anything about it until we saw a finished copy. Obviously there had been some consultation with Phil at an early stage, but I don't recall even seeing proofs."

The album received unexpected and very significant airplay on Kid Jensen's Radio Luxembourg show. Jensen would prove to be an extremely useful ally in the early days, as Ted Carroll recalls. "The major bonus for this record was the fact that Kid Jensen worked so hard to promote it, making it his No.1 album on the Radio Luxembourg charts. That was a great break for us. John Peel was also instrumental in hoisting it upon the unsuspecting listener. Those guys gave Lizzy the kind of break you needed back in those days."

Rodgers' recollection of which DJs supported the band through the early tides of their musical voyage slightly contradicts Carroll's telling of the radio support that the band received, though it's in no doubt that even occasional plays assisted in establishing the band in the public's consciousness. "On the way over [to live in England] the band met John Peel on the ferry and Phil asked him to give them a plug but he never really played much of their stuff on his show," recalls Rodgers.

No plans were in place to issue a single to promote the record, as this route had yet to be agreed by the band as a promotional tool. The strategy was to put the band on the road, as was usual at the time. One positive thing was that Decca didn't meddle in the presentation of the material the band was recording. They had a folky edge but they were allowed to go into the studio and get down the material their way. In the light of Radio Luxembourg's support of the album, and specifically David Jensen, Lynott in particular made many visits to the tiny Grand Duchy.

"He came over to Luxembourg quite frequently, usually with Frank Rodgers; music became his passport," Jensen reflects fondly. "One time we were sitting outside a café and he took his bass out and just started practising right there and then. He had real heart, and so much enthusiasm that he just couldn't sit there and not take the bass out. Phil was certainly a more frequent visitor to me than Eric or Brian Downey. I always liked Downey, he kept this kind of low profile, very self-effacing kind of guy. In fact the three of them seemed to work very well together. Another time, he was on the show and we were playing Van Morrison. He loved Morrison's stuff. Specifically, I was playing 'Sweet Thing', and of course he knew the lyrics inside out, so as the record is playing I look across and see him singing along to the tune."

During this time, Frank Rodgers arranged for Acorn Artists to represent Thin Lizzy, as he had a good working relationship with some of the guys there. Brian Longley, one of Acorn's directors, managed Marmalade and Junior Campbell, who were signed to Decca and Deram respectively. Longley also managed a band named Arrival while John Salter and Keith Rossitor, between them managed The Equals and Middle Of The Road. Colin Johnson, Status Quo's manager, worked there, as did a guy named Chris Morrison, who had recently left Peter Walsh's Starlight Artists to set up Acorn.

Both Salter and Morrison became key allies for the duration of Lizzy's career and Lynott's solo endeavours thereafter. Meanwhile, Ted Carroll had returned to Ireland with Skid Row as the band were obliged to complete an Irish tour, lasting until the middle of January.

Skid Row soon returned to England to continue intensive touring and by the end of February Carroll handed over the reins of tour manager to Frank Murray. Carroll's departure led to his affiliation with Lizzy:

"While we were in Ireland, I was invited to dinner at Peter Barden's house just after New Year's Day 1971. Peter and Brian Tuite, both good friends of mine, played me the acetate of the Lizzy album. They said that they had heard that I was leaving Skid Row and they invited me to come to work for them, looking after the band when the boys moved to England. Although I was impressed by the sound of the band, especially by Phil's compositions, I turned them down initially, but decided to come to work with Lizzy when they agreed to make me a partner in their management company [Chord Management], which also managed Ditch Cassidy, Mellow Candle and Elmer Fudd."

The addition of Carroll to Lizzy's management team was an astute move, given the friendship established several years before. Carroll was someone the band could trust and also rely upon for input on their material and direction. Once work was completed on the album the band returned to Ireland and played a few dates. The necessity to move to London full time was paramount to gain Decca's confidence. "They had to accept that this was where they needed to be as it was no use to us [Decca] for them to be in Ireland," says Rodgers.

Though Downey and Bell were by far the most accomplished instrumentalists in the band, much of the material that was written came from Lynott's boundless imagination. Once he brought the ideas in and got some input from the other members, the material was then developed between them.

When asked about the writing process for their debut album, Eric Bell has this to say: "Writing as a band wasn't really around that much during those days. Another big factor was that me and Brian didn't realise how much money you could make from writing songs. A lot of musicians didn't realise this. To be honest, the difference I find about today and these times is that back then we hadn't got one eye on 'How much are we gonna make here?' or 'When are we gonna get famous?'; we'll give it six months and if we're not fucking millionaires we're gonna pack it in.' There was nothing like that at all with Thin Lizzy. It was music, that's what it was, it was the love of music. That's why we were together.

23

"A Protestant from Belfast and two Catholics from Dublin. Through the power of music we had no problems, 'cos music is bigger than all that shite, the politics and religion. What I'm trying to say is that the music was very sacred to us and we were very passionate about it."

Following the band's permanent move to London they undertook a punishing tour schedule which began with dates in March through until November – though they did take occasional breathers. Touring meant that the band were losing routine time to work on new material, but by keeping on the road it at least meant that their name wasn't too often unheard of by the booking agents.

A key factor to their early survival in England lies within how the band worked as a whole, road crew included. They assumed a "band of brothers" motto. With the tiny promotional budgets they worked to in those early days, often the band couldn't afford more than a road crew of two or three, but it wasn't long before this changed and improved the overall stability of the set-up.

"A guy named Paul Verner was Lizzy's first roadie," remembers Carroll. "He was a friend of Phil's and was doing an apprenticeship in the electrical engineering trade when he started working with the band in the very beginning. In fact, he probably had worked with Phil and Brian in Orphanage as well. Lizzy and their road crew hung together and looked after each other and there was a kind of gang mentality in the bond between members of the band and the crew, especially while on tour."

Six months earlier, a guy named Pete Eustace was about to leave England to start work as a lighting engineer with a mobile disco operation in Northern Ireland. On his way to Belfast, he stopped off in Dublin with his step brother Ashtar, who had worked as Skid Row's lighting man a couple of years previously. The pair stayed with Lynott at his flat in Clontarf for a few days, which concluded when Lynott asked Eustace if he fancied working with Thin Lizzy, as they needed additional support. It wasn't long, however, before Eustace was laid-off, as the band wasn't earning enough money to pay wages for two road crew. However, just prior to the release of their debut album Verner was forced to quit, as Ted Carroll confirms. "To his great dismay, he was forced to drop out, as his parents insisted on him staying in Dublin to complete his apprenticeship, though he did later work in the industry with Horslips and The Pogues."

It was when Lizzy were in final rehearsals for their debut English tour that they were joined by Mick Tarrant, who was offered the job by Carroll. Despite having no experience as a roadie, Tarrant was an avid music fan, and previously worked as a bus driver, and so could be depended upon to get the band safely to and from gigs.

About a month after the band moved to London, Pete Eustace turned up to visit and was promptly invited to join up again by Lynott. Soon after, Mick Tarrant decided that life on the road with a struggling band was not as glamorous as he had been led to believe, and decided to leave. Eustace, at that time, was unable to drive so a variety of people pitched in until a replacement was found. The band were due to make their British debut at Sisters Club on Seven Sisters Road, Holloway, North London, but the gig had to be cancelled as Lizzy were unable to leave Ireland in time to make the gig. Their eventual UK debut was Upstairs At Ronnie Scott's on 23 March 1971, for which they were paid just £10.

Lizzy had an unfortunate London music scene baptism when, on the occasion of their third UK date, supporting Status Quo at the Marquee on Saturday 27 March 1971, their van, which had been parked in an alley behind the club, was broken into and much of their gear was stolen. This included some of Downey's drum kit, Lynott's much-loved Fender Jazz bass and several mikes. Quo kindly saved the day and Downey borrowed John Coghlan's drum kit, while Alan Lancaster lent Lynott a bass.

Though heartbreaking for the band and an obvious frustration for the management, as the bills were piling up, every cloud has a silver lining. Ted Carroll recalls the impact that the replacement instrument had: "Well, Phil's first bass guitar was that [stolen] battered old Fender Jazz bass. Those early models are now highly prized. Phil picked up this bass in Dublin, which had a large hole the size of a fist that the previous owner had carved out of the body just below the bridge. As no one could afford to buy another decent bass outright, we had to get a replacement on hire purchase, and Phil's mum agreed to stand as guarantor.

"Phil looked at various bass guitars and eventually chose a model, designed and manufactured by Dan Armstrong, whose innovative range of instruments had just come on the market in the UK. This guitar was rather unique for the time, as it had a clear perspex body with a stainless steel plectrum guard. Phil soon discovered that the stainless steel plectrum guard acted as a mirror and using it as such, he could reflect a narrow beam of light from a spotlight in the back of the hall onto anyone in the audience. This was to become one of his trademark gimmicks and in the early days he used to shine it on any girl he fancied in the audience to attract her attention."

While the band were on the road, Decca finally released their debut album, wisely changed from *The Friendly Ranger* to *Thin Lizzy*, on 30 April 1971. It met with mildly positive reviews and marked the band out as a curiosity worth keeping an eye on. Breaking the band on the road was the order of the day. One downside to this was Decca's perceived lack of investment in promotion. Lynott habitually checked the local record stores of the towns or cities they were playing and more often than not couldn't find the album they were promoting which led to frequent heated exchanges with Decca.

The album didn't sell enough copies to make a dent in the charts in the UK but the release did elevate the band's profile in their native country, with them frequently undertaking sell-out Irish tours to replenish depleted coffers. This cash helped them to survive on the club and university circuit in England.

Coinciding with the release of the album, Frank Rodgers had cause to travel to Luxembourg, where he ended up acquainting himself with David Jensen. As previously outlined, the DJ was instrumental in providing frequent airplay for the band's debut album. In a time when radio airplay was gold dust to a band bubbling under, this kind of support was essential on many levels, not least for boosting morale. Jensen first came to prominence as the presenter of *Jensen's Dimensions* on Radio

Luxembourg, a pirate station which appealed to an audience bereft of the kind of music which was reflecting social and political change.

The freedom afforded Jensen at Radio Luxembourg is something that he gained a better understanding of only after leaving the station. "I liked Lizzy's debut album, and made it my album of the week," he says. "When I was doing the show it was unlike others, in that there was no committee in place who would vote on what the best recent album release was. I had that freedom to choose what I felt was the strongest release. The music papers of the day (*Record Mirror, Disc* or *Sounds*) would then be given a list of something like my Top 20 or Top 30 records and print them in their next edition."

Though Lizzy's debut didn't garner any chart success, it gave the band the inside knowledge they needed to understand how the recording industry worked in the UK. It also paved the way for their exploration of life on the road in Great Britain. With a little luck, the combined experiences would enable the band to develop a harder carapace when it came to bringing their brand of rock 'n' roll to the masses, albeit rock 'n' roll with a heady dose of Irish folk.

Decca knew it would take time and road work for the band to dent the public's consciousness, but it still took Lizzy's management some time to convince the label to bankroll further studio sessions. Unconvinced by the debut, a compromise was reached. Instead of putting the band back into the studio to record a new album Decca agreed to finance the recording of an EP.

Recording the EP, soon to be titled "New Day", was Nick Tauber's first official engagement with the band in his role as producer. He was assisted by engineer Dave Grinsted. "As with many acts at that time, they came to Decca virtually unknown by any of the engineering staff, but presumably previously monitored by a member of the A&R Department," recalls Grinsted. "I have no bad recollections of the sessions, but they were essentially another gig. I was not aware of plans for them, nor did I monitor their subsequent development."

Grinsted was kind enough to review his diary entries for the sessions, and confirmed that all four tracks that were recorded for the EP were recorded on 14 and 15 June, with 12-hour sessions for each day. On the first day, the band recorded at Decca Studio 2 while the following day they took up residence in Decca Studio 1. All four tracks were then mixed during a marathon session on 17 June.

Lizzy's management asked Decca to release the EP in a picture sleeve, but they refused on the grounds of cost, so the band decided to produce their own. Ted Carroll recalls, "A guy named Rodney Matthews was recommended to us by a friend who worked for a booking agency in Bristol." Matthews has since gone on to produce some classic artwork for the rock band Magnum and here he recalls how he got to be involved in Thin Lizzy's early career: "At one of the Lizzy gigs, at Redland College in Bristol, they saw one of my event posters advertising a future event at the Commonwealth Institute Theatre, featuring a collection of Bristol folkies. It was the Thin Lizzy manager who spoke to my graphics associate, the late Terry Brace, at Plastic Dog Agency. It was Terry who passed the request to me, and I remember thinking, 'What a break, an actual record cover job, for 40 quid'."

Matthews later met the band to talk about the job, along with Brace, and after the discussion all adjourned to a regular watering hole, The White Harte, across the street on Park Row. Matthews again takes up the story:

"I seem to remember at our meeting that Phil led the conversation more than Eric or Brian, but they all struck me as agreeable personalities. Of course, at that time, no-one knew who they were, and the level of conversation was quite relaxed and informal. As we continued drinking at the White Harte, I'm assuming we were eventually as relaxed as newts. After the meeting, Thin Lizzy, including Phil, helped push Terry's obstinate car around the Park Row multi-story car park when it refused to start.

"At some point, I was given a lyric sheet and the title 'New Day'. From the lyrics I did three pencil drawings for the inside of the unusual gatefold sleeve. These drawings depicted a Moses-like character, a caricature of the three band members, and a cop taking notes in a little book. For the front cover I painted a stylised scene of a sunrise in acrylic gouache on canvas, and hand lettered the title separately. I think the artwork was done the same size, but as it was never returned I can't be sure. The small dimensions of the artwork would not have been a problem, but later in my career I made a rule of doing album artwork larger than the vinyl size, so that when printed, it would be reduced in size and thus look sharper. I was credited on the back of the 'New Day' sleeve as Hairy Rodney from Bristol."

The sleeve itself was printed in Dublin by a friend of the band named Tony Bradfield who they knew from around the club scene. 2,000 covers were printed and shipped to the Decca pressing plant in New Malden, Surrey, but they arrived late resulting in the first 500 copies going out without the picture sleeve.

As the band ventured far and wide across the UK, playing the club and university circuit, it helped hugely to be away from the spotlight and bustle of London as Lynott by this stage was still far shy of the bass player he later developed into. It was also at venues outside of London where the band earned much higher wages. The only way to learn stage-craft was to play, and it was best done away from the pressure cooker environments of places such as the Marquee, so as to build up confidence. Kirby Gregory, guitarist for a band called Armada, met Lynott during this period of Lizzy promoting their debut album, and the pair would later work together on a number of sessions over the next few years.

He recalls: "I first met Phil in 1971 when Lizzy and a band I was playing in at the time [Armada] played together at a gig in Manor House, north London. I remember the poster said 'debut of two great bands'. When I joined Curved Air the following year, I met Phil again as we had the same publicist – Tony Brainsby. At some point after I left Curved Air, Phil invited me to play with him and Brian [Downey] at the Country Club in Haverstock Hill. We spent the afternoon running through some songs, and I remember that there was another guitarist who arrived at some point and for a while we both played together. I'm afraid that I don't remember who the other guitarist was. Phil recorded it all on a reel-to-reel recorder."

A few days after playing the prestigious Rainbow in London, supporting Canned Heat, the "New Day" EP was released on Lynott's birthday, 20 August. It contained four songs: "Dublin", "Remembering (Part 2)", "Old Moon Madness" and "Things Ain't Working Out Down At The Farm".

It didn't bother the charts but the release was useful in letting the public know that the band was a going concern. Frank Rodgers concludes: "'New Day' came about as a result of the promotions department. They felt that if they didn't have product to work on for the band, they wouldn't be able to increase their profile. With only one album out every year, the hype will only last so long, and with Lizzy on the road it was hard to keep their name on the lips of the public."

Once more the band found a useful ally in David Jensen upon the release of the EP: "I picked up on that when it was released, and the romantic quality of the songs was there and very unique," he says.

Towards the end of the UK leg of the tour the band took time out to record their first BBC session at Maida Vale, before returning to Ireland at the end of July to tour. On some of the Irish dates the band was earning more than £100 a gig, even as much as £300 in some cases, which came in very handy.

September and October found the band gigging through Scotland before departing to Luxembourg on 5 October on a short promotional stint, where they once more met up with David Jensen: "My first clear recollection of seeing Lizzy on stage was at the Blow Up club though I did see them playing in England before that; I didn't see their full show on that occasion though." It wasn't a particularly memorable concert according to Ted Carroll: "Not a great gig at all due to sound problems, but they did do a radio interview afterwards".

By chance, Carroll ran into an old acquaintance from Dublin, Pete Sellwood, in a music shop on London's Charing Cross Road. Sellwood had recently been laid off by The Grease Band and was looking for a job, and ended up working with Thin Lizzy for a weekly wage of £12. "Pete Sellwood stayed with Lizzy for over a year and did a great job at all times, teaching Pete Eustace along the way how to get the best out of Lizzy's aging PA," says Carroll. "He [Sellwood] eventually left over some trivial matter. We tried to persuade him to stay but, with Pete, once his mind was made up, that was it. He was replaced by a friendly long haired young Scottish guy, Charlie MacPherson, who took over the driving duties as well as assisting Pete Eustace with the equipment. This team remained in place until 'Whiskey In The Jar' became a hit."

Before returning to Ireland for a Christmas tour, the band completed several dates in England, the last of which was on 13 November at The Pavilion in Bath. Again Ted Carroll states: "That was down to the promoter Mel Bush. He liked Thin Lizzy and had given them dates at a club near his home outside Bath. The band had been rebooked several times and Mel had recently given them a support slot with Canned Heat and also a gig with Slade in Boscombe at The Ballroom." In the meantime, given the incessant touring the band undertook in promotion of their debut album, it didn't leave an abundance of time to work on material for the follow up. Negotiations for the second Lizzy album didn't start until after the release of the "New Day" EP, but as yet no studio time was used to work on material.

Once Decca agreed to finance the recording of a new album the band made overtures to producer Martin Birch, but this would entail using a different recording studio if it was going to happen. The band managed to convince Frank Rodgers to talk his superiors at Decca into agreeing to it. It meant the band would record their new album away from Decca's beady budget-driven eyes. Carroll recalls: "In the end, the whole thing turned out to be a disaster as Martin Birch was not available and we had problems with the new De Lane Lea studio, as we were the first band to use Studio 2, which had just been completed."

The debut album hadn't sold too many copies but the band was being worked on the road heavily and, in lieu of royalties coming in from sales, the band was just about keeping its head above water due to constant touring and Brian Tuite's deep pockets. One of the major let downs was the slender promotional budget allocated by Decca. Lynott later confessed to Gay Byrne on RTE's *The Late Late Show* during April 1981 that he was "Handed fifty pounds to promote their record".

However, if the post-production work on their debut album had been trying, it would pale into insignificance when compared to the follow up record. Next stop, De Lane Lea studios!

3

SHADES OF A BLUE ORPHANAGE

Having failed to secure the services of Martin Birch, producer of "New Day" Nick Tauber was drafted in to handle production duties for album number two. Tauber was assisted by engineers Louis Austin and George Sloan. Austin had started at De Lane Lea just three years before, but this was the De Lane Lea Kingsway Studio. In its day it was a fairly hip studio facilitating the likes of Jimi Hendrix, Eric Clapton and Fleetwood Mac. Not long after Austin started at Kingsway, the owners decided to build a big complex in Wembley, and called it the Music Centre, though there was also another facility on Dean Street in Soho, which is still operating today.

The Music Centre was opened to a big fanfare with Princess Margaret in attendance for the launch. The majority of technicians working at Kingsway were soon transferred to Wembley – much to their dismay, as Louis Austin confirms: "The studio itself was an unmitigated disaster from the point of view of recording rock music. It just didn't work, and I had a lot of hassle with bands like Queen who were essentially used as guinea pigs. They'd be moved around from Studio 3 to Studio 2 and Studio 1 to test things like sound separation."

As the winter of 1971 approached, the Music Centre should have been fit for purpose – but when Lizzy arrived they found themselves in much the same position as Queen. "It was absolutely bug-laden with horrible problems, one of which was the separation between rooms," confirms Austin. "You could hear people in adjoining rooms recording. Also, if you moved a chair across the floor there were metal ducts, so if you touched them with a wheel on your chair it put a clip on the tape; actually not a clip, more like a huge bang."

As happens with many bands, the time afforded to developing new material after recording and touring a first record was insufficient.

Reviewing their tape log confirms the glaring fact that their rehearsals yielded ideas but these ideas were seldom even recorded to demo form before the band ended up in the studio trying to work out the arrangements in quick-fire time and then recording them. Little or no demos survive from the band's Decca era and, in many ways, some of the material that ended up with an eventual release on their follow-up could be viewed as demos, such is the lack of development in the material. Also, it was a classic case of "second album syndrome", when a band use up their best material for their debut, tour incessantly to promote it and before long find themselves having to write to order for the follow up.

Songs rejected from a band's debut often find their way onto the follow up. It hadn't helped that the band chose to issue an EP with four new songs just a few months earlier, thus lessening the options for track inclusion on their new album. Plundering and re-working older material to fill out the album was the only solution.

"The rehearsals for *Shades* were done at Peter Webber's place," remembers Tauber. "They were a very hard working band and when they were rehearsing they had a very very clear idea of what they wanted to do with the material. But the pressure was always on Phil to come up with the ideas. Bands are not democracies and in Thin Lizzy's case it was Phil who drove the band. Bands are dictatorships, like Townshend in the Who, it was Phil in Lizzy. The closest to a democracy that I've seen in a band was probably Queen but there aren't many others."

"Chatting Today" was recorded for the second album, though was a contender for the debut before failing to make the final cut. It was one of a number of songs that Lynott had played for Bell when he first visited his flat in Manor Street in Dublin prior to the band's launch. In its form on the album it still sounds unfinished, with Lynott scat singing the lyrics and sounding like nothing more than a jam that somehow found its way onto the album. Tauber explains: "The budget for *Shades* was around £6-7,000 and Decca moaned about having to give us that amount of money to make the album. But Decca were mean with everyone."

The first recording sessions at De Lane Lea were conducted on 17 December 1971 where the band worked on the title track and "Brought Down". The following day work was done on "The Rise And Dear Demise Of The Funky Nomadic Tribes" and "Call The Police" before the boys enjoyed a short break, recommencing work on 22 December and putting down the backing track to "Buffalo Gal" and also working on "Sarah". Further work was done on the 23rd with "Buffalo Gal" being finished and work also done on "Babyface". The group then took a week off before returning to the studio on New Year's Eve to do some more work on "Call The Police" and "I Don't Want To Forget How To Jive".

The opening track, "The Rise And Dear Demise Of The Funky Nomadic Tribes", which clocks in at over seven minutes, also includes a 40 second drum introduction. It is an inaccessible nightmare. It's a painful excursion that needed a strong armed direction, and perhaps, in the hands of a more experienced producer, an arm around the shoulder of the band might have helped in deciding on a collective aim.

Confidence plays such a key role in the recording environment, but here the band are so wide of the mark they were wandering off down side-streets and ultimately becoming side-tracked in terms of what kind of band they wanted to be. The disjointed opening number is pushed aside by another highlight of Lizzy's Decca dalliance in the form of "Buffalo Gal", credited to Lynott. Its warm glow and superbly controlled vocal delivery hints strongly at the commercial leanings that the band might have explored further in order to get some chart action. Heavily influenced by cowboy matinée movies in his youth, Lynott allows this fantastical tale to canter with ease and grace across his own imaginary landscape.

The difficulties at the studio tried the patience of all involved – not least the band – and at one point abandoning the sessions and returning to Decca Studios was discussed. Such was the chaos, everyone in the control room had to remain motionless while a take was going on, as engineer Austin confirms: "I nearly deafened Phil one day because the talkback control on the desk had a tendency to make a huge explosion in the headphones if you let go of the switch too quickly, and I did on this occasion. It made a huge crack in Phil's headphones and he came back into the control room, moaning like fuck about that," recalls Austin laughing.

Studio 3 at De Lane Lea was also used by the band, and had "the most God-awful acoustics," according to Austin. "It was as dead as a dodo in there," he recalls. "Now this is pre-software days where you had to have a room that had decent reverb time. It was all about the sound of the room, so you had to go and get the sounds for yourself. If the room was dead, then the sound you'd come up with was reminiscent of "Hotel California" by Eagles, with these thumpy drum sounds. They certainly weren't Led Zeppelin sounds for sure. When Queen were using Studio 1, which was a huge room that could cater for over a hundred musicians, even that was dead. You'd have to have microphones ten metres away to get any sense of space, so that was another constraint in recording the *Shades* album for sure."

As the studio continued to cause frustration, the band forged agonisingly ahead in trying to get material together to flesh out the album. The well-intentioned but filler-reeking Elvis Presley tribute "I Don't Want To Forget How To Jive" is one of quite a few discouraging moments on the album. Devoid of sensibility and structure, its inclusion serves no purpose and, if the band were trying to establish an identity with the public, songs such as these were not aiding their cause.

A little while later in their career when the band started touring in the USA one supporter, Jeff Marvel, decided to approach Lynott backstage having got passes to meet the band: "I just wandered over towards him. Now here I am standing right in front of my hero and I don't really know what to say. We just shook hands and asked how things were going but then I sort of clammed up and began to turn away but for some reason I went back and said to Phil, 'You didn't forget how to jive did ya?' Here I am singing one of his songs to him and then he just looked at me and maybe figured I was a genuine supporter. He took a few steps back, then grabbed one of his poetry books, signed it and gave it to me right there on the spot."

"Sarah (Version 1)" was a conciliatory caper written by Lynott for his granny. The piano-freckled song, buttressed by the resplendent poetry of the lyric, spotlights the writer's ability to tap into his deepest emotions during these early days of the band. The richness in the raw delivery would later give way to rowdy rock 'n' roll scenes but, here on these early Lizzy songs, the audible honest, low key reverence is revealing.

The album continues with the simple yet precise "Brought Down", featuring some tantalising vocal harmony work from Lynott. He later funnelled some of the lyrics in live performance on the soon to be written "Still In Love With You". He even finds time to namecheck "Dr. Strangely Strange" during the fade out, a band which, of course, featured some friends of his, namely Tim Booth who was soon to design the first Thin Lizzy logo.

Interruptions were still commonplace during the recording, with the band forced to walk away from the studio on occasions while the technicians ironed out the problems before recording could continue. Also defective were the fluorescent control room lights, which rather ironically couldn't be controlled. "You could turn down a certain series of lights but not everything completely," recalls Louis Austin. "So, it gave the impression when you were sitting at the desk and looking out, like you were in a factory. The purple and orange theme didn't help. The designer, we later found out, was colour blind."

The experience proved to be such an upheaval for Austin that, not long after the Lizzy sessions ended, he, along with three other technicians, quit Wembley and returned to the delights of De Lane Lea Kingsway. The producer that Lizzy initially wanted for the album, Martin Birch, was working there with Deep Purple. In turn the boys ended up getting friendly with Ian Gillan, who eventually bought the studio from the owners of De Lane Lea, without them ever knowing the true identity of the purchaser. Soon after it was christened Kingsway Recorders.

With just over half the album completed, the band once more tried to make the best of the studio before another technical interruption ruined their momentum. Generally starting work around lunchtime, the group often found themselves working until early the next morning due to the constant downtime experienced with technical difficulties. Remarkably, within three weeks they had a finished cut of nine tracks.

"Baby Face" was a straightforward rocker though lightweight in some respects. It at least adhered to the image that the band were trying to put across to the public. Not interested in being perceived as a folksy or psychedelic rock band, their rootsy use of the blues to propel their rock 'n' roll intentions is all apparent across "Baby Face". "Call The Police", an album highlight along with "Buffalo Gal", complete with Bell's addictive riffing, had solid musical structure. The reduction in experimentation allows the listener that bit more access. Containing, as it does, the ferocity that was soon to be developed across other material by the end of the band's liaison with Decca, it's a very subtle, though then unknown hint as to the direction that the band was later to take as a four-piece. Material with a harder edge and a more accessible vibe was starting to be written as the band recorded and gigged more.

"I think the folky element in Lizzy was less successful towards audiences in a way, because when Phil looked and saw what the crowds in England wanted he realised he could write a much harder type of rock 'n' roll song," explains Tim Booth. "He understood that this would go down well."

The album closes with the personal lyric of "Shades Of A Blue Orphanage", describing Lynott's childhood or, more pertinently, how he now perceived it as a young adult. The underage drinking, lurking on street corners, looking for trouble in the backstreets, gazing at heroes up on the silver screen. Larger than life figures held a close association for the young Lynott, and it would be one of the most intensely autobiographical songs to ever appear on a Lizzy album as Lynott teases out the landscape of his youth. Few glimpses are to be had which spotlight Downey's or Bell's train of thought, as Lynott alone handled the lyrical content.

Louis Austin sums up his experiences of the album: "My recollection of the conditions doing the Lizzy album are that it was horrendous for all of us involved. Phil was a really top guy, smoked a lot of dope which wasn't unusual for its time. I had never worked with Nick Tauber before and he seemed OK. I'd say he was a bit out of his depth with the band, in the sense that Lizzy were a rock band and, to me, he was more a pop producer possibly. I just think that Nick didn't quite fit into the genre, he seemed a bit straight: a nice guy but the band were very much a rock band.

"Also, I didn't have much of an awareness of Lizzy as a band prior to starting work on the *Shades* album, and I don't think they had any hits at that point, I'm not sure. But I certainly had no pre-conceptions, much like Queen, in that I didn't really know who they were. My clearest recollection from the sessions, in working with Phil and Nick, is they both treated me very well. I think they realised that I was confronted with a lot in the studio which took up much of my time and thoughts."

In a promotional interview for the soon to be released album, Lynott confessed to Robert Brinton of *Disc* magazine on the songs and direction of the band:

> I am into developing the melodic side. It's important. But that's not to say I'm – or the band are – going to do it at the cost of the feeling we try to put into our music. *Shades* was really an experiment with a number of sad and blue songs, relating to a certain time. (*Disc*, 1 July 1972, Robert Brinton)

Once the album was recorded, Tauber remained behind at De Lane Lea to mix it, as he confirms: "The whole album was mixed at De Lane Lea and also everything on the album was de-clicked due to the technical problems we had with the studio. I think the recording turned out pretty good in the circumstances. It could have been better sound-wise but it felt like a good record to make."

Ted Carroll remembers: "The guys put a lot of work into this album, and several songs that did not sound as if they would amount to much improved considerably in rehearsals and in the studio. At the end of the day, we were not totally delirious with the sound. Nevertheless, I think at the time, Brian, Eric and Phil were quite satisfied with the results and felt that it was probably better than they had expected, given the lack of time and studio problems."

The band enjoyed an extensive combination of taxed and untaxed substances to see themselves through the experience of De Lane Lea. The early days were mainly spent enjoying dope, alcohol and the occasional experimentation with mushrooms and LSD.

Given the technical disadvantages the band experienced, it was a wonder they managed to cobble together an album at all. Later in their career, when technical difficulties in a studio occurred and the vibe was being killed by such circumstances, the band bade farewell to said studio. During these early days they didn't have the clout to be able to do that, and simply had to work through whatever difficulties they were faced with.

"A lot of people I know liked the album and had a lot of good to say about its content," says Frank Rodgers. "Again, Jensen loved it and played it to death. But it was really an interim album; it was a step forward for the band but not a very big one." The budget for the album was in the region of about £6,000, though considerable concessions were given by De Lane Lea due to the technical problems and delays experienced by the band. In an interview some years later, Lynott tried to explain to the late Philip Chevron what the band were trying to achieve with the *Shades* album:

> What we were trying to do, as opposed to say, Horslips (who later developed into something different) was to write modern Irish songs. Like "Shades Of A Blue Orphanage" was a modern Irish song. If people wanna know what it was like in the late sixties, when we used to hang around St. Stephen's Green and just pull chicks and drink bottles of wine, it's there in the song. Similarly, traditional music represented an earlier part of Irish history. (*Hot Press*/Chevron Interview)

To reflect the melancholic title and downbeat tone of the album content, the band agreed on an orphan-themed sleeve while the Decca Art Department started researching various photo archives to try to find a suitable image. Although it may be laudable that they tried to do an arty shot for the cover, it's unfortunate that they couldn't use a straightforward image of the band so that those who knew what the guys looked like would have something familiar to see in adverts or in-store, and those who didn't know much about the group would at least recognise them in the future.

However, this wasn't to be and the band eventually chose a photograph of three street kids, taken shortly after World War II, which was among a small selection sent by the Hulton photo archive. The image was shot by Paul Martin, who had titled the photo "Street Urchins, Lambeth".

John Slater, who worked in the Sleeve Department at Decca, confirms: "I found this photograph of a few children posing in rags, and they went with it, but the guy who was in charge of European marketing objected to it. He felt that the cover resembled people, or in this case children, from a concentration camp. Of course this subject hit a little too close to home, for the man was Jewish, and that idea was rather quickly deleted. However it did remain for the British prints and the band felt happy enough to go with it."

Shades Of A Blue Orphanage was released on 10 March 1972 while the band was still in rehearsal for their upcoming UK tour dates, which would begin on 2 February at Coventry's College of Further Education, and take them right through until 26 June at Wall City Club at Quaintways, in Chester. At Quaintways, the band picked up an avid supporter in Dave Manwering, who also photographed the band during this period in an unofficial capacity. He had first seen the band the previous year.

"At Quaintways when I first saw them, they were supporting Edgar Broughton," recalls Manwering. "They played on a tiny corner stage which was about 9" high, and I just couldn't believe a support band could be that good. Phil was very quietly spoken in those days, in fact Eric did quite a lot of the talking onstage. Phil was as thin as a lath with sweat covering his clothes in no time at all. Eric was a very inventive guitarist while Downey could play a solo that never bored me. At the time they were a strange cross between blues and folk and I made it my business to get the first album as soon as I could. I made a point of seeing them a lot, and it was easy to catch them playing from week to week as they were frequently in the area. In all, over the years, I saw the band perform 34 times."

Again, no singles were issued from the album in order to promote it. As with their debut, the strategy on how to break a band like Thin Lizzy was to work them on the road and build up word of mouth. Given that the band were against issuing singles at that stage – they wanted to be an album band, maaannn! – touring was the most viable option for promoting them.

However, they soon wised up as Lynott explained to *Disc* magazine...

Some bands shy away from making singles, but I think it's becoming more important for any band. Personally, I like the challenge of trying to write a good short song – packing it all into three minutes or whatever. The climate has changed towards this. There's a new market nowadays that's unaffected by the old image stigma. The young people are into sounds. Most places we play we get a really great response. When you're on the road it gives you a chance to pick up on it. (Robert Brinton, *Disc*, 1 July 1972)

In support of *Shades Of A Blue Orphanage*, the band toured across the UK from February through until May. A short break followed with sporadic dates in June. An Irish tour was completed in July, but a planned tour of America in August and September with Skid Row was abandoned.

This aborted tour led to some key developments in Thin Lizzy's career. During the band's July Irish tour, Brian Tuite and Ted Carroll decided that the latter would try to find someone in the UK to take over from Tuite as co-manager. Tuite was eager to concentrate on his business interests in Dublin and, although Lizzy were still popular at home and slowly starting to build up a following in the UK, progress was exceedingly slow. The financial burden in having to continuously loan money to the band was also a strong factor to Tuite's planned exit.

A sea change was imminent, and with that came the first real challenge to the band's existence. Firstly they needed to overcome the hurdle of Tuite's departure and, with it, his financial support. Carroll initially tried to entice Status Quo's then manager Colin Johnson to become part of the team. He expressed an interest but wanted to see the band play live, whereupon Carroll asked Lizzy's booking agent Chris Morrison to arrange a gig as soon as possible at the Marquee in London. Carroll was somewhat taken aback when Morrison himself lobbied for the position, and seeing how hard Morrison worked for the band he was then managing, a band called Danta, was convinced enough to agree to Morrison coming on board as co-manager.

The duo's first major management decision was to try to get the band a release from its contract with Decca Records so that they could secure a new deal and raise money to help finance the band. With the commercial failure of their first two albums came a somewhat unwelcome suggestion from Decca that they record a cover version to release as a single, though which song was suggested is not known

After discussions with Frank Rodgers at Decca, it was decided that Lizzy would record a single and, if that was not successful, then the band would be given a release. A recording date was set and Thin Lizzy started rehearsing two songs that they were going to cut. The A-side was going to be a heavy-ish but melodic song of Lynott's called "Black Boys On The Corner".

"Phil suggested that they might record 'Whiskey In The Jar' for the B-side", recalls Ted Carroll. "This was an old Irish folk song made popular about 20 years earlier by The Clancy Brothers. Lizzy had been including the song in their stage set for some months and Phil thought that it would be a good idea to include it as it had been going down quite well at gigs. I turned up at the final rehearsal before the band was due to go in the studio; when the band got through playing 'Whiskey In The Jar', Phil asked me what I thought, and I replied that I thought if the band could go in the studio next week and play it just like you have now, it would probably end up as the A-side. Eric's incredibly catchy guitar figure repeated twice on the intro and his flowing guitar solo in the middle complemented Phil's hoarse vocals so perfectly that the combination seemed irresistible."

On Saturday 23 September 1972, the band made their first recording at Decca's new Tollington Park Studio, which became known as Decca 4. During the period that the band recorded *Shades Of A Blue Orphanage*, the studio was being built. Nick Tauber again oversaw production and was assisted by Derek Varnals and Dave Baker. The session began just after lunchtime, and the first track to receive work was "Whiskey In The Jar".

"As it was a simple track it would be ideal for setting sounds and getting headphone levels set for the band," says Varnals. "The basic track had one electric guitar (Eric); acoustic guitar (Philip) and Brian on drums. There was no bass on the track at all. On the first run through, bearing in mind there was no vocal, it seemed endless. In fact on the first run through, I had got everything set very quickly and interrupted them just over half way through. The trouble with a long track is that three takes and three playbacks take the best part of an hour."

Both the "Whiskey In The Jar" and "Black Boys On The Corner" backing tracks were completed on the Saturday, though the sessions overran and didn't finish until after 1 a.m. Again Varnals recalls, "A lot of the overdubs were also done on Saturday, mostly guitars on 'Whiskey In The Jar'. Sunday was taken up with the 'Black Boys On The Corner' overdubs and all the vocals".

On the Sunday sessions, Varnals was assisted by Alan Leeming rather than Dave Baker, and again those sessions ran over and weren't finished up until around 4:30 a.m. on the morning of the 25th. On 30 September, Tauber and Varnals oversaw more overdubs and also mixed the two songs, and had completed their work by 8 p.m. It's not known if it was Dave Baker or Alan Leeming that assisted Varnals during this final stage.

Ted Carroll came storming into the office on Tuesday 26 September with the latest edition of *Sounds*. Although *Sounds* officially came out on a Wednesday, you could pick it up in Soho around lunchtime the previous day. He had spotted a small news item about a forthcoming Slade UK tour in November, though no other information or dates were included. Guessing that Mel Bush was going to be promoting the tour, as he had already handled some major Slade dates in the south west of England, he got Chris Morrison to phone Bush, who promptly asked the latter if Lizzy could have the support slot.

"Word came back within a week that Lizzy were on the Slade tour with no 'Buy On' [no need to contribute to tour costs]," remembers Carroll. "It was customary for the support act or their record company to pay a substantial sum towards the cost in order to secure a place on the tour and the exposure it would bring. However, as Slade were using a new prototype PA system specifically built for them by Charlie Watkins of WEM Amplification, Thin Lizzy would not be able to use this PA and would have to carry their own."

In early October, it was announced that Suzi Quatro had been added to the bill and, in a cut-throat piece of business, Lizzy's management allowed her to use their new PA system while charging £300 a week for the privilege. Over the five week period this more or less paid for the band's outlay on upgrading their equipment. Quatro remembers, "Mickie Most used to produce The Animals, and Chas Chandler, Slade's manager, was the bass player in that band. So Mickie asked him as a favour to let me be the opening act. I was allotted 15 minutes at the beginning of the show where we did all original material, stuff that I had written. We played stuff like 'Monkey Mama', 'Ain't Ya Something Honey' and 'Curly Hair For Sale'."

Frank Rodgers has vivid memories around the time of the Slade/ Lizzy/Quatro tour and its announcement: "We were all out at Finsbury Park at the Rainbow waiting to be taken to the launch reception when this limousine pulls up. We all jumped in laughing at the thought until later, when we realised that it was after being laid on for Slade and not Lizzy. Of course Slade then had to make do with our little banger and arrived in considerably less style than we did." Whoops!

On Thursday 2 November 1972, the band could be found having a final rehearsal in a church near Stamford Hill in north London. The new PA had been delivered, set up, linked to the new mixing system and everything was working fine. The tour was due to commence the following day, so it was to much relief that everything was fully functional and, once rehearsals were completed, the equipment needed to be packed up. According to Carroll, Pete Eustace maintained that there was no chance of getting everything into the Lizzymobile.

Carroll thought otherwise: "I said that I was certain everything would fit in, as I had calculated it all down to the last inch very carefully. Now it was time for the acid test. With a lot of puffing and panting we finally managed to get the back doors closed and locked everything inside. I heaved a mighty sigh of relief as, for a few minutes, I had thought that I had miscalculated and it was not going to fit. Eric and Brian shared a cosy little tram seat for the entire tour, squeezed in beside a giant PA cabinet."

It was a tough tour to begin with for Lizzy as they struggled to get any reaction from the Slade audience, notorious for their boisterous behaviour. After a couple of nights, Slade's manager Chas Chandler was annoyed by Lynott's lack of showmanship, and gave them a shape up or ship out ultimatum. The feedback was noted, adjustments to the set were made and the performances improved. It was a valuable learning curve for the band now established in the bigger leagues of playing, albeit as a support act.

Quatro recalls her time on the tour: "I had no problem whatsoever. Noddy always says the audience completely took to me, which they normally did not do to any support act, maybe because I was a girl... I don't know. I was different, a rock chick and no threat to Slade. I didn't even think about the bigger venues, as I had been playing since 1964 and played some big festivals too, so it didn't daunt me at all. Phil was a nice man, we were always close. The whole band was nice and we did some gigs together through the years. Slade were very big and [we knew] we had better come up to scratch on that stage during the tour. I liked him [Phil] best in the 'Whiskey In The Jar' phase, although 'Sarah' was great too; he did progress... I think he wanted to be the bass version of Jimi Hendrix."

A brief promotional trip to Dublin to launch "Whiskey In The Jar" also took place with Ted Carroll accompanying Lynott to the event. By the time that the Slade tour concluded, the band were once more ready to return to Ireland to build up the bank balance, and took in a number of shows when they returned on 19 December in time to witness, to their amazement, that "Whiskey In The Jar" had gone to No. 1 on the Irish charts. They returned to the UK early in 1973 to find that the song had also entered the charts there. The management combo of Morrison and Carroll had undertaken a second stream launch to wring as much promotion as they possibly could from the single's success in Ireland. This involved coming up with all sorts of gimmicks to lure DJs into playing the song and gaining it wider exposure.

On 30 January, engineer Derek Varnals spent the day working on a mix of the song for the band to use on an upcoming appearance on *Top Of The Pops*. Varnals expands on the work done in the studio that helped make "Whiskey In The Jar" a hit. "As it was the band's first experience of a 16-track studio, they had to get used to the fact that the playbacks sounded less like a record than with 8-track," he recalls. "On 16-track, all the instruments are separate: the drums were on four tracks, no reverb/echo or effects were on the tape. Monitor echo was very simple. On any playback the sound on the monitors would vary from day to day as everything was infinitely variable. It only sounded like a record during the mix. On 'Whiskey In The Jar' the reverb at the start was not on the tape, the vocal delay/double track gimmick was done on the mix."

Tim Booth and the band helped with the promotional materials: "I dragged up this logo out of my subconscious and I also did this little comic strip for 'Whiskey In The Jar'. I also made a whiskey bottle strip which went to all the DJs. I did a poster which I didn't think was very good, but Ted liked it and the logo. Soon after, Jim Fitzpatrick became involved: now Jim and myself were friends and occasional rivals, I suppose, at the time. I got a message from Jim asking for permission to use some aspects of the logo I created and I sent back an OK saying 'Do what you wish with it'."

The second stream promotional wave instigated by the band's management soon had a positive impact when "Whiskey In The Jar" started gaining momentum. It eventually peaked at No. 6 in the UK charts, resulting in the band making an appearance on *Top Of The Pops*. "Being on *Top Of The Pops* was great," muses drummer Brian Downey. "It meant to us that we'd made it. It was also where everyone wanted to end up because it meant you had a hit."

In February, London Records released "Whiskey In The Jar" in the USA, though no record exists as to how it fared. The band had at last achieved some commercial success and, given that they were two thirds of the way through their contract with Decca without having had much commercial success thus far, it was very welcome. Encouraged by the success of the song, recording a new album was given the go ahead but, before that, a follow up single was requested to try to build on the ground made with "Whiskey In The Jar".

"The success of that song saved their asses," says Nick Tauber bluntly. "Lizzy were in a very tricky situation at this stage. Decca didn't really want to invest that much money in them and they hadn't had a hit. In fact, the *Vagabonds* album probably wouldn't have got made if 'Whiskey In The Jar' hadn't been a hit."

4
VAGABONDS OF THE WESTERN WORLD

The next recording sessions carried out by the band concentrated not on a new album but a suitable follow-up single to "Whiskey In The Jar". The success of the song guaranteed that the band would record the third and final album of their initial contract with Decca; that much was secured. The choice of follow-up single being bandied about was a matter for concern. "Randolph's Tango", written by Lynott, was the song the band wanted. They recorded the song at Air Studios on Oxford Street in London on 1 March 1973, with Nick Tauber again producing. Incidentally, the band also commenced work on two other songs: "Suicide" and "Vagabonds Of The Western World" on the same day. They worked at Air Studios again on 20 March where work was done on "Slow Blues".

All parts for "Randolph's Tango" were successfully recorded and mixed at Air and it even got to the test pressing stage. However, it was brought back to Decca Studios for additional work on 29 March. "I did some overdubs and mixed it again, this is the issued release," says Derek Varnals. "Broken Dreams" [the B-side] was done at Tollington Park [5 April 1973] by me [As was "Cruising In The Lizzymobile"]. It was very like a John Mayall track [slow blues] and it took me back five years when I last worked with John Mayall [after hearing it]." Overdubs were done on 6 April, as were the final mixes for both tracks, with Varnals and Alan Leeming assisting Nick Tauber.

On "Randolph's Tango", Lynott's penchant for crooning was starting to emerge. There is an audible shift in this new material that the band recorded, but they were given time to develop the arrangements leading to a much more focused outcome.

A mystery surrounds "Randolph's Tango" as the choice of follow up to "Whiskey… ". It is by no means a poor song: if anything it shows just how much the band had advanced in their understanding of how to arrange new material, while showing off Lynott as a keen wordsmith in the making. The sophistication of the song also contributes to its undoing; it is too left field to be a follow up to a rocked up traditional Irish folk song. It failed to find an audience in the UK but did make the Top 20 in the Irish charts.

David Jensen recounts a conversation with Lynott: "After 'Whiskey In The Jar' the band came up with 'Randolph's Tango' and I recall asking Phil, 'Why Randolph and not Rudolph', and he said 'Exactly', nobody would ever remember Rudolph. The romantic quality of the songs was there and very unique."

Although the cash from "Whiskey…" was slowly rolling in, Decca, on occasions, would advance the band five or ten grand to keep the momentum going, as Frank Rodgers confirms, "They (Decca) knew that they could recoup that". On the success of "Whiskey In The Jar", Rodgers continues: "The band was happy when it hit the charts. It got them on *Top Of The Pops*, which is where they wanted to be, and Phil realised that he really enjoyed being a pop star. The thing with Phil was that you knew he was going to get there someday, and so did he. It was just a matter of time. All the women used to home in on him wherever he might show up and Phil, being Phil, lapped up all the opportunities it presented."

The failure of "Randolph's Tango" to replicate the success of its illustrious predecessor didn't present too many problems, as the band had by now got a firm commitment from Decca to proceed with the difficult third album in their contract. However, that contract was due to expire in November 1973, so it was very much in the band's interest to hone the material they had recently written to such a degree that they could present their most powerful album yet to the record label, to ensure a stronger bargaining position when it came to negotiating a new deal.

On the failure of "Randolph's Tango", Rodgers laments: "'The Rocker' should have followed 'Whiskey…' as their next single. You see, I think Phil didn't want to be pigeon-holed. Phil talked the record company into releasing 'Randolph's Tango', but it just wasn't the ideal follow up to a Top 10 hit. I had an inkling of what he was up to; he was scared that he was going to get pressurised into recording another rocked up Celtic song, so he went the other way altogether. Although it did get airplay it didn't sell enough to breach the Top 40."

Sessions for what was to become *Vagabonds Of The Western World* began in earnest on 11 April, again with the technical support of Tauber, Varnals and Leeming. The recording sessions were spaced out to allow the boys to fulfil a series of live obligations. It proved useful as the band would road test some of the new material at gigs. The first sessions, which took place on 11 April, yielded two songs, "Here I Go Again" and "Mama Nature Said". The band returned to the studio on 12 and 13 May to record overdubs for the material, and purposely took time out on 24 May to record their next single, "The Rocker". "Little Girl In Bloom" was also recorded that day while "The Hero And The Madman" received work on 25 May. "Gonna Creep Up On You", recorded 26 May was the final song to receive any kind of work during this period.

"The Rocker", engineered by Varnals and Leeming, displayed a new intent by the band. Varnals comments on the guitar phasing that was done to get that sound on the song: "When recording the basic track, they had to learn that it is the performance, rather than the sound, they should worry about. The engineer makes it sound like a record on the mix, the musicians supply the ingredients."

After reviewing the rough mixes done on 20 June, further recording took place on the 26th, with some gigs squeezed in too. As their profile had increased since the success of "Whiskey..." larger fees could be commanded for live performances, and therefore the band undertook the gigs to keep the cash flowing.

Two new key ingredients to the pot, collaborations that would be sustained throughout Thin Lizzy's recording career, happened during this period. Composer and arranger Fiachra Trench brought the strings, while artist Jim Fitzpatrick began a steady and fruitful contribution by creating their album and single sleeve artwork along with promotional posters and such.

The album featured eight songs in total and came in just shy of 40 minutes, opening with the Lynott-scribed "Mama Nature Said". Full of bluster and blues with Lynott's bass high in the mix, it's a significant change. On the previous albums, the instrument is seldom to the forefront and, with the new material, a new Lizzy was beginning to emerge. Lynott, who always attempted to make his lyrics much more than Moon and June type-rhymes, shows signs of a wider awareness as he highlights ecological problems caused by mankind's interference.

The Lynott-credited "The Hero And The Madman" follows, draped shamelessly in all its curios. Though meandering in parts, it's a number that warrants repeated listens due, in no small part, to Bell's guitar solo which closes out the song. That solo alone is worth the price of admission. It's a highly experimental track and features long time band advocate David Jensen phased in and out of the track on some spoken word passages.

Jensen recalls: "I got a call, probably from Ted Carroll, and was asked to go to London as the band wanted me to do this thing on their album. I was flattered to be asked and didn't have to think twice about it. I'm not sure if it turned out the way that they wanted it or the way they intended it to be. It turned into a performance piece, though I recall that they initially wanted my spoken introduction to sound, or to have the same vibe, as that of a newsreader." Engineer Varnals oversaw the recording: "Kid Jensen's bit was done one evening as a quick overdub in April or May."

"Slow Blues", a Lynott/Downey composition, brings the album back down from the somewhat overblown "The Hero And The Madman". Lynott's vocal follows Bell's screeching guitar refrain while suitably backed with Downey's pipe band-style drumming origins. Lynott bellows pain from vocal cord to microphone with unashamed sincerity in a fashion reminiscent of Peter Green-era Fleetwood Mac. Soon enough the album unveils "The Rocker", the first of many of Lynott's lyrics to catalogue his exploits with the girls.

Lynott's lyrical tongue is firmly squatted in his cheek as he revels in the primeval posturing and sexually primitive overtures he presents. The album version features another memorable Bell solo, disappointingly omitted from the single release version for reasons of

51

length. It's another significant signal of the direction the band were soon to take. It also became a live set mainstay throughout their career.

The title track "Vagabonds Of The Western World" launches Side 2, the title being a wordplay on *The Playboy Of The Western World*, written by Irish playwright John Millington Synge. It's an early indicator of the band's thirst for forlorn tributes to Ireland, and is one of the first instances of Lynott multi-tracking his vocals. It's not just Lynott, however, playing with vocal harmonies, as Bell had also taken to layering guitar overdubs – something that was to become a real Lizzy trademark before long. The next song, "Little Girl In Bloom" is another one of those early ballads that shows the emotional accessibility Lynott had in song. From Bell's sustained opening note, Lynott's bass playing punctuates the luscious lyrics perfectly. It's unfortunate that it didn't have a longer life in their live set. It's a warm and reflective piece, and from its glow it heaves a melancholic sense of wonder. Aged just 24 when he committed this lyric to tape it's a highly autobiographical piece.

"Gonna Creep Up On You" follows, and brings with it an ascending darkness. From the opening bass line it's the perfect contrast to "Little Girl In Bloom"; just when you think the band have softened up for a wimpish closure to the album, this emerges complete with Lynott's double-tracked vocal whispers. The band were at least keeping the fan base guessing and, with such diverse and accessible songs at their disposal, they once more offer a surprising climax to the album.

Downey's percussive propulsion amid Bell's gloomy guitar grindings, blended with Lynott's threatening delivery, perfectly mixes the three ingredients for this classic number. Thin Lizzy drag the listener across their own emotional spectrum and, as the album finale "A Song For While I'm Away" begins, it's immediately clear that this band's soulfulness is expansive.

Lynott's harmonically whispered and slightly Irish accented vocal is tumble-dried with Fiachra Trench's first contribution to a Thin Lizzy album. Trench recalls his work on the album's closer, "I'm not sure if it was the Irish connection or it was through Nick Tauber that I came to be involved." However, Frank Rodgers confirms: "It was Phil that suggested Jim Fitzpatrick for the artwork and Fiachra Trench for adding strings to the records. To me, it was Phil that gave Fiachra his break into popular music and a very unusual move as well, to have that dimension added for songs in the rock 'n' roll genre".

"It was my choice to have a string group," remembers Trench. "It usually took between 10 days and two weeks, between me having a sit down to discuss the work and the arrangement being recorded. I'd usually take a walk and think about how to do the arrangement. I do a lot of writing away from the drawing board, as it were. I didn't get my first piano until 1975 so until that point I relied on my inner ear. Phil gave me some reel-to-reel tapes as I had a machine and speakers and I would work off the tracks like that to think how best to put an arrangement to the song."

Trench also has some enlightening comments on the differences between classical and rock musicians: "The actual recording of strings or brass is a very fast process, with sessions being in three-hour blocks. We could get through three or four tracks in a session; the arrangements having been worked out beforehand as the actual recording itself is a very quick process. It was always a source of amazement with the rockers because they could spend all day on one track, or maybe even just getting a snare drum sound. I don't mean to sound cynical by this, but it's just a very different way of working. When you're laying down tracks, you're recording over and over again to make it perfect. But when you bring in something like a string section, the standard of reading music is just so high that sometimes I would say to the engineer before the first run-through: 'record this' and often that was it – the first take was used."

Trench's contribution to the album was a late addition. Recorded on 18 July and completed within an hour, he also contributed oboe to the song. The album was compiled and mixed over 17-19 July but further work was done on "The Rocker" and its B-side, "Here I Go Again", on 8 August. "The Rocker" was to be the first ever song that the band pruned from an album for release as a single, though it appeared several months after the album was released. Had it been used as a taster and released prior it may have had the desired effect and slid the band back into the singles charts.

Varnals recalls: "The industry was still, at this time, in transition from singles acts who made an album if they had a hit, to album acts who issued a single to promote an album. As the band wrote all their own material, there would be a limited supply of songs. I don't know if there were any spares not recorded. Some of the longer tracks would obviously not be suitable as a single, so there was little to choose from."

In a *Record And Radio Mirror* interview Lynott relayed his vision on what Lizzy could and should not do when it came to releasing singles.

> When a song comes up that sounds commercial, we will release it as a single. But we don't want to be dependent on the charts and I don't write songs with the charts in mind. (Peter Harvey, *Record And Radio Mirror*, 29 September 1973)

Once the recording of the album was completed, and a title decided upon, a tender was put out to artists to supply artwork. In the end, it was Jim Fitzpatrick whose submission was accepted and ultimately used on both the sleeve and numerous advertisements, as well as posters for live dates. However, Hairy Rodney [Matthews] from Bristol, who had not been approached for Lizzy's second album artwork *Shades Of A Blue Orphanage* even after his intuitive work on the "New Day" EP, did submit some work.

"It features caricatures of the three band members seated upon various critters and riding across the Western World on a globe," says Matthews. "I can't remember the significance (if any) which can be attributed to the frog (Eric) and the mouse (Brian), but I do remember that Phil had at that time the nickname of spider man (I think this came from Ted) so he is shown seated on a spider.

"On the night, Jim's design was chosen rather than mine – no hard feelings, he's a great artist! But I was asked to draw graphics for the shamrock that appears on the reverse of the album and that rounds up my total dealings with Thin Lizzy. I would say that for Thin Lizzy (and the work I did do), the commissioning of a stylised image from an unknown, hairy artist from Bristol was certainly a step of faith."

The eventual cover art used by the band is credited to Fitzpatrick, but the sleeve draws from work already completed by Tim Booth, who coincidentally was a school friend of Trench. "He's a fantastic musician, greatly overlooked," enthuses Booth. "His younger brother Brian was a member of Strangely Strange for a while. For someone of Fiachra's calibre to play on those Lizzy songs was a real high point. I don't know who actually decided to get Fiachra in – be it the producers or record companies – but it certainly was a very positive move for Phil. They got on quite well as he did work with him over a number of years."

Booth also explains how he himself got involved with Lizzy: "Phil knew me as an artist and illustrator from way back and knew that I was into various aspects of the medium. The first piece of work I did was a poster for him which was for a [Skid Row] single called 'Old Faces, New Places'."

Following the completion of the new album, each member headed in separate directions. In August, Lynott made for Ibiza, Bell to North Africa while Downey returned home to Dublin for some much-needed downtime before commencing rehearsals for the upcoming tour in September and October.

The new album, *Vagabonds Of The Western World*, was released on 21 September 1973, mid-way through the tour. The band had now fulfilled their recording commitment to Decca, so while they were on tour, negotiations were ongoing between their management and the record label. Reviews for the album were quite positive. Writing in 1974, *Sounds'* Mick Rock considered Lizzy "a band whose work rewards closer attention".

As the boys concentrated on promoting the new album on the road, Ted Carroll and Chris Morrison trod carefully in contract negotiations, knowing full well that the band wasn't best placed to get a good deal due to their lack of commercial success. *Vagabonds Of The Western World* had also failed to gain a foothold in the charts, weakening their bargaining position. In the end, the band and label reached an agreement for a contract extension of six months with a view to issuing two singles.

"By now, Phil had the whole thing down," Nick Tauber recalls. "He was singing really great. Downey's drumming was synonymous with Lizzy. Eric was up alongside Rory Gallagher as one of the best guitarists to ever come out of Ireland. They had finally got it right and made a rock 'n' roll record and as a complete album it really worked. Phil was also great in that he went to every party or reception and album launch. He was one of those guys that would talk to everyone and one of the best to give people the blarney. He was very natural like that and would do what he had to do to promote his own album or single or whatever was being released. It's not easy to do all that stuff, but he did."

On 9 November, "The Rocker" was eventually released as the lead single, but didn't sell enough to breach the Top 40 in the all-important UK charts. The failure of the single was a shock as it represented the pace at which Thin Lizzy's music was now racing. The slow removal of the shoe-gazing and the emerging shift towards an aggressive and participatory show was now the angle.

Lynott in particular, since the previous year's tour with Slade, was starting to up his game as the focal point of the group. The late Philip Chevron recalls a later conversation he had with Lynott: "He told me about his own experience supporting Slade. He claimed it was one of the most difficult experiences of his professional life: the audience yelled for Slade throughout Lizzy's set. Philip said they could have collapsed under the pressure or else risen to the challenge. He told me that tour taught him about professionalism... everything."

During November, the band toured in Germany before returning home to Ireland for the Christmas tour. It was at a New Year's Eve gig in Belfast's Queen's University which saw the band unravel when Eric Bell broke down on stage. Hurling his guitar in the air and walking off, he had had enough of the Lizzy merry-go-round. The band quickly turned to Gary Moore to fill in the next series of dates, waiting to see if Bell would have a change of heart. By 16 January 1974, Bell decided not to return and Gary Moore agreed to be a temporary fill while Lynott and Downey figured out how best to proceed. Incidentally, Moore had just six hours of rehearsal time before his first gig.

Brian Downey remembers:

He [Moore] was superb. We didn't really have time to rehearse. He was one of these musicians that just knew instinctively what to play. He had heard some of the tracks on the albums but he didn't have much time to learn them. He picked them up really quickly all the same, because he was so talented. In fact, it was unreal. I remember asking him how he managed, not having played the songs before. He said he looked at Phil's hands. Anytime Phil changed to an A or a B or whatever, he'd follow it. To do that and carry it off is amazing. That's how we winged it on this particular tour. (*Hot Press* – "Remembering Gary" article, Feb 2011)

On Bell's exit, producer Nick Tauber says: "Eric left because it was all getting too mainstream for his liking. Eric's thing was the blues and whereas Phil wanted to take the band to the mainstream, Eric wanted it to get more eclectic. I think that's the main reason he ended up leaving."

The band played the National Stadium, Dublin, before proper rehearsals could be made for another UK college and club tour, commencing 1 February 1974 at the Central London Polytechnic, where they were supported by Shearwater. It was also at this gig that Richard Williams, head of A&R for Island Records, saw the band perform and was interested in signing them to Island, knowing full well the circumstances with Decca. Negotiations took place between David Betteridge (Island's MD), Ted Carroll and Chris Morrison, but Island decided not to sign the band as some of the senior staff members didn't feel that the band was an Island Records type act.

Encouraged by their management's continuing faith in them, though disappointed that "The Rocker" hadn't become the hit single they were hoping for, the band continued to work on new material. Songs such as "Little Darling", "It's Only Money", "Showdown" and "Still In Love With You" emerged, with Gary Moore working with the band in a variety of demo studios.

The second single that the band decided upon, as part of the extended six month period of their contract with Decca, was "Little Darling". The song was first put to tape at Tollington Park (Decca 4) on 24 January 1974. Overdubs work was completed on the following two days, with Kevin Fuller and Alan Leeming engineering. The mix was completed by Derek Varnals on 17 and 19 March. It was released as a single on 11 April but again it failed to make a dent on the charts.

"Sitamoia", was also recorded on 24 January but didn't surface on any studio album to follow. There was also "A Ride In The Lizzy Mobile", which featured as the B-side to "The Rocker" in some territories. Again, this would fail to find a suitable home on any studio album but sat quite comfortably as a non-album B-side.

The recording of "Little Darling" and "Sitamoia" represented the last time that the band would record with Nick Tauber in the producer's chair. However, after Lizzy left Decca, numerous compilation albums were issued in the wake of their success on Phonogram, for which Lynott, and an assorted crew, would re-record some parts to clean up the songs before release.

"I remember 'Little Darling' as the last thing I ever recorded with Lizzy and I think Midge Ure might have played on it," recalls Tauber. "Of course, Gary Moore was also on the recording after taking Eric's spot in the band around then. It actually didn't do so badly in the charts and I think might have got to the Top 50."

Despite the record buying public's indifference to "Little Darling", it was a popular number in the band's live set and endured through several tours. The tale in the lyrics highlights a theme Lynott would return to over the years: the chick, the wide boy, too cool to be controlled. It's a classic tale of someone that Lynott may have met on the road, and his passionate delivery of the vocal might suggest it was more than lust. The underbelly also suggests disapproval of their liaison by her parents, and culminates with his acceptance that their tryst has to end.

With its angst-ridden riff ably lacerated by Lynott's lyrics, the song seems conceived as a genuine attempt at writing a hit for radio. It never quite found its audience, and one wonders, if it had been the hit they had hoped for, would Gary Moore have stayed? He had grown tired of the lifestyle and, having aspirations himself to lead his own outfit, quit the following month, leaving the band in the lurch for a German tour they had already received the deposit for.

Frank Rodgers muses: "I always thought 'Little Darling' should have been a hit, which Fiachra played on. Little known is that Midge

Ure plays on the original recording for it. He wanted to join Lizzy in 1974 when they were undergoing a reshuffle after Eric Bell's departure. In the end it didn't happen and, as the phrase coined sometime later goes: Eric was so good that when he left Lizzy they had to get two guitarists to replace him."

The German tour had to be completed, so in May the band quickly recruited Andy Gee and John Cann. The tour was a disaster and drummer Brian Downey decided to quit, though he later had a change of heart after meeting with the band's management. Around the time of the German tour, their contract extension with Decca lapsed and, unable to agree new terms, Thin Lizzy were in recording contract limbo and their future uncertain.

Frank Rodgers sums up the Decca years: "I don't think we lost money on the band but I know it wasn't a huge profit by any means. It was unfortunate that we didn't come to some agreement, but then I think we all felt that the relationship between Lizzy and Decca had run its course and that the experience had helped the band a great deal. They were certainly in a more favourable position for having gone through the experience with Decca."

The early part of 1974 was a turbulent time for Thin Lizzy, and they very nearly imploded entirely. However, the recordings made with Gary Moore signified a change: "Little Darling" was a big advancement, a postscript in some ways to "The Rocker". These were the songs that signalled the sea-change, though the loss of Bell reverberated strongly with some close to the band.

"After Eric left, there was a little downtime where Gary Moore was on board for a while, but soon enough Lizzy changed up as Robbo and Scott joined," reflects David Jensen. "They became a very different band to the one that I initially saw and heard. When you heard this new incarnation of Lizzy it became more a case of 'Let's get the party started'. I didn't see Lizzy on stage around this period and soon they were regularly doing worldwide tours. They were a fantastic band, but not quite the band that I fell in love with."

5
NIGHTLIFE

The first recording sessions to yield material which would end up on the album that became *Nightlife* took place at Saturn Studios, Worthing, West Sussex in April 1974. Though initially recorded without a destination in mind for the songs, while Gary Moore was still a temporary member, the songs recorded represented a lifeline of sorts for the fading Irish outfit. New arrangements of songs such as "It's Only Money" and "Showdown" emerged. There was also a duet on "Still In Love With You" where lead vocals were shared by Moore and Lynott.

Moore's guitar playing had certainly edged the band toward a heavier musical terrain. While Bell and Moore shared many blues-based influences, stylistically they were different players. The structure and athleticism of the arrangements on these new songs indicated a strong evolutionary pulse within the band, though as a trio this wasn't to last. The audible evidence from these April demo sessions highlighted the musical distance travelled since their Decca debut. The Thin Lizzy of the Decca period was a very different beast though, and while it produced strong material in places the commercial highlight remains the solitary "Whiskey In The Jar".

The sessions at Saturn are often easily overlooked in the bigger picture that became the Thin Lizzy success story, as the songs documented would eventually secure a new record contract. Tony Platt was the engineer on the sessions. Having started as a tea boy at Trident Studios, within six or seven months he had moved onto Island Studios around the beginning of 1970. He worked as a tape operator at their Basing Street address in London.

Platt recalls Island's forward thinking ways of working: "They were one of the first independent studios, along with Olympic and Trident, that actually encouraged their engineers to go out and do sessions elsewhere because it expanded Island's reputation. In fact, probably around the time of doing the sessions [for Lizzy] at Saturn I was still an Island engineer. I did an album with Ducks Deluxe down there; I think that was the first time I went down there. That was with a producer who was a regular producer using Island Studios. We recorded the album at Saturn and took it back to Island to mix it. That was the sort of premise: Island reckoned if their engineers went out and recorded stuff elsewhere the likelihood was that we'd take it back to Island to mix, so it was kind of an income generating policy really."

Platt worked with Lizzy over several sessions during this transitional period with Moore, but lurking in the background for the band was the spectre of having to secure a new record deal. "When they first came in we got some tracks down and there was a certain amount of writing going on at the same time," Platt recalls. "It was sort of 'posh demos' in a way. The recordings were of master quality but they were not necessarily the finished versions of the songs. Then they came back later to do some overdubbing work."

The boys were averaging 12 to 14 hour working days at Saturn, though the passage of time has made it tricky to identify the other tracks that the band worked on during this initial burst of creativity. Platt's routine was to arrive at the studio late morning while everyone else would pitch up around lunchtime to start work. One of the main reasons for going to Saturn was that it was a cheaper studio to use. "Lizzy were using it as a 'one step up' from a rehearsal room'" as Platt confirms. "We could actually get what could be masters out of a rehearsal situation if things went really well."

Several different labels had been courting the band on the sly, paying for demo sessions at studios outside of London just to see what the new material sounded like. The addition of Moore to the band wasn't to last, not that any of the record labels knew that at the time. Although Lizzy had been solidly building a reputation in England, Platt was largely unaware of their existence when it came round to working with them. It didn't take long for the Irish trio to make an impression though!

"I think with Gary in the band, it opened up the possibilities," claims Platt. "I had experience, for instance, in working with Free, another three-piece band [instrumentally], and I liked that format. But, only certain guitar players can get away with doing that. Paul Kossoff was particularly good at it. If you saw Free live when Paul started playing a solo, Andy [Fraser] would step into the space and you wouldn't notice that the rhythm guitar had gone. There was no drop in dynamics or anything like that, it was brilliant the way they orchestrated those things. What I was really taken by with Thin Lizzy was the way Phil played and especially Phil's sound... it had the same kind of vibe [as Free], he sort of slipped in there".

While the band enjoyed the short term security of the extension paid for by Decca, and knowing the union was unlikely to go beyond this, the management were trying to secure a new deal. It wasn't unusual for the band's management to play off any prospective deal offered against the "supposed" assurance they had from Decca. It was all mind games and tricks to try to secure the most money to clear the band's debts and start afresh.

In addition to managing Lizzy, Ted Carroll ran a record stall, *Rock On*, in Portobello Road market, London. A chance encounter there proved key in getting the band the new deal. Nigel Grainge, A&R man at Phonogram, remembers: "It was a Saturday morning down at the market, and I went to Ted's little hole in the wall. I asked him, 'What do you do for the rest of the week?' and he said, 'I manage a band called Thin Lizzy' and I went 'I don't believe it'. This would have been 1973-ish and I said, 'I love Lizzy but they're on Decca and they're crap', So he said 'Make me an offer'. I said, 'Let me see what I can do'."

Grainge was a relative newcomer to the A&R role, and proved instrumental in securing Lizzy's signature to Phonogram. Prior to A&R, he was working as their display manager, scouring the country with his staple gun, creating a list where he would document the best DJs in each town, based, of course, on what they had on their playlist. Gung-ho and keen to move into A&R, he took his chance when the label cleared out a lot of dead wood, and knocked on the marketing manager's door and asked for the American Labels to look after as, in his words, "The guy that did it before me was a complete brainless idiot who just happened to be the nephew of the chairman of the company. So, this meant I was looking after Mercury, Chess, Avco and Westbound, all of the labels Phonogram distributed from America."

Grainge arrived into his office the Monday after meeting Ted Carroll and met with his own boss. Grainge, within a relatively short amount of time, had acquired a sizable amount of hits for Phonogram, ensuring his ravings about Lizzy got an audience: "I said to my boss, 'Shit! I think I can get us Thin Lizzy,' So his words to me were, 'Go and get us Thin Lizzy'. So I got to thinking, how the fuck do I negotiate a record deal, I've never done that in my life," says Grainge. "So, I called Chris Morrison and Chris O'Donnell, who were the managers with Ted, but Ted's bowing out to run the record shop full time. So they made an appointment and came in to see me, and I asked if they had any demos; and they said they have this one song they could play for me, a brand new song. So they play me 'Still In Love With You' and I'm sitting there freaking out thinking this is utter genius, and I'm raving about the guitar playing and, as I only found out years later, O'Donnell was kicking Morrison on the leg, not to tell me it's not the new guitar players, Scott and Brian. So they kept that quiet.

"I went to a gig that they had set up at the Marquee; it must have been sheer naiveté on my part, because I know Miles Copeland [who had probably just launched his BTM label at the time] was also there sniffing around because he wanted to sign them too, but somehow I got a really good vibe going with them and I don't think the band trusted Miles Copeland. So I asked the band what they needed and they said they needed about £15,000. They thought they were being clever about lying to me about the guitarist and we ended up doing a deal, and I didn't really know anything about A&R, and of course I was responsible for them."

By May, Moore departed but the band still hadn't been offered a deal with Phonogram, though they had been picking up the tab for the demo sessions with Tony Platt at Saturn Studios. With Moore bowing out, Lynott and Downey were now obliged to find a new guitar player. However, instead of directly replacing Moore, they decided to add two new guitarists. The direction of the material that Lynott was now writing didn't really suit a three-piece and to reflect these changes it was agreed that a second guitarist had to be found.

Thin Lizzy auditioned guitar players in Hampstead where the band was in residence at the Iroko Country Club in Haverstock Hill, London, then run by African drummer Ginger Johnson. Very soon, a three-piece drawing influence from the Jimi Hendrix Experience and Cream evolved to a four-piece courtesy of Scottish Brian "Robbo" Robertson and Californian Scott Gorham.

Many guitar players were auditioned including the late Mick Cox. Kirby Gregory also rose to the challenge: "When I played with Lizzy at the Country Club I had just left Curved Air, and been listening to a lot of Zappa and John McLaughlin," says Gregory. "I was still playing my Dan Armstrong/Ampeg perspex guitar (Phil had the bass version) and I was experimenting a lot. Although my playing was still blues/rock based, I was trying loads of other stuff. Later on, I remember him saying that he [Phil] and Brian had gone back and listened to the recordings of the Country Club session, and thought that I had been playing 'interesting stuff'. I would have loved to have joined the band at that time as I thought that Phil was really special."

At the behest of one of Lizzy's roadies, the late Big Charlie MacLennan, the band agreed to audition Brian "Robbo" Robertson who was born in 1956 and still a teenager at the time. Multi-talented, he had already made his way from Glasgow to London to audition as a drummer with a band called Slack Alice. He got the gig with Slack Alice but before taking the position he agreed to try out as a guitar player with Lizzy.

"It was Downey who gave me the nod, and that was how we started," remembers Robbo. "We started talking about the group set up and it turned out that Phil didn't want to get somebody else in, he wanted to get back to a three-piece. Three-pieces were dead: I said it straight out to him. It wasn't that I didn't have the confidence to play as a three-piece, it just wasn't the time. I felt that if I was going to have some input then we needed to change it. What Phil was writing at that point didn't really suit a three-piece. In the studio it would've been fine but touring would've been impossible."

A couple of weeks passed before Scott Gorham, born 1951, came through the doors of the Country Club, finding the band at a low ebb after going through countless guitarists. Gorham had recently travelled from California to London with the express intention of trying out for Supertramp, though the audition didn't happen in the end.

Needing some dough, he quickly put together a band for the pub circuit, aptly named Fast Buck. He landed the Lizzy audition via the late Ruan O'Lochlainn, a fellow musician with pub rockers Bees Make Honey. With his visa due to expire in a matter of weeks Gorham strode in and proceeded to audition like his life depended on it – which in some respects it did – playing songs such as "The Rocker" and "Suicide". Scraping a living on the London pub circuit hadn't left much disposable income to hand, and many gasps were heard when Gorham unleashed his Japanese Les Paul copy. "Everyone's jaw dropped as if to say, 'What the fuck is that piece of shit?' confirms Gorham. "And it really was a complete heap of shit but it was the only thing I had."

At Gorham's audition, Lynott had his poker face on, but after each number was played there was a pause while he exited the rehearsal room before coming back to start over. He was, in fact, recording the proceedings, as he had with all who auditioned over a number of weeks. Once the audition was complete they exchanged phone numbers, Gorham feeling slightly down as he couldn't gauge whether or not he had impressed the band enough to secure the gig. He was only on tenterhooks for a day, as within 24 hours a brand new Thin Lizzy was formed. "When they called me back to ask would I join the band one of the first things Phil said in his deep Irish brogue was, 'Oh by the way, we'll have to get rid of that fucking guitar of yours'," laughs Gorham.

On 9 July 1974, the new look band played the Marquee in London with Phonogram representatives in the audience. It was this performance which swung the deal, and Lizzy had found themselves a new label. An Irish tour followed before the new band were booked to record a new song titled "Philomena" on Lynott's 25th birthday, at Olympic Studios in Barnes during August. Following the completion of the Irish tour, Ted Carroll relinquished his interest in Thin Lizzy, leaving Chris O'Donnell and Chris Morrison as co-managers. The band completed two more dates, their first at the Reading Festival on 24 August, appearing halfway through the day's running order.

In addition to fine guitar playing, Robbo and Gorham brought something else to the party too – additional material to work on. Gorham contributed an idea he had, called "Jesse's Song", also known as "Scott's Tune". It was developed up to the stage where a guide vocal was put on it, containing just two verses. Further work on the song was abandoned, but Lynott later commandeered a verse and included it in a different song not planned for inclusion on the album, "King's Vengeance".

"Jesse's Song/Scott's Tune" is an interesting number, reflecting the transitional period the band were going through as the new members were bedding in. What was surprising was that it was never revisited by Lynott for a solo project, as it would have fitted well. If it was to have found a home on a Lizzy album, then *Nightlife* was the release that could have accommodated it. Robbo plays some very atmospheric piano, while Lynott double-tracks his misty-eyed vocal to superb effect. For the recent deluxe edition release of the later album *Johnny The Fox*, an instrumental version of the song was included, indicating that the version where the guide vocal Lynott put down might be considered for inclusion on a proposed Thin Lizzy box set.

Robbo also brought a song called "Blues Boy" to the table, which he initially conceived himself, before Lynott helped him with the lyrics. Again, a recording was made and ultimately unused but the song would be revisited on numerous occasions over the following years. It's a fairly straightforward blues rock song that the band used to jam on prior to recording to get the musical muscles pumped. Lynott later re-recorded his vocals for the track with Huey Lewis in Compass Point Studios, Nassau during the spring of 1978, for consideration on his solo album, but again it failed to make the cut.

On one of their many visits back to Saturn Studios throughout 1974, engineer Tony Platt met the band once more – though this time he was surprised to find a Lizzy minus Gary Moore. He calls it as he sees it in his assessment of the new guys, particularly Gorham. "If I remember rightly, there was a little bit of a space and then they came back again and, all of a sudden, Gary wasn't there but Scott and Brian were there," says Platt. "I was somewhat taken aback when they suddenly arrived with two guitar players, and I was also taken aback because it was two guitar players that were doing what I would term as 'twiddly twiddly' things with the dual guitar, and all that sort of thing. Whereas what was happening with Gary was much more blues orientated and so on. To be honest I didn't get on with Scott at all... I got on with Brian [Robertson] and in later years we became very close friends but Scott, I just thought... it was a pointless waste of time frankly."

As previously mentioned, the time spent at Saturn both while Moore was in the band and later with Robbo and Gorham was key in developing the new material. The brash template established by Moore was little deviated from by Robbo and Gorham in the presentation of material such as "It's Only Money" and "Showdown".

Platt rationalises what was going on: "The point of the whole exercise really [at Saturn] was that here was a band that had had what was essentially a pop hit and then changed their line up, and those are the kind of things that made record companies jittery, so the point here was to get some tracks out. I think the sessions were even paid for by Phonogram, and that wasn't an unusual thing.

"When I was at Island Studios, for instance, there was a period of time when Stephen Stills was booked in, and he just had a block booking for months and months and every now and then he'd take a weekend off. Atlantic Records, who were paying for the sessions, would put acts in there that they wanted to do some demos for them, to see how they responded in the studio. I spent one weekend doing stuff there one time, on a Saturday, with a little known band called Yes. They came in to do some demos and on the Sunday another little known band called Osibisa.

"This wasn't an unusual thing for a record company to do, especially if the band has a decent manager – and of course Thin Lizzy certainly had aggressive managers. It wouldn't be unusual for the management to get the record company to pay for some time for the band to go in, do some demos and see how it came out, and that could often be the thing that would seal the deal."

For the production of the album, the band brought in American Ron Nevison. Three different studios were used: Saturn, Trident and Olympic. "I think he had done Jefferson Starship and they fancied doing something with him. I said 'OK, sounds like a plan'," recalls Nigel Grainge on Nevison's appointment. "I went to the studio one day and they were recording the track 'Night Life' and I just went along with the programme – I just thought, it's pretty good you know, I'm liking it. I wasn't even thinking in terms of hits or singles. Another thing was, I hadn't been what I would call a huge fan of the Lizzies. I loved 'Whiskey In The Jar' and 'The Rocker', I could never believe why 'The Rocker' wasn't a hit.

"I didn't particularly like their albums on Decca nor did I like the artwork. I thought it looked a little like cheesy rock, so I felt that they were being badly handled – and I certainly wasn't sophisticated enough within my role and should have put my foot down."

Nevison had gained a reputation for being able to pull off big sounds for bands, something which Lizzy found impressive. What they found in the studio, however, was someone that appeared to be not overly keen on their music and going through the motions of producing a record. Nevison has accepted his share of the blame over the years on the production values of the album, but the band and their management too have to shoulder some responsibility.

The four-piece Lizzy was together less than three months when they started to record with Nevison and needed more time to get their act together, literally. More time spent touring and writing was needed, but when Phonogram came knocking they wanted the group in the studio. With 50% of the band being new boys it was unrealistic to expect the members to come up with a killer album so early in their career as a four-piece.

Nightlife is a transitional album in the band's canon. It offers tantalising glimpses of various avenues down which Lizzy could have sauntered musically but (as was the problem during the Decca period) the material simply wasn't sufficiently developed enough yet to be recorded to the standard required. To complicate matters further, the material that did exist was very diverse and not conducive to building a new identity with record buyers.

Sure, Lizzy had been pulling in the punters to their live shows but this wasn't translating through to the ringing of cash tills at record stores. By the time of *Vagabonds*, their third album on Decca, the band had reached a musical plateau. It would take the group a further three albums on the new label for them to click with the masses. Patience is a virtue; one that most record companies don't possess. However, in Phonogram they had a record label which would nurture their development, as they could see the evolution apparent in Lynott's songwriting, so they deserved to reap the rewards that were to come their way eventually.

Drinking in *Nightlife*, the curate's egg of their creative oeuvre, is (at times) a frustrating experience. It clocks in at just over 37 minutes and contains 10 songs, eight of which are credited to Lynott alone, while the remaining two feature him as a co-writer. The album opens with "She Knows", a Gorham/Lynott accredited collaboration which features some of Lynott's best new-look Lizzy lyrics.

Its acoustic origins remain prominent on the track and, while the guitar playing is impressive, it is bone without meat. The spiritual essence and message in the lyric is never quite matched by the production quality and never elevates itself to the powerhouse song it could have become. It sounds like the band are treading water, just. The audible anxiety apparent on the recording of the track only serves to highlight the inexperience the band had as a quartet. Robbo would have liked a bit more help from his producer: "Nevison, Jesus I nearly stuck the fucker out. He was really off his tits at the time, I mean we're friends now but at the time he was… it was a joke. There we were in the studio and we didn't know what we were doing or I didn't know what the hell I was doing. It was my first album and I felt I was treated like a piece of shite."

The title track of the album follows, a somewhat risky inclusion that serves as an early indicator of the dichotomy of the material to come. It has a weariness about it, a contagious melody maybe more at home in a cocktail lounge bar that in effect only further muddies the direction taken by the band on "She Knows". This soulful air, though apparent throughout Lynott's writing, is later revisited on "Downtown Sundown", a close relative of "Night Life" in terms of style and jazzy overtones. Lynott recorded a home demo of the song with keyboard player Jan Schelhaas, a startling early blues version featuring lyrics that were mainly discarded on the eventual recording with Nevison.

The haunting melancholy of the demo, brought superbly to life by Schelhaas' organ playing, was unfortunately cast aside during the development of the song. If anything was to be discovered on the multitude of demos for the album, it's Lynott's continuing penchant for crooning, and his efforts are at the very least interesting to behold (he later crooned to mighty effect on the almost forgotten Lizzy gem, "A Night In The Life Of A Blues Singer"). "Night Life" is by no means a poor song, though questions need to be asked regarding its suitability for the band's direction. It also features a contribution from keyboard player Jean Roussel, with strings by Jimmy Horrowitz.

Roussel's involvement came about as result of his friendship with Lynott. "Any pre-production work was done directly in the studio, Trident Studios I believe," recalls Roussel. "We would rehearse the songs through and then record the same day, so there wasn't really pre-production done as such. I found the band very easy to get along with, wonderful human beings, very respectful and excellent musicians."

"It's Only Money" follows, one of the songs initially demoed with Gary Moore earlier in the year. Each of the songs demoed with Moore sound and feel superior to the rest of the album, simply because sufficient time was allowed for their development. The more polished final version again loses its fire under Nevison's stewardship. It's certainly one of the songs that marks the band's intent and direction, and features some classic early interplay between Gorham and Robbo.

"He [Phil] was writing stuff as... (if I remember rightly) when we first put the backing tracks down there weren't really many lyrics to the songs," recalls Tony Platt. "When he came back later, there were more lyrics, and Frankie Miller was around as well, and of course he's a great lyric writer. My memory is that when we were doing 'It's Only Money' Frankie was around on that one, and probably contributed quite a lot of lyrics to that."

"Still In Love With You" appears, and brings with it Gary Moore's incandescent guitar solo, originally recorded the previous April. Neither Gorham nor Robbo felt the solo could be bettered and so the pair only contributed rhythm guitar to the track, leaving Moore's performance intact. It's without doubt Thin Lizzy's early masterpiece, a song that remained in their live set for the duration of their career, and was something of a highlight at each show as Lynott welcomed the input of the audience at various points throughout the song.

The emotional high water mark of the lyric is something Lynott would try to reach with varying degrees of success for his entire career. He successfully re-enacted the same sense of loss on another song years later, "With Love", from the *Black Rose* album. Written about, and alluded to in the lyric, is Lynott's then girlfriend Gale. Lynott, though, was wise to the fact that if he didn't mention a name, then the song could be adapted by more people who used music to interpret their own lives. So, in effect the song could be written about anyone who has experienced the trials and tribulations of love, be it fumbling into it or tumbling your way out.

"He was very clever like that with his lyrics, unlike me when I wrote a song about a similar situation to what he was going through called 'Borderline'," recalls Robbo. "I mentioned the girl by name and I think that kind of restricted the reach of the song in a way, but I still love the song." Multiple versions of "Still In Love With You" exist, alternate takes with alternative lyrics. The song was performed as a duet with Gary Moore on the demo and features some devastating couplets that were surprisingly discarded for the finished version. Moore's vocal, always intended as a guide, was later replaced by Frankie Miller in a joint lead vocal with Lynott on the version that made the album. The alternative takes that exist with Miller pining for some beer and wine are priceless, showing the banter at the recording sessions; with Miller at one point falling off the stool he was sitting on while singing.

The album has its shortcomings in places and "Frankie Carroll", a nod to roadie Frank Murray and ex-manager Ted Carroll, is reflective of this. Clocking in at just over two minutes, it indicates a threadbare cupboard of songs to draw from and, though it's also an acknowledgement of gratitude to two close friends, it does little by way of progression for the band. When Lizzy laid down a filler, it was seldom interpreted as anything different. Within the Lizzy archive the song exists in demo form, performed on an acoustic guitar, unlike the piano-led album version, though the existent demo is without vocals.

"Showdown", a song that didn't survive beyond the band's *Fighting* tour of the next year, follows the throwaway "Frankie Carroll" and has the band back on track. It's the strident side of the band let loose, and is another to spotlight Lynott's ever increasing cleverness with a lyric. This was another of the demos worked on with Moore earlier in the year, and all the better for it, as Gorham and Robbo seldom shift from the template worked out by Moore other than dropping the tempo. The over-cleansed production by Nevison doesn't quite do justice to the song, whereas with Moore it was hot and heavy under Tony Platt's guidance.

It comes over as a song from a "Blaxploitation" movie as it stands on the album. The female backing vocals are an unexpected and unwanted intrusion and sound like they've just walked off the set of the *Shaft* movie and into the vocal booth at Olympic. What could have been a great rocking number (which it later became in their live set) is nothing more than a floundering flame as it appeared on the finished album, complete with Downey's bongo filling in the bedding of the backing track.

The understated instrumental "Banshee" follows, clocking in at a less than impressive 1:27. It's clearly an unfinished song that somehow managed to crawl its way onto the album. It's also a monster peeking out from beneath the hem of the band's Celtic roots. Fortunately, the band did return to the song to finish it, with Lynott also recording a complete vocal. The finished song never featured on any Lizzy album, though if it had, its tone and style is more suited to the Decca era material. Lynott later whittled away some of the lyrics for the *Black Rose* album track "With Love". It is a song that deserves a wider audience with Lynott's lyrics painfully etched across the rather less than full backing track, which works perfectly. The Banshee of the title could be interpreted as an analogy for Love and Ireland or, deeper still, love for Ireland.

Recorded on his birthday in August, "Philomena" was initially worked on by Lynott along with Jan Schelhaas at his flat in West Hampstead and then titled "Home Boys It's Home". With Lynott on bass, acoustic guitar and vocals, and using an old reel-to-reel recorder, Schelhaas backs him on organ and Clavinet D6. Lynott refined the focus of the song, and many of the lyrical ideas done on the demo would also feature on the completed song with Nevison producing. The pair achieved the inclusion of multiple instruments by bouncing tracks on Lynott's reel-to-reel tape. Though the well-intentioned song is admirable, it's really another track that doesn't particularly feel at home in the Lizzy ballpark. The demos with Schelhaas are available for repeated listening on YouTube. It was also amongst a handful of songs that was worked on at Saturn Studios in Worthing with Tony Platt at the desk.

The penultimate track is a Lynott/Downey collaboration by way of "Sha La La", another song that featured strongly in the band's live set over the years. There isn't a whole lot of substance to it, though it's no surprise the song was a live set mainstay for so long, as it showed what an accomplished drummer Downey was. Lyrically, it's a scat job and one of Lynott's lesser efforts. He conveniently let the instrumentation do the talking for the song. Much like "Boogie Woogie Dance" a few years later, a song that might have been a good choice to warm up the audience as an introductory song or even in live performance, "Sha La La" hardly warranted immortality on a studio release.

The album closer is the poignant and panegyric "Dear Heart". The sense of the emotional spectrum within Lynott's lyrics at this relatively early stage of his career is an indicator of an artist on the ascent. "Dear Heart", a long since forgotten piece in Lizzy's armoury, is worth its weight in wonderment. It's highly unfortunate that the mix was approved by the band, as the barely audible Lynott's near-whispered vocal is mainly buried, making it a struggle for the listener to follow the tragic tale. The song was recorded for a BBC Session at a later date, which was subsequently released on their multi-disc set in 2011 where the song can be enjoyed in all its unravelling lament. "Dear Heart" is a bewitching behemoth, a somewhat forgotten file in the Thin Lizzy dossier.

Nightlife was officially released on 8 November 1974, but didn't see any chart action. Jim Fitzpatrick's cover sleeve is open to interpretation, just the way Lynott liked it. His growing affection for subtlety was mischievous, but given that the band were still relatively unknown, and just added two new members, a straightforward group shot (as also mentioned about *Orphanage*) might have better served them.

Fitzpatrick, who went on to produce an enviable amount of artwork for the band, says of it: "I was a real propagandist for black music and culture, and it's actually something we started on with the *Nightlife* album cover where the panther is gazing out over the city; not that we said anything like that at the time."

The generally tepid reaction by critics upon the album's release was mirrored by insiders at Phonogram. Though there was some positives to take from the experience of making the album, such as initiating Robbo and Gorham into Lizzy as a recording entity, it caused A&R man Nigel Grainge much dissatisfaction: "*Nightlife* didn't really develop them in the way they needed to be moving forward. By the time we got to the *Fighting* album, which was probably about a year later, I was still learning as I was going along myself. Also, Lizzy's managers were feeling their way as they'd never really managed anyone before; they were both agents really. It was the blind leading the blind. So the album came out and I didn't really like it. This was really an A&R guy learning his trade the hard way."

Scott Gorham echoed the frustrations of Grainge about the making of the album: "When you're in this situation you look to these guys [producer Nevison] to help you through the rough spots, and it seemed that it was just a gig for him, and something that he wanted to get through and get done with. He wasn't that enthusiastic about the music, and probably rightly so because it wasn't a great album. We hadn't found our feet yet so it really was a bad experience for all involved. It's probably why the next project *Fighting* was taken on by ourselves regarding production – which was a big mistake because we weren't ready to do it by this point."

6

FIGHTING

1975 was shaping up to be a busy year. Part of January and February 1975 were spent nestled into Olympic Studios in Barnes to rework some songs that hadn't made the cut on *Nightlife*, as well as putting down some new material. Also, rehearsals were being put in for their debut American tour which was due to begin in the middle of March. The band were going to be shacked up with some label mates, Bachman-Turner Overdrive and Bob Seger.

In the band's archive a number of "works in progress" exist which were later filtered and developed into fully fledged songs. A demo with the working title "After All This Time" was worked up, but soon succumbed to a new working title, "He Was A Friend Of Mine". Decorated with a drum machine, bass and 12-string guitar courtesy of Robbo, it finally emerged as "Try A Little Harder". The song was a collaboration between Lynott and Robbo. The early demo suggests that Lynott was unsure of which hook worked best.

It's also around this period when the band started putting in solid time in developing their material, as the demos in their archive confirm. Somewhat fragile after the experience of working with Nevison, Lynott decided to produce the new album with assistance from the late Keith Harwood. However, Lynott's input as producer appears to be a lot less significant than the subsequent album sleeve credit suggests. It was an unwise decision, but understandable perhaps in the light of his experiences with Nevison. It's also an early indicator of the slack which his own management team were prepared to cut him. The shift in control from the early days with Eric Bell was now nearly complete.

By the end of February, the band had as many as seven songs in various stages of development. "Ballad Of A Hard Man" was worked up to a complete backing track though it lacked vocals. The reggae-ravaged "Half Caste" was in the final stages of completion. "Mumbo Jumbo" was an instrumental work in progress and essentially an early backing track of "Fighting My Way Back". Once the song was developed, it was properly titled and an amusing demo exists in the band's archive with alternative lyrics.

"Cadillac", a Brian Robertson song, existed as a backing track only; the band's archive suggests that no lyrics were ever written. "Leaving Town", a Lynott ditty, was worked up to the point of having a vocal. Multiple takes exists in the band's archive suggesting the number was a contender, each with alternative lyrics as Lynott is feeling his way through the piece. The last song from these primary sessions to have some graft done was "Spirit Slips Away", though not all of the special effects were added by this point.

The first half of 1975 saw the group capturing a wider audience. They undertook the planned US tour with BTO, who were riding high on the back of their No. 1 hit in America, "You Ain't Seen Nothing Yet". Once the North American leg was completed, the band returned to the UK and undertook the second round of recording sessions with Keith Harwood. Much was achieved during this short burst of activity in April before the band were back on the road for the European jaunt of the BTO tour.

During these April sessions the band worked on four songs, "Rosalie", "Wild One", "King's Vengeance" and "Bryan's Funky Fazer". BTO also happened to be a band that Grainge had inherited as part of his A&R role in Britain with Phonogram. During this era, using outside promotion wasn't a common practice in the UK, but Grainge hooked up with an old school friend which helped change his perception on how to break a band. "This guy I had known from school had gone to California and had weaselled his way into the record business," says Grainge. "I remember this guy 'cos he was born with three fingers on one hand and he was a drummer. He was a lovely guy and he'd gone to work for a label called Mushroom, who had a band called Heart. He became their promotion guy and he actually broke Heart in America.

"He decided to come back to London around 1974, and he came to see me and said, 'Look, one of the biggest things in America is this independent promotion thing' and he explained he was independent, didn't work for anybody, but that he goes out and does deals with companies to handle the promotion as an independent rather than just in-house. So, you pay me and give me a bonus if we have a hit. So, I said fuck, my promotion department is shit. I mean they were all a bunch of jobsworths. I said they don't 'get' bands like Thin Lizzy and stuff like that. So, I explained that I had this band, BTO, who'd had a great single with 'You Ain't Seen Nothing Yet' in America. My thinking was like, if those guys go into the BBC it would be a disaster and be like my uncle's promoting it.

"So I employed him, and, of course, the record went to No.1 in England. So when they came over to tour we decided that we were going to put Thin Lizzy as the support, and that's when the Lizzies broke. They bust wide open 'cos the tour was sold out. It was big halls and the Lizzies, they had some songs that eventually appeared on *Fighting*, and the live versions were fantastic. Phil had learned to be a really strong frontman at the time and that's when it all blew up. So by the time they finished on the road with BTO, I think they were asked to leave the tour before the end, 'cos the punters wouldn't let them go.

"By the time they were ready to record the follow-up to *Fighting* there was huge anticipation. It was ready and that's how it happened, everything was primed and all it needed was a great record, which came when they released *Jailbreak*."

Though memories of the tour and the reactions on both the US and European legs are positive, interaction between the support and lead act was confrontational at times as Robbo sums up: "They were Mormons for Christ's sake – no sex, no drugs, no drink – and then Thin Lizzy happened along. They were convinced we were off our tits, which we were, but at the end of it when it came to playing we kicked their ass night after night. We did get the drummer fucked up on one occasion [BTO drummer Robbie Bachman]. Basically he was being told what to do, who to be and where to be by Randy Bachman. So we hired four hookers and stuck them in his room just for the hell of it."

Little time elapsed before the band returned to the recording studio and worked out which songs were contenders for the new album. Though

Lynott was credited as co-producer, guitarist Robbo maintains that his input on the sound was minimal.

"Keith Harwood didn't just help out on *Fighting*, he produced it," says Robbo emphatically. "Phil wasn't really doing it. At that point, Phil wanted to be a producer and wanted to control the band, so that was part of the whole thing. He just wanted to control the whole thing. I was pissed off, but from day one I didn't get annoyed because I realised that Phil wasn't producing it at all. It was Keith Harwood sitting behind that Olympic desk. Phil didn't know how to work the desk so he just sat back and mumbled suggestions about bringing the bass up or something. Harwood is sitting there going all right, all right, trying to be receptive. Philip's suggestions, to me, weren't really reflective of what a producer was meant to say or do."

After the first batch of sessions earlier in the year, the band brought in a series of rough mixes to A&R man Nigel Grainge, who was less than impressed with their efforts, as he recalls: "They went in and recorded *Fighting* and then all of them came into my office to play it to me. So the guys and the two Chris's are there and I remember saying 'This isn't going to get us any further than *Nightlife*'; so there was this kind of deathly silence. I said 'There's nothing like a single on here and what are we going to do?'. So they asked 'What do you want us to do?', and I said 'I'll give you more money and I want you to go in and write the best four songs on the album – all up tempo, and just go out and do what you know you gotta do, otherwise you're just treading water.' So they went away and did 'King's Vengeance' and others, and all of a sudden I had the makings of an album when they came back in."

In the light of Grainge's input, Lynott relaxed his perceived role as producer to concentrate on developing some of the earlier skeletal ideas. Acknowledging that he had bitten off a little more than he could chew, Lynott's concession was a healthy move, and he spent less time mumbling at the desk and more time writing. The change in the material for consideration on the album took a positive turn. It wasn't long before the band dumped the lightweight "Try A Little Harder" and "Leaving Town", leaving space for the punchier material to take flight.

The album opens with a cover of a mid-tempo rouser, "Rosalie", written by Bob Seger. Having toured with Seger in the USA, the band co-opted the track and put some very basic dual lead guitar on it, which really doesn't do it justice. It's to the album's misfortune that the sequencing of tracks made this the introductory tune on the new Lizzy record. The arrangement sounds underdeveloped, the track sounds constrained, almost like some of the *Nightlife* tracks, where the studio experience bled the Lizzy life out of it.

It sounds like a demo and, on the available demos of the track, it's quite evident that either the band didn't have time left to re-coordinate the track or, perhaps, this was the best they could have played it at this time. The song might have been rescued by another mix that could have elevated it beyond its purgatorial outcome. A couple of years later, in live performance, the defects so audible on the album version were superbly corrected, allowing it to become the lead promotional single for the band's bestselling *Live And Dangerous* album.

"For Those Who Love To Live", a Lynott/Downey offspring, straggles in after the malnourished mix so audible on "Rosalie". Lynott publicly admitted the song was in part a tribute to the wayward ways of footballer George Best who was indeed past his brilliant best by this stage. The amusing lyrics reflect Best's amorous stealth, and while the song has its appeal it's not exactly top drawer material. The band, as exemplified on all their albums to date, could never resist throwing a few odd ideas against the wall to see what might stick. The song, however, isn't without its appeal. It has a fledgling funky feel that macadamised the route to ensure that songs such as "Johnny The Fox Meets Jimmy The Weed", "Dancing In The Moonlight" and latterly "Fats", surfaced on Thin Lizzy product. The song is a very subtle hint from a bunch of guys anxious to explore genres not normally associated with a traditional rock 'n' roll band. Remove the electricity, the jigs and reels, and what you'll discover is an ever-exploratory band on the cusp of something big. Thin Lizzy were beginning to announce themselves.

"Suicide" finally manages to find a home on a Thin Lizzy album, having been in development since the latter days of the Eric Bell era. Originally titled "Baby's Bin Messin'", Gary Moore also played on an early incarnation of the song. The early demo of the song suggested it might unravel as a merciless ode to infidelity, but somewhere along the line it became a very different feast. As the song was developed a lyrical element of ambiguity shadowed it, so much so that the listener ends up rooting for the mystery to continue rather than the case to be resolved.

Lynott later revisited the concept of deception on a demo of a track titled "Don't Play Around", a seldom-mentioned reject from the *Chinatown* album sessions. On the mastered version, which appears on the album, "Suicide" appears as a straightforward rocker with Lynott's revelatory lyrics spotlighting the murky background of a suicide case that was lamented only by him, in song. Lynott's storytelling by now was gathering a much stronger dimension, as was his sometimes sparse use of words to convey and deliver a mood to the listener.

On "Wild One", the band reaffirmed their affection for the ballad format. Though a completely different emotional strain in every way to the previous album's "Still In Love With You", it stands as one of their most graceful laments to date. Lynott, a known scribbler in his notebooks all the time, frequently used historical events embedded in the Irish mindset as part of the DNA of his songs. If his Irish heritage was a canvas, he was only too willing to sketch his own scenarios into a song juxtaposed against the historical backdrop to convey the sense of struggle he sang about. It was also a nod to familial surroundings and a reminder that those you love the most have within them the ability to hurt you the deepest. The free spirit of the song runs deep with its themes of departure, particularly from Ireland and the timely reminder that there may never be a return to the Emerald.

The album's title was drawn from the aforementioned "Mumbo Jumbo" which in turn was developed and completed as "Fighting My Way Back". It might have been a contender for a single release in the UK, and certainly fitted into the image that the band wanted to convey to the masses. The tale of excess as outlined by Lynott in the lyric, and the subsequent rebirth of the title character, could easily be used as a metaphor for the band's own fractured history, slow build recovery and larcenous intent for the UK charts.

"King's Vengeance" is one of the lesser acknowledged diamonds of four-piece Thin Lizzy's early recording career. When the band presented a rough cut of their new album to Nigel Grainge, this track was missing from the selection. By now the band were developing some very intricate and melodic guitar lines and, not interested in being considered as a heavy metal outfit, they purposely and cautiously attacked their accusers by writing harder melodic licks while also dressing the songs with lyricism that was sophisticated to the point of being challenged as "conduct unbecoming".

Lizzy were by now outgrowing their critics at an alarming rate. The depth of song and lyric that the band was offering was becoming impossible to sidestep. A beefing up of their sound was now imperative and it was mainly a production responsibility to get the balance right.

While Harwood was trying to rescue the album in progress, given its initial snubbing by Grainge, he was also having to deal with claims by Ron Nevison that he was at fault for an error made during the recording of the recent Led Zeppelin album.

"Harwood was actually being taken to court by Ron Nevison," says Robbo. "He [Nevison] was phoning up 'cos there was a Led Zeppelin track that got wiped and it was recorded at Olympic. While we were in the studio, the phone kept ringing, and it was for Harwood. Ron Nevison is shouting down the phone 'I'm gonna fucking sue you for saying that I wiped the song'. Nevison was blaming Harwood 'cos he was the engineer and let me tell you something – there was no fucking way it was Harwood. All he did was drink Earl Grey tea, but Ron was from LA and he'd be wearing a silver fox fur coat in summertime in London just to look cool."

Next up is the Lynott-credited "Spirits Slips Away", a daring and darkly delicate offering from the band, it's one amongst a bunch of songs that offer glimpses as to their collective prowess. The restrained yet pulsating playing from Robbo hits home like a spiritual spear, while Lynott's mortality-tinged words convey his innermost thoughts on the cessation of life and what follows. The introspective nature of the song, made accessible by Lynott's very poetic lyrics, no doubt aided their growing appeal – but aside from their own burgeoning fan base catching up, the band's urgent need was for new acolytes to cotton on. Various demos of the song exist in the band's archive, all of which show the song at various degrees of development, some with and some without the variety of special effects used to create the ominous vibe it offered.

Fighting was also the album where Robbo felt he could contribute more than just guitar, having gone through the *Nightlife* experience. Feeling more comfortable in the studio environment, he began by having more input on the arrangements of songs and, having built up his relationship with drummer Downey, he would confidently make suggestions and the creative friction generated often led to the pair spurring each other on.

The combustible Scot also began throwing songs like "Sneaking Sally Through The Alley" at the band in rehearsals. Featured on the late Robert Palmer's debut album with backup being provided by Little Feat, a favourite band of Robbo's, his suggestions were sometimes met with confused faces. Robbo is solely credited on the next track, "Silver Dollar" which began life as "Bryan's Funky Fazer".

It's a song that also features the late Ian McLagan on keyboards. Robbo recalls: "The feel of 'Sneaking Sally Through The Alley', that's where 'Silver Dollar' came from and where a lot of space between the lead and the riffs, elongating the space in the rhythm section, came. There was quite a lot of influence from this style, this New Orleans kinda thing that I tried to get into the band, but not a lot of it was taken on board; a certain amount was. Scott couldn't get his head around it but me, Phil and Downey got into it a bit."

"Silver Dollar" was largely devoid of the rough and tumble of other album tracks. It's, at best, another sideshow on a slightly schizoid album. Given the strength of songs such as "Suicide" and "King's Vengeance" and the direction this material was taking the band, "Silver Dollar" is a confusing addition to the album. It showed the influences that Robbo held at the time and, in much the same way as a 12-bar blues rendition of a song on their following album, "Running Back", it just doesn't quite fit into the Lizzy format.

The second and final Gorham/Lynott credited track was "Freedom Song", their third collaboration to date, as per album credits. The lyric-free chorus is a humming riff that nearly rescues the song. It has the feel of a tune that might have been recorded with a view to release as a single, but with an instrumental chorus this was unlikely to pass muster. The duo came up with a number of commercial riffs in the intervening years though this one wilts in the steam stakes to take it over the line. Chiming in with lyrics laden with a call for liberty, its moral message is strong, with Lynott using a loose back story about the fictional Jack MacDuff. The message that sacrifice is required so that moral fortitude can be achieved is all well and good in the post-hippie free love era, but cliché is riddled all over the piece. A slightly different alternative take exists in the band's archive though the musical arrangement doesn't vary hugely from the final version.

The album exits with the Gorham-only credited "Ballad Of A Hard Man"; in fact it's the only song in the entire Thin Lizzy catalogue to solely feature him as the songwriter. It's a stubborn number and keeps the mood of the album title in check, but also one of the lesser numbers. In the early days of the four-piece Lizzy, Lynott's lyrical assistance wasn't always required (though this would soon change). It may have helped in the instance of this song, as the banal lyric adds little to the strong riff employed by Gorham. Lynott's early attempts at rapping over the riff sounds ahead of its time, but the vocal delivery leaves a lot to be desired. So the album closes on a downward spiral with the finale sounding like an inbred cousin of "The Rocker".

An extended version of the song exists in the band's archive. The album outtakes such as "Leaving Town", "Song For Jesse", "Blues Boy", "Half Caste" and "Try A Little Harder" all received various re-workings but ultimately none were deemed fit for inclusion. The lyrics for "Leaving Town" were disassembled and used on a variety of different tracks over the following years.

Having exhausted all of Phonogram's budget for the project midway through the sessions, Grainge had subbed them an additional sum to return to the studio, and it certainly helped round out the album in a superior way to *Nightlife*. However, the album sleeve produced suggests that the band didn't have enough money to be able to re-employ Jim Fitzpatrick to contribute to the third Lizzy album cover on the bounce, and what resulted was a confused message sent to fans of the band.

"It was supposed to be the first time they were going to use this logo I had done, but which originated from the single 'The Rocker', says Fitzpatrick. "The lettering on that sleeve was what I used to develop the logo. I understood that we were going to be using the logo on the front and that there was going to be a band picture on the back. I remember telling Philip that I thought they just looked like thugs, that there was nothing appealing about it.

"They had this reputation as rockers, coolers and to be seen with iron bars in your hands just wasn't an image I felt served them well. I think it was driven by the record company but there were other voices. Philip was beginning to become a strong voice around this time and he could have told them to fuck off. They had already done some work with Mick Rock who was a genius."

The image used of the four members on a London side street fell short of the expected sophistication exemplified by the band on earlier sleeves, though it wasn't just Jim Fitzpatrick who felt the band sold themselves short by the chosen cover shot. It's very literal interpretation was ill-conceived and certainly drew criticism from all sides.

"Well, I hated the title of the album and thought it was completely naff," states Grainge. "Also we had the worst Art Department in the record business. I thought the cover art was shit and began thinking 'I'm getting fucked at every turn'. The American company, Mercury, in New York, were the worst and they did a cover design that was even worse than the UK version. As good as the record was, an improvement on *Nightlife*, it still wasn't a great record."

Fighting was released on 12 September 1975 and eventually made it to No. 60 on the UK album charts. It was at the very least a charting album and, given the responses to live performances when supporting BTO, the band had good reason to be quietly confident when they undertook a promotional tour that took them through until Christmas 1975.

"Rosalie" and "Wild One" were issued as singles from the album in the UK though neither made any chart inroads so, even though they had an album that charted, the band had yet to achieve the commercial acclaim that could secure their future. Phonogram were also obliged to fulfil their contract with the band, which was initially a three album deal with further options, depending on success.

While the band were touring, their management team had set up a meeting with a producer named John Alcock, who agreed to meet with them and catch a performance before deciding whether to work with the band. It was probably the most important audition of their musical lives to date, which they passed when Alcock was impressed with what he saw on stage that bitter English winter night, "somewhere in the sticks," as he recalls. Soon after, he met with Lynott to hear what material the band had been working on for the new album, to see how developed it was and, suitably encouraged by the demos, he agreed to work with the band.

On *Fighting*, Robbo says "By this time we had gelled a lot better. It's a very underrated album. Maybe it's the cover; the worst cover ever to grace an album sleeve. We were taking on board a lot of influences, and playing with people is a very personal thing. If it isn't, you're in the wrong band; it just so happened that we didn't have that problem."

7

JAILBREAK

Five albums in and Thin Lizzy had experienced one solitary hit single. Though they had conceded by now that hit singles were a necessary evil for the greater good of the album, thus far chart success was limited to "Whiskey..." in the UK and some Top 20 hits back home in Ireland.

This isn't a new problem for most bands, of course. If anybody could write a hit single, anybody would, but it's not that simple. One thing was apparent though, the Decca albums suffered due to a lack of time for song development, whereas the *Nightlife* early sessions spent with Tony Platt showed the benefits of routine time for writing and then song development in the demo studio. The Platt sessions which yielded "It's Only Money" and "Still In Love With You" are easily the strongest that emerged on that album. *Fighting* also benefitted from this approach.

Alcock insisted this discipline be employed, which the band agreed to. They then decamped to Ramport Studio on Thessaly Road, Battersea, south London to record their new album. Alcock, along with John Wolff (A.K.A. Wiggy), worked on the construction of Ramport Studio. The space was initially utilised by The Who as a storage facility for their equipment. Wolff was the project manager, while Alcock was the recording consultant, with input on the design of the recording room, the control room design and the equipment.

As a studio, Ramport brings back fond memories for the people that worked there, whether it was visiting musicians or full time staff. Originally a church hall, there was a pulpit in the studio, though this wasn't an original fixture. It was situated in the live room of the recording studio and, if the notion took you, you could stand in the pulpit where you were raised about four or five feet from the ground, making it ideal for use by a conductor in an orchestral session. On a smaller scale it was equally ideal for adding strings to a record. The live room was actually big enough to comfortably fit a 40-piece orchestra.

"It had a great live room," remembers Robbo. "It also had a very nice grand piano in there. It was a great studio. It was more down to the feel of the place for me. All of The Who's roadies were there, they loved us and we loved them. We had some great times, shall we say."

"Pete [Townshend] and I had started a company named TrackPlan, which was a company set up to build private studios for 'rock stars' in their homes," says Alcock. "It wasn't successful, ultimately, as it was literally years and years ahead of its time. But look at the music business now... we were right! Sadly, 30 years too early. Shit."

"I talked to Phil about TrackPlan and I know he was interested by it," adds Alcock. "I said, down the line when he had money he could walk out the door of his house, into the studio and lay down whatever ideas he had in his head as opposed to worrying about having to pay someone to have these ideas put down on tape by going into whatever studio he chose. With this investment he could do that for free at his own whim and it wouldn't cost him a thing. And being as he was, a poet, I think he saw the value in that freedom."

Alcock's recording studio experience was crucial, as was his ability in helping to define Lynott's vision for the new record. A frequent collaborator with Who bassist the late John Entwistle, Alcock's interest in recording equipment and studios dated back to his teenage years. He also had varying degrees of involvement with Cat Stevens and The Rolling Stones, and these liaisons certainly weren't lost on the Lizzy boys.

Alcock significantly reduced his going rate in order for the record to be made, accepting an advance of only £2,000. His regular wedge at the time was anywhere up to five times this figure but with the budget of the album between £15-20,000 he agreed to the reduced fee as he had "a feeling that this could be quite a big selling record."

The technical team behind the *Jailbreak* album consisted of just three people: Alcock in charge of production, engineer Will Reid Dick and tape operator Neil Hornby. Reid Dick was the in-house engineer at Ramport by the time that Thin Lizzy started working at the studio. While working previously as a porter/cleaner at CBS Studios on Whitfield Street, a money saving swoop saw him lose his job along with others, but this quickly led to his first chance at being a tape operator at the then yet-to-be-finished Ramport Studios in 1973. He applied for a job there after a tip off from a friend, and within two weeks began his apprenticeship.

John Alcock had worked the band hard in rehearsals and all involved were aware that whatever album they came up with, it had to have chart potential.

"The first point was to figure out the backing tracks; later on we'd book Ramport. The fine print for the contracts took a few weeks, but I do remember a lot of urgency about the record, which should indicate that the budget wasn't overly generous," recalls Alcock. "It was never a case of going into the studio and seeing what happens, as time was such a priority. It can be assumed that Lizzy didn't get a huge amount of money from the label as they had already released a number of albums. You have to understand that unless a label thinks it's going to make at least its money back then there are going to be restrictions."

So, with this in mind, the band bedded down at Ramport Studios during January and February 1976. "Generally, the first day is getting acquainted with everybody, making sure everybody is as happy as they can be," Reid Dick explains. "*Jailbreak* was better than *Johnny The Fox* in that they had most of the material fairly well organised, I think. It was different also because they were in a different scenario. They needed to make something happen with the album, because there was pressure from the record company, as far as I know. It's always a bit nerve-racking when you've never met anyone before. Obviously I knew John Alcock and Neil [Hornby] my assistant, but I had never met any of Lizzy before. I can certainly remember meeting Phil for the first time in the control room, and he just said 'Hi' basically."

The first sessions for the album were completed over three days, beginning on Thursday 8 January, with Sunday designated a rest day. Once the initial recording sessions ended on 6 February, the next stage of the process began with overdubs. Given the possible outcome should the band not come up with a hit album, the recording sessions were tense. It can't be overstated enough just how the technical trio of Alcock, Reid Dick and Hornby helped the band to realise their ambitions.

Alcock explains: "Will Reid Dick was an integral part of those Thin Lizzy records. He was the quiet guy: just working away while chaos [sometimes] erupted around the sessions. He'd just shake his head at some of the antics, and carry on doing what was necessary to make the session run as smoothly as possible. I think it was Downey that occasionally referred to Will as 'The Professor' as he had that kind of quiet demeanour. [The production team] was very small, just Will, a tape op named Neil Hornby and me. Neil was great too – not that he contributed to the sound, but he was diligent and had a good way with people – important in a session where there are volatile personalities. Will gave him the nickname of Pike from the television series *Dad's Army* and often used a catchphrase from the show: 'You stupid boy, Pike'. Of course, Neil soon became known as Pike by everyone involved in the albums."

Aside from the technical team supporting the band, there was also the staff at Ramport, a gregarious bunch who helped to alleviate any strain setting in as the recording process continued. Gerry Leitch, brother of Donovan, worked at Ramport. John Wolff was considered a strange sort of character, and also suffered with alopecia which rendered him completely bald. Another of Ramport's characters was Dave Matthews (A.K.A. Python) who was convinced that John Wolff was most definitely from outer space. The joking seldom stopped when Python was in the room, as Reid Dick confirms: "Python was a lovely character, he was very funny, got the nickname because he was incredibly funny. Anyone could get on with him; very jovial and naturally a very funny guy. He was part of the building crew, and once it had been built, Gerry Leitch did maintenance."

The remaining staff were rounded off by an electrician named Bernie The Bolt, a chap called Harry and another guy, Gary Skillman, "who was a maniac, but they were all maniacs in their own way", recalls Reid Dick. Python, Bernie The Bolt and Harry did the night shifts, with one of them there every evening until everybody left for the day. As they were responsible for the place, it followed they were responsible for getting the beers in and getting as fucked up as possible until dawn broke. As the initial sessions progressed, the band were getting through a steady amount of backing tracks and things were running to plan.

Robbo in particular was immensely happy with Alcock and Reid Dick's contributions to the proceedings: "Alcock had good ears for the band. I know for a fact he listened to *Fighting* before he attempted work with us. There's a lot of *Fighting* influence in the guitar sounds for *Jailbreak*. But, by that point, I knew what guitar sounds I wanted. Alcock came on board, it was our third album and we had a better understanding of our job. I knew what kind of sound I wanted and what parts I was going to be playing. So Alcock was basically an orchestrator and he had a good set of ears. I didn't have any clue about miking when we were doing those Lizzy albums, but you learn as you go along. Around the *Jailbreak* time I was learning from people like Will Reid Dick about how and why to mike things as they should be."

The first series of sessions yielded backing tracks of newly written songs, in some cases with working titles used, as the lyrics were incomplete. Songs such as "Jailbreak", "Fight Or Fall", "Kid Is Back" and "Funky Job" emerged by the time the initial sessions were completed on 10 January. In the band's archive, "Kid Is Back" is listed as the instrumental version of "The Boys Are Back In Town". Three of the first four songs worked on would eventually make the album cut. No further work was done on "Funky Job" during the *Jailbreak* sessions, though it was developed and finished later in the year for the *Johnny The Fox* album.

"As we began the work on *Jailbreak*, it was easily noticeable how greatly improved they were at their craft, having spent so much time on the road," says Alcock. "The *Fighting* album was good, showed great style, and they also had the image, but they needed a couple of songs that could break them to a wider audience."

The band had a remarkably short period of time in the studio to make the album, but the graft put in during rehearsals ensured that they made inroads, and fast. As soon as the sessions for the album were done they were booked to tour the UK in late February and March.

The big one was to follow when the band were booked for America, where they would be playing on various bills with Aerosmith, Rush, Journey and Rainbow amongst others.

By 21 January, the band had worked up a significant number of backing tracks, and one curiously overlooked epic in the band's archive is titled "Brian's Number", which was never afforded lyrics but features Robbo on piano. Multiple versions exist clocking in at various lengths. It's a sprawling ballad, though perhaps not an obvious choice for inclusion on the album. It's extremely surprising that it wasn't revisited and finished. By 23 January, the band had added more backing tracks with "Cowboy Song", "Warriors", "Romeo" and "Running Back", with lyrics in differing stages of development for each song.

"I seem to remember it [*Jailbreak*] was all recorded fairly smoothly," says Reid Dick. "There would be the usual tinkering around with things, but once your gear is up and running and everyone is happy you'd be looking to record maybe two or three songs a day probably; backing tracks that is. And possibly, if everyone is in a good frame of mind and everything is working, you might get two or three backing tracks and rehearsal on a fourth – that would be a pretty good day. I don't remember running into too many problems in getting the backing tracks down, though it did get trickier once we got into the overdubs."

Both "Emerald" and "Warriors" were worked up during rehearsal, though Alcock recalls them as being "very rough at the time". His job was to take that material in its embryonic form and "figure out how to make it as good as possible, to listen to it, to break everything down and essentially to try and help translate it from the point of a backing track to the record, and then it was up to the band to take it further". Alcock continues, "'Emerald' as a song always flowed superbly and the same with 'Warriors'; one of my other favourites, though I have heard others say it wasn't one they were keen on."

Certainly the most divisive song on the album proved to be "Running Back". The story of the recording of "Running Back" has been well documented over the years but highlights, above all else, pressure amidst the passion that the band faced when trying to save their career, as if this album wasn't a hit with the record buying public, a very strong possibility was that their record deal would be terminated. Robertson: "The Butchers Arms pub was where I fucked off to when I had that argument with Phil about 'Running Back'."

Reid Dick explains how this troublesome track got laid down: "Tim Hinkley came in and played the Bösendorfer grand piano on 'Running Back', which was enclosed in a recording booth. As you looked out from the control room window the booth was on the left hand side of the studio. The control room had three glass windows, one massive one at the front and two slightly smaller ones at the sides. The booth was just big enough to get the grand piano in along with some mikes. The booth had glass panels all the way around, so the musician could look at whoever else was playing, and you could open the door if you wanted to have a bit more connection. On 'Running Back', I'd imagine it was just Tim, Phil and Brian on the backing track. I'm not really sure why Tim Hinkley was brought in to play on the song; maybe Phil did it just to piss Robbo off [laughs]! Certainly as recording [of both *Jailbreak* and *Johnny The Fox*] in the studio went on, the relationship between Phil and Robbo deteriorated."

Tim Hinkley, who has worked with so many people – such as Humble Pie, The Rolling Stones, The Who and Whitesnake to name but four – recalls: "When it came to doing the work on the *Jailbreak* album it was Phil who wanted me to repeat the riff over and over on keyboard, as he liked the vibe it gave the song. I was only talking to John Alcock about it recently and he recalls the same story, in that Robbo and Scott were not keen on it at all but they were overruled, and my contribution to the sessions stayed."

In Alcock, the band had the right man to disperse the frustrations being experienced, and also a man unafraid to wield the power his position allowed him. "There were some fairly strong characters in Lizzy; Phil and Brian Robertson," says Reid Dick. "John Alcock could be pretty forceful if he wanted or needed to be. At this point in Lizzy's career John would have had the ultimate say as Lizzy still hadn't reached the point they wanted to get to, and their future was slightly questionable because of that. I think they respected John and they pretty much did what he said as far as I remember. Although Phil, obviously, had a big say in a lot of stuff. But if it came down to decisions on whether more time was spent on a problem or move onto something else, I think John would have made that decision, pretty much."

Top left: Guitarist Eric Bell during the Decca years. (*Dave Manwering*)
Top right: Decca era shot of Phil keeping rhythm. (*Dave Manwering*)
Above: Drummer Brian Downey during the Decca years. (*Dave Manwering*)

Above: Eric Bell is a great blues guitarist.
Note the Marc Bolan poster to his left. (*Dave Manwering*)
Right: Lynott stopped using a Rickenbacker bass soon after the
Fighting album was recorded. (*Dave Manwering*)

Top: Brian Robertson playing a rarely seen Flying V
during his Lizzy tenure. (*Dave Manwering*)
Middle: Scott Gorham playing a nicer Les Paul than the one he used at his
Lizzy audition. What the hell, he still got the gig! (*Dave Manwering*)
Above: Engineer Kit Woolven describes drummer Brian Downey as
"a fantastic drummer". He's not wrong. (*Dave Manwering*)

Top: Once work in the studio was complete, Lizzy were always on the boards.
Scandinavian Tour early 1980s. (*Jan Koch*)
Above: Manchester Free Trade Hall. Roadie Big Charlie runs across stage
to provide assistance. (*Dave Manwering*)

Scandinavian Tour early 1980s. (*Jan Koch*)

Top: Having fun at Ramport Studios. (l–r)
Will Reid Dick, Big Charlie, John Alcock,
Neil Hornby, Frank Murray. Dave "Python"
Matthews seated at front. (*Erica Echenberg*)
Above: Brian Downey at Ramport Studios
1976 during the making of *Johnny The Fox*.
(*Erica Echenberg*)
Right: Honestly, some work got done at
Ramport! Producer John Alcock (with beard)
chucking some "arrers" with Mark Dodson.
(*Will Reid Dick*)

Top and bottom left: Phil with local Bahamian. Phil with friends including a long
haired Huey Lewis by his side. April 1978. (*Will Reid Dick*)
Top and bottom right: Scott Gorham with Will Reid Dick. Huey Lewis,
Phil and Will Reid Dick in Compass Point Studios,
April/May 1978. (*Will Reid Dick*)

The album was completed by the end of February with a planned release date of 26 March, by which time the band would soon be rehearsing their live set for the American tour. Vibrations at their record label were strong, with a feeling that the album was the best they had ever come up with, but confusion hung in the air as to what song might make the best single. Contradicting the usual process in releasing a single as a taster for the album to come, the band, management and record label couldn't agree on which cut should be the lead single. The celebrated George "Porky" Peckham was the mastering engineer sounded out by Alcock: "As far as George Peckham is concerned, he was the best mastering engineer at the time. I remember taking the mixes to him and he cut *Jailbreak* but I don't recall if it was actually used. The reason may have been that the sequencing of the album changed at the last minute and the label got the album recut. I don't think much had to be done, as the mixes were good, but I know there was less bass on the released vinyl than the test pressings I got at the time. Later on, the CD mastering wasn't good, and even worse on the compilation CDs. The whole point of mastering is to take a well-mixed song and add some subtle enhancements that make it sound even better. Mastering is adding sparkle and gloss to your music."

Peckham is perhaps best known for etching funny messages on Stiff Records releases which helped add to the label's zany reputation.

The album opens with the title track, "Jailbreak", initially worked on before Alcock came into the fold. The band had demoed the song with engineer Lawrie Dipple the previous November at Free Range Studios in Covent Garden, London.

"I was naturally aware of Thin Lizzy at that point, but had no connection; it was just another booking that came in, a one day session," Dipple recalls. "The band, except for Phil, showed up early; the guitarists were really friendly and took a real interest in getting the sound together. The drummer was very grumpy and sat outside in his car all day! Phil showed up in the evening and the tracks came together quite quickly. Brian came in from his car and away they went.

The tracks had definitely been rehearsed to some extent beforehand. I was very impressed with how tight they were. There weren't many overdubs, mainly the vocals by Phil (I can't recall the others singing at all) and some extra guitar parts. I didn't have the luxury of assistants in those days, no tape-ops or anything, I did the whole thing. It finished with the mixes late that night."

Three songs were demoed that day with Dipple; "Jailbreak", featuring lyrics that never made the final cut, "Cowboy Song", again with incomplete or alternative lyrics, and a third song which was an untitled instrumental. However, by the time the band recorded them at Ramport they were developed even further with additional changes made to the arrangements and lyrics. As an album opener, "Jailbreak" displayed all the collective musical intent the band could muster. With twin lead guitar gusto, the duo's playing was perfectly perched upon the benevolent bedding of Downey's and Lynott's rhythm section. It signalled a new era, a new Lizzy, and it was all about those two twin leads.

"When we started on *Jailbreak* it was pretty obvious where the focus should be when recording the band – the guitars," says Robbo. "We were really a live band at that time. We were recorded in the studio as we were on stage. I'm on the right, Scott on the left and whoever took the solo, well that's obviously in the middle. In a live situation when it was time for the solo we'd use a little delay, 'cos then it sounds like there's two guitars when there's actually not."

Gorham comments on the virtues of the title track:

> With the song itself it was love at first sight due to the hard-edged guitar riff and the great lyrics. That was the song that fitted the best to our image, which we tried to protect throughout our career. Bottom line, this was a very characteristic song for the album. (*Classic Tracks* Interview, April 2002)

Reid Dick explains how he set things up in the Ramport Studio: "If you can imagine a church hall, it normally has a stage and a big area where people can dance or have an audience. The stage area (of the church hall) was where the control room was, so it was slightly raised so you could see down, not by a huge amount, maybe two or three feet. The live room in length was probably the size of a tennis court, something like that. We would probably only use the front half for the band stuff and I used to move the positioning of things around to see... like sometimes I'd have the drums right up against the control room window with the drummer with his back to me, so that he was facing outwards as it were... the other people facing him, so you'd have a circle.

"On the Lizzy stuff, though, I pretty much had the drums in the middle of the room and we'd have Phil on the left hand side and the guitars on the right hand side of the drums (from my perspective in the control room). I'm pretty sure we had Phil's amp on the left, because I can remember him doing his Pete Townshend windmill impersonations with both guitars on the right. We tended to only use one guitar at a time, I think. We didn't do a lot where they [Gorham & Robbo] both played as far as I remember, because we had this business of getting sounds for everybody and we struggled a bit with their guitars.

"What we ended up doing was getting Steve Hackett's guitars, as Phil lived with one of their [Genesis] roadies, a guy called Tex Read. He had access to these guitars and we were allowed to borrow them. Some of them were very nice, so that's what we used for the recording. Whoever was playing rhythm on a track would use one of the borrowed Les Pauls and most likely use one of their own amps. I think it was Marshall amps used for *Jailbreak*."

The album opener was followed by the Lynott/Robertson credited "Angel From The Coast". It stands out as a slight curiosity when heard alongside the other tracks on the album. Robertson's drive to expand the band's guitar sound is evident, while Lynott's lyric calculatedly captures the shady netherworld landscape of his own imagination. It's one of a number of songs heavily inspired by the band's US visit the previous year. It was unlucky to only feature in the band's live set for a very short time, though there are some rousing bootleg versions available online.

Alcock says: "I liked that very much but always... it has sounded 'light' to me compared to the other songs. I would have liked to have mixed that once more." Reid Dick adds, "'Angel From The Coast' I always rather liked, but maybe not as a single. The same with 'Fight Or Fall', another one I really liked, though again not really as a single."

The much maligned "Running Back" follows; with its handclaps and ooh la la las it certainly sounded like a blatant attempt at recording a single. For all its poppy pretensions, its lyric features Lynott at his most poetic and for that reason alone it's difficult to easily dismiss the song. Though Robbo is quick to deride the song as "utter bollocks", perhaps its undemanding arrangement can in some way be attributed to the ire it causes within the guitarist when he is confronted with speaking about the track.

However, Robbo does have an ally. "'Running Back' was suggested as a single by someone at some point," remembers Reid Dick. "I don't recall everyone in the band being overly happy with the way 'Running Back' turned out. It was a bit too soft and didn't have enough balls in it. It was designed as a single with the handclaps. I'm glad really that it never made it out as a single, as I think 'The Boys Are Back In Town' was a much stronger choice."

"Romeo And The Lonely Girl" is up next, the second song on the bounce solely credited to Lynott. It was also another song considered by the record label as a possibility for a single release. Curiously, as the band were finding their musical identity, their record label Phonogram was considering the more experimental efforts, such as "Running Back" and "Romeo And The Lonely Girl", as potential single releases. The song was later covered and released as a single by the late Ernie Graham, who played with Eire Apparent, Help Yourself and Clancy. The song was also featured in the band's live show for a short period, though the arrangement was slowed down significantly and provided an alternative to the one slow song in their live set in "Still In Love With You".

Side 1 closes with the morbidly foreboding "Warriors", a Lynott/Gorham hybrid with its sparse lyric and twin lead guitar. Inspired by the drug related deaths of Jimi Hendrix and Jim Morrison, it isn't slack in its use of Lynott's ever increasing lyrical ambiguity. The "warriors" of the title is an analogy of sorts, for those who had gone to the edge, peeked over and ultimately lost their balance. However, aside from the lyrics and pummelling guitar work, what stands out is Downey's inexorable drumming which drives the song to its bloodied conclusion.

"The Boys Are Back In Town" opens Side 2, and underwent many changes between the time it was rehearsed and recorded at Ramport.

Early working titles included "Kid Is Back" and "GI Joe Is Back" before Lynott eventually revised the story of the song. At one time, the theme was that of a soldier returning from war. That theme was later resurrected, albeit very loosely, on "Soldier Of Fortune", a song on a subsequent album release. Amazingly, the song very nearly didn't make the final cut, as Gorham explains:

> We loved this song but at that time we had doubts whether we would put it on the album or not. I personally thought the lyrics were better than the music. Phil did a great job. Then our manager decided this was a fantastic song and definitely should be on the album; we all consented. (*Classic Tracks* Interview, April 2002)

Though the song found a home on the album, its commercial potential wasn't apparent to some though producer Alcock can recall discussions being held as to which song should be the lead single. "I vividly remember as we were trying to find the single from *Jailbreak*, Downey leaning across the console saying, 'Don't discount "The Boys Are Back..." as a possibility for a single'. In many ways, it was the label who picked the single and then got input from the band."

When asked about the alternative themes being explored for "The Boys Are Back In Town" and its alternative titles in development, Alcock was unaware of any such temporary titles: "Well, Phil had this big book, his lyric book. I have no doubt he had many over the years. When you refer to the song as 'GI Joe Is Back', well that working title doesn't really mean anything to me, but maybe it was how Phil had started off the initial idea before I became involved with recording it.

"Also, with Phil, if he was working on his lyrics while we were in the studio I wouldn't be able to gauge how new or old those lyrics were. He would refer to it if he thought there was something appropriate for whatever song we were working on at that time. For all I knew, some of the things suggested could have been noted down years prior to me working with the band; on the other hand, it could have been done the previous week. All I can say is that I only ever knew the song by its eventual title, 'The Boys Are Back In Town'."

97

With its invitational vibe to become part of the Lizzy gang, albeit from a distance, the song's sentiment is a lyrical reflection on how Lynott viewed his band members, road crew and fans. What the band captured in spirit in this song, the fans felt in spades. It was the connection Thin Lizzy badly needed to make with an audience. Multiple versions exist in the band's archive with alternative lyrics and arrangements, a couple of which have been released on the deluxe re-release in recent years.

"Fight Or Fall" follows the band's breakthrough song, and couldn't be further from it in terms of commercial leaning. Lynott had visited the subject of race, colour and creed on previous albums and this rather subdued affair sits well in his stable of songs that address the issue. It also served to moderate the tempo of the album, allowing the band to take their foot off the gas before the next assault.

One of the first tracks written for the album was "The Cowboy Song", a Lynott/Downey hangover distilled from the band's American tour experience the previous year supporting Bachman-Turner Overdrive. The band had been playing it live occasionally, testing its impact as a work in progress and, as late as November 1975, it was referred to in title as "Derby Blues". Gorham says:

> We had just ended the US Tour and everyone had fallen in love with Texas, especially Phil, who went berserk in Dallas and Houston. When the tour ended we went straight to the recording studio and Phil wrote "Cowboy Song". (*Classic Tracks* Interview, April 2002).

"Cowboy Song" was another song that helped Lizzy's public identity. Robbo reflects: "'The Boys Are Back In Town', 'Jailbreak' and 'Cowboy Song' were three songs that should have been singles in the UK, maybe in that sequence. I think they were strong enough songs, instead of putting 'Jailbreak' on a B-side like happened in the States. We should have put demos or outtakes on the B-side, throwaway tracks. Strong songs on a B-side was stupid."

The album closes with the only composition credited to the whole band, "Emerald". After Lynott's lyrical lust for Americanisms was satiated with "Cowboy Song", he returned his focus to Irish history for the album's climax. Again, like "Warriors", its focus was on the musicianship while the lyrical content was streamlined to allow for this. Gorham says:

> Phil was proud to be Irish and especially proud to be able to write Irish songs, but he did it in his own way. He wrote with vengeance about certain Irish issues; "Emerald" is a perfect example. (*Classic Tracks Interview*, April 2002)

Lynott later confessed to *NME* journalist Harry Doherty on the inspiration for "Emerald":

> I used to share a flat with an African fella from Lagos and he used to play African sounds all the time. What really freaked me out was that I had all me Irish albums, me Sean O'Riadas and that; the one connection between the Celts and the African man was the tempo – 6/8.

While the band gigged across the UK, their dates for the US leg of the *Jailbreak* tour were being confirmed. *Jailbreak* was released on 26 March 1976 and made positive strides up the UK charts, peaking at No. 10, without any assistance from a single being released. The band alternated between top billing and supporting in the States, and had worked out their set list to accommodate the changes as the tour progressed. Though no single was issued prior to or during the UK leg of the tour, one song was gaining traction in the States on FM radio: "The Boys Are Back In Town".

With Lizzy on a US tour, the timing couldn't have been better. The knock on effect from the exposure of the live gigs cemented the song in American consciousness and the band found themselves with a song that just stalled short of the *Billboard* Top 10, peaking at No. 12. Shortly after, the song was released in the UK and succeeded in breaking into the Top 10, though going no higher than No. 8. It was, though, more than just a significant turnaround in the group's fortunes, financially and creatively speaking – it was the breakthrough they needed to ensure their survival. Ultimately, the album stayed in the UK charts for two weeks shy of a full year. For a band that had very limited commercial success up to that point, it was certainly a remarkable achievement.

Thin Lizzy's luck, or lack of, has been well documented over the years. There was to be no luck of the Irish when the band were just about to start the final leg of the American tour with Rainbow. Feeling unwell over a number of days, Lynott was diagnosed with hepatitis. He was quickly flown back to England to recuperate while the remainder of the band lamented the loss of momentum. It was a savage blow at a particularly crucial time. Without the necessary promotional tour to push the album it never quite hit the heights it might have if the band had managed to complete the dates.

The curtailed tour wasn't without its entertainment value though. "REO Speedwagon: Jesus, they were so shit they were thrown off the tour," laughs Robbo. "We were also playing with Rush at the time who were a great bunch of guys. We were down the bill on that one and REO Speedwagon were second. The gigs were massive, some 20 or 30,000, and they were arguing constantly and pissing Rush off no end with their performances, so they threw them off and we were put up to second on the bill: what a great bunch of guys!"

With Lynott *hors de combat* and recovering his strength, a decision was made to get the band back into the studio to record a new album. The cancelled dates from the American tour were rescheduled for the following December but these dates too were to end up on the cutting room floor. Before that, however, the band once more planned to reunite with producer John Alcock and engineer Will Reid Dick to try to replicate the success attained with *Jailbreak*.

John Alcock, back on board as producer, had his reservations: "Clearly, Lizzy should have lived on the road for a year after *Jailbreak*, and only returned to the studio when they had a substantial pool of material; had a chance to evolve and endured more rehearsals. But this was the 1970s when bands typically released LPs much more frequently than now. Who was at fault is difficult to say. I wasn't involved in any meetings with the label and I have no way of knowing what financial or contractual influences were in play."

Robbo too was sceptical about going back to the studio so soon: "It seemed such a short time had elapsed then we had to get started on the *Johnny The Fox* album. Back then you could end up with two albums coming out in a year. Some bands take two years to do half an album these days. We were doing a lot of work each year and touring it. We just started getting very used to getting into the studio and going out on the road and repeating that cycle. It was mapped out as we were doing it, that's just the way it was then".

As *Jailbreak* continued to solidly shift the units, particularly in the UK, Lynott was laid up recovering from hepatitis – the markings on his face a result of the illness. It wasn't all doom and gloom, however, as the band had gained two hit singles from the album in the UK and set themselves up in a strong position for negotiating a contract extension with Phonogram.

Jailbreak as an album was rounded out by artist Jim Fitzpatrick's artwork contribution – arguably his most famous and recognisable piece of work for the band. The album was Lizzy's closest shave to that very 1970s beast – the concept album, though there was never any mention of this for the duration of recording. The spirit captured on the songs recorded certainly lent themselves to the concept of breaking free from a controlled society and/or breaking through to the mainstream. Tapping into some loosely inspired ideas from Orwell's *1984* certainly assisted in presenting a readily identifiable image to the public, "breakout" being the operative word.

Fitzpatrick assisted Lynott on the concept: "We were both very influenced by HG Wells' *The War Of The Worlds* and American Marvel comics. Philip wanted something that reflected these influences, and together we worked on the imaginary story of 'The Warrior' that Philip had in his mind, and I reworked the roughs to reflect this idea until it all held together".

On the back-story of "The Warrior", Fitzpatrick continues: "If you read the sleeve notes on 'The Warrior', I felt they were a bit clunky so I re-wrote them, but Philip didn't use my re-write. Sometimes when Philip wrote prose they could be very clunky but they just needed fixing, like an editor would do."

101

The band, by and large, left Lynott to his own devices when it came to coming up with an idea for the sleeve art, and with his ever increasing position of power he retained Jim Fitzpatrick as often as possible for the work involved. Gorham, Downey and Robbo all played second fiddle to Lynott in these matters as the latter confirms, "Phil was the one with all of the contact sheets."

8

JOHNNY THE FOX

Apart from the seriousness of the illness, one of the main problems with hepatitis – for someone who likes the odd drink and drug – is the patient has to lay off the sauce and recreational substances. Manfully, Lynott managed the former (to a certain extent), but was damned if he wasn't going to smoke weed.

A side benefit though, with touring being out of the question, was that Lynott had time on his hands to work out a few new song ideas. He was informed that recording sessions were planned with the old Ramport team of Alcock and Reid Dick (though Neil Hornby wasn't involved this time around).

At the rehearsals for the album that was to become *Johnny The Fox*, alarm bells began to ring almost immediately for Alcock, due to the paucity of the material. Although Lynott had come up with song fragments whilst recuperating, there wasn't enough studio time to develop the material as they had done in demo studios for the *Jailbreak* album. "In the mid-'70s it was common for LPs to be released by an artist annually, if not more frequently," reflects Alcock. "The band was rushed in to *Johnny The Fox* because *Jailbreak* broke Thin Lizzy, so because of the greed of the record company and management, eager to recoup their losses and pull in revenue, the creative wishes and nurturing of artist talent took second place to making money.

"Artists like Elton John were churning out album after album, but Elton and Bernie [Taupin] apparently could write amazing material at the drop of a hat. Lizzy couldn't, so it was a struggle. Nowadays artists put out an album every two or three years. Had that been the norm back then, Lizzy would have had a run of three or four great records, simply because Phil would have had the time to write them. And the producer, including me, would have had the luxury of being able to pick the best contenders, as opposed to frantically finding something that would fill up a few minutes on a record, like the awful "Boogie Woogie Dance."

On the plus side, the purse strings were loosened considerably by Phonogram for the follow-up to *Jailbreak* given its commercial success. The budget was in the region of £35-40,000 and this is also taking into account the abortive experience that the band and crew were to experience at Musicland Studios in Germany.

Plans were in place to record their first album outside the UK. The band and crew flew out to Munich on a 10:30 a.m. flight on 2 August 1976, enjoying a few drinks and playing cards during the journey. Lizzy recorded over three days at Musicland Studios in Munich before deciding it wasn't working out as envisaged.

Recording outside of England was a then common way to sidestep the tax burden on high earners, but it wasn't to be as Will Reid Dick, who flew out with the band just a few days earlier, recalls: "I can't honestly remember any of the work we did in Munich and I don't have any tapes of the work done there either. We were only there for two or three days before we realised it wasn't working very well. But we did record some things because I do remember doing some editing, or attempting to, on the 24-tracks. We must have recorded some stuff."

Reid Dick didn't bring any tapes back that he can recall, nor has he any recollection of listening back to the material once they left Munich, as he continues to recollect: "The annoying thing is I had a lot of cassettes of this kind of work, run-throughs and other studio bits that I used to keep in my car over the years; I've had about four cars stolen around this time, and a lot of these tapes disappeared along with the cars. I had some pretty bad luck with cars".

Reid Dick wasn't happy with the studio; the band struggled to get the sounds they wanted, while Alcock wasn't overly impressed by the mixing desk or monitors, but ultimately he was nervous about where the direction of the record was headed. It's a view substantiated when the band's tape store reveals they didn't have a full album ready to go and thus were going to have to write to order in the studio when the time came.

Enquiries were made as to the availability of Ramport Studio, and the band were lucky to be able to secure a four week block to make the new album and still be within the original schedule and budget allotted. The band took an afternoon flight back to England on 6 August and started fresh on sessions in south London on the 9th. Neither Alcock or Reid Dick can recall which tracks received any degree of work at Musicland Studios, but viewing the band's recording log suggests that at least three backing tracks were attempted while there: "Fool's Gold", "Sweet Marie" and "Borderline".

Alcock does recall transferring the recordings made in Munich upon their return to Ramport but they were in such poor condition that the band decided to start from scratch. The oxide was literally falling off the 2" tape brought back from Munich, thus reducing the high frequency responses each time the tape was played, "It turned out it was a particularly bad batch of BASF tape," recalls Alcock. "That particular nightmare will stay with me to the grave."

Given the successful sound obtained on *Jailbreak*, with one keen eye on the American market, the band were keen to explore this further on the new album. The trailing problem was that they didn't really have the material in place to focus a genuine attempt at making an album aimed squarely towards succeeding in the competitive American market. Without sufficient time to rehearse and develop the new material, with Alcock making suggestions as was done on *Jailbreak*, the band faced an uphill climb to a summit they could never conquer. Though the budget allowed for the recording of the new album was more generous than *Jailbreak*, the band simply didn't have the time to be able to record the type of album that could follow up the cohesion so apparent on that record. This was evident on some of the early attempts at recording the new material.

A wide range of working titles were used as the band listened to various jam sessions and extracted the best ideas to develop. "Funky Job", begun earlier in the year during rehearsals for *Jailbreak*, was fully realised as the track "Johnny The Fox Meets Jimmy The Weed". Another song called "Give It Up", an instrumental based around a Scott Gorham riff, was worked on but discarded with no further work done after 17 August. It's also logged in the band's archive as "Biryani Tango". A jam session given the working title of "Weasel Rhapsody" yielded two songs for the band. Having sifted through what worked well, "Weasel Rhapsody" was deconstructed and provided the band with "Son Of Warrior" and "Johnny".

"Son Of Warrior" was itself a working title and received sufficient development through the second burst of sessions between 16 and 21 August. The song eventually morphed into "Requiem For A Puffer" before the band eventually tidied it up and settled on the final title of "Rocky". On another of the band's rehearsal tapes, a jam lasting just over five minutes reveals another early version of "Rocky", a soon-to-be discarded piece, before the band settled into the bass groove of what later became "Dancing In The Moonlight", though neither Alcock or Reid Dick recall that song being presented for development prior to or during sessions for *Johnny The Fox*.

As it stands, during the summer of 1976, the song is without lyrics and is little more than an idea toyed with in rehearsals. When informed of its existence, Alcock was rather surprised. "I can't imagine that 'Dancing In The Moonlight' was in existence at that time in even an embryonic form, simply because we were very short of material and had that song been around it would have been grabbed at once to substitute for some of the crap that made it onto *Johnny The Fox*." It's very possible that Alcock was never made aware of its existence during rehearsals and, as previously mentioned, all that really exists on the recording is Lynott's bass riff.

Another of the ideas Lynott outlined from his hospital bed was a song he temporarily titled "Little Big Horn". Once the song was brought into the studio and developed under Alcock's guidance it eventually became "Massacre". In total, the band recorded their new album at Ramport from 9 August to 10 September; a remarkably short space of time, particularly given they lost a week in Munich.

It was clearly evident that the band's canon, having been sufficiently depleted by the songs recorded for *Jailbreak*, was not in a healthy enough position for the boys to begin recording. On *Jailbreak*, decisions were made fairly quickly on which songs were definite, probable or unlikely to make the cut.

"As for *Johnny The Fox*, there really wasn't enough material, so this part of the decision making process was easier in so far as there was very little to choose from," says Alcock. "After the choices were made, we went through all the songs to talk about structure and a 'map' of how each of these would be recorded. I made notes on each song, so I could plan what each song would need, although this often changed in the studio. When it came to actually recording, it would start with all four members and we'd concentrate on getting the right backing track down. We'd make the decision on what was a good take and stick with it. Rarely, we went back and rerecorded a backing track if we discovered something wrong with what was thought to be a 'keeper'. Maybe a guitar part was out of tune or we decided to insert an extra section because we had an idea after listening to it. 'Warriors' would be a good example of this; we put in a section for the whole choir part later."

With the twin guitar sound now identified as the band's strength and a key part of their musical identity with the record buying public, the template established with *Jailbreak* was once more adhered to. Stylistically opposites, both Robertson and Gorham recorded their work in very different ways. Engineer Reid Dick comments on the challenges faced with recording them: "We did do a lot of doubling up of guitars and vocals, so by the time you've got double rhythm guitars plus a third rhythm normally, I think we had three rhythm tracks going on with Lizzy, then you'd have the lead, and certainly Scott's leads were often doubled. Once we'd done that with Scott, we liked the sound of it. I think it was John [Alcock] probably, who suggested it was doubled. Once we heard it we thought it was a pretty good sound.

"It could only really work with Scott because he worked his solos out, you know, like once he knew where his solo was in the song then he'd take a cassette away and go away to work out the solo. Whereas with Robbo he'd just have a few drinks and whack it out and whatever came out, came out. So with Scott it was fairly easy to say: 'As you know exactly what you're going to be playing every time, can you double it?' Certainly on a number of them we'd have two tracks of his rhythm guitar; whether we actually used them all the time I'm not sure, but we certainly did it on some of them. So there would be at least two tracks of lead, then you've got all the backing vocal bits. Phil was quite keen on his backing vocals so there was a fair bit of those. So, you could fill up the tracks fairly easily if you wanted to keep everything separate. When 24-tracks came in, it was nice to have those extra tracks as you didn't feel you had to start sticking random bits of vocals on guitar tracks or whatever."

By the time Lizzy recorded at Ramport it was a 24-track recording studio, having been upgraded from 16-track sometime in 1974. Though it was an added luxury to have the extra eight tracks, it was also something that engineers are wary of. Having a whole bunch of tracks open without anything happening on them risked extra noise and hiss. Again Reid Dick: "If I'm mixing, I've only got two hands. 24-track is quite a lot of stuff to be doing at one time, so probably Phil was also doing stuff at the desk during mixing. I certainly remember him moving faders during the mix. John wasn't overly keen on that but would do it if necessary. Phil quite liked it so he'd be quite happy to move faders around."

Jim Fitzpatrick was again recruited to provide the sleeve artwork, once more based around a concept devised by Lynott. A lot of their communication was done over the phone, particularly when things were heating up during recording sessions. Once Lynott had conveyed his idea it was left to Fitzpatrick to interpret as best he could. It was the same with the band, if Lynott arrived into rehearsals with an embryonic idea he would convey what he felt the song needed to his bandmates. "I'm not quite sure if we ever interpreted some of the ideas that Phil brought in as well as he heard them inside; sometimes it was hard to identify how he wanted to develop songs, not all of the time but it happened," remembers Downey.

Once Fitzpatrick had identified as much as he possibly could with a commission over the phone, he would begin work on the first draft of roughs where the initial concepts come together, before developing the idea further. On many occasions, Fitzpatrick found himself running down to a local photocopying shop in Dundrum, a suburb of Dublin, making the copies and getting them in the post or faxing them before waiting on feedback on additional ideas he had while the cover art progressed.

"The original idea for *Johnny The Fox* was a completely different cover," remembers Fitzpatrick. "Within the Celtic border I had drawn, I had come up with a *War Of The Worlds* type scenario involving a warrior, but Philip was really stuck on the border and just told me to draw the border. It was a neo-Celtic border and he didn't want anything, no picture inside it at all. I left a section in the centre blank where I thought they might put a band photo in.

"A little later, Chris O'Donnell sent me a photo of a stuffed fox head, especially arranged for me to draw. I did the work but they didn't like it and thought it was as scary as shit. Again, this left the empty space until late on when Philip, who had only recently settled on the album title, asked me to include the fox. It had to have the feel of the outsider looking in; it had to have that feel and it did. Philip was always an outsider and he identified with all of that."

The new album began with the solely Lynott-credited "Johnny", an assured and positive opener for those so fanatical about the *Jailbreak* record and how it sounded. As previously mentioned, this was plucked and developed from a conjoined idea the band initially titled "Weasel Rhapsody". Buried in the mix is Fiachra Trench's contribution to the song. In the band's archive a different version of the song exists with Trench's brass contribution highly audible in all its glory.

Upon hearing the mix where the brass is prominently featured, Reid Dick commented: "It must have been Fiachra, it brought it all back to me. It reminded me that The Who used brass quite a bit on their songs. Someone must have decided not to have featured the brass section high in the mix. I think we decided in the end that the horns used on 'Johnny' were to be used, but not to make them too prominent. I think there's an element of fear on using brass and strings for a band like Thin Lizzy. Phil must have decided it was a good idea or else it wouldn't have got through. Adding something like strings may not have gone down that well with everybody, I can't remember exactly but I can imagine that not all parties may have been happy. I also think that John may have made these suggestions. Fiachra, John and Phil would have worked out where the addition of strings or brass were best suited."

Though Lizzy had worked with Trench previously on the *Vagabonds Of The Western World* album, he had yet to contribute to the four-piece

Lizzy. "I knew Scott before he joined Lizzy," remembers Trench. "His brother-in-law was Bob Siebenberg from Supertramp. Before Supertramp, Bob was in Bees Make Honey at the time of pub rock. That was a great band. Scott was already in London and he used to sit in with Bees Make Honey at their gigs in The Tally Ho in Kentish Town, which incidentally is where I met my now wife."

"Rocky" follows, a number credited to all except Robertson. It's further testament to the band's unflinching commitment to taking the best elements from the *Jailbreak* album and evolving the established guitar sound. It's a playful paean lyrically as they disentangle the inspiration of its origins. All is laid bare about whom Lynott has in mind when he reveals the adventures of "Cocky Rocky".

"When I heard the lyrics I sort of went... mmh hmm... I think I know who this is about, but he never said anything and I didn't ask," says Robbo. "Later on we were sitting down drinking whiskey and we were chatting, messing about really and he says, 'Cocky Rocky, shut the fuck up'... and I said, 'So you did write that song about me'. I kinda always knew he wrote it about me but he never really admitted it until that point. It was a nice thing, a kind of brotherly thing in a way. It wasn't like a slag off and I didn't take it that way. I actually took it as a compliment."

Robbo's first credit on the album swings into view with the broken down balladic "Borderline". When the song was initially worked on it was preliminarily titled "Borderline Case" and featured slightly different lyrics. The song was a direct call-out to Robbo's then girlfriend, Jeanette "Jeannie" Melbourne. Lynott later amended some of the lyrics and earned a co-writing credit in the process.

Melbourne had first met the band while working at Harlequin Records on the King's Road in Chelsea, as she recalls: "Actually, I knew Phil before I got to know Brian. A friend of mine knew one of the Lizzy roadies, I think his name was Tony. He then went on to introduce me to Tex [Read]. One evening Tex invited me over to the flat he shared with Phil. Phil and I clicked straight away and became good friends. I spent a lot of time at the flat as Phil was recovering from hepatitis. I remember making him drinks of fresh orange juice with added glucose. We used to go shopping together in Kensington

High Street for stage clothes. In fact, looking back we used to spend a lot of time shopping.

"I first started dating Brian after a gig in Guildford, Surrey, which is my hometown. I was visiting my family that day and dropped in to see the band backstage. Brian and I headed back to London and went to the Speakeasy which was one of our favourite haunts and was always full of people from the music industry."

Jeannie describes the back-story to the "Borderline" song after she received a phone call from Lynott to discuss it, prior to recording sessions at Ramport: "Phil asked me to come round to his new flat that he had in West Hampstead. When I arrived, he put some paper on the table that had Brian's lyrics written on them and asked me how I felt about them. He made some tea while I read the lyrics and, from our conversation, I knew he had reservations about the words. Phil had a very different way of mentioning people in his songs or lyrics and what Brian had written he was struggling with; struggling may not be the right word, it's just that Phil did that kind of thing differently.

"He told me about a girlfriend of his called Gale and he mentioned a song he had written for her called 'Look What The Wind Blew In'. So, we talked about the song he had written for Gale and how he normally approached songs like this. He just had a very different way of doing these things and he was trying hard to get it right. I think he was surprised at what Brian had written and wasn't entirely sure what might be the best way to approach it. Though I don't remember specific words that I read that day, they were an outpouring of Brian's feelings. I don't think I heard the song before it came out on the album. I felt quite sad when I first heard it and I felt very sorry that I hurt someone in that way and made someone feel like that. I was also very young at the time, we all were.

"I was heading toward a bad place in my life back then, and relationships weren't at the forefront of my mind. I wasn't showing the commitment needed and the relationship just faded out. As I said earlier, my life was going to a bad place. I continued on this road for a while until I decided to move away from London and fix myself. Phil really helped me a lot during my last year in London. I still feel he was my inspiration to clean up my life and I often wish he was around now to see I did it in the end."

"Don't Believe A Word" is up next and, while clocking in at a little over two minutes in length, remains one of Lizzy's most recognisable tunes. Like "Running Back" on the *Jailbreak* album it was also one of the more divisive numbers that emerged around this time. When Lynott initially brought in the idea it had a distinct slow blues feel. Both Robertson and Downey rejected the initial arrangement proposed by Lynott and reworked it when he left the studio aggrieved at their critical feedback.

A little known fact is that Robbo played the song using a Stratocaster. He recalls how it led to being used instead of his beloved Les Paul: "Big Charlie [MacLennan} broke my guitar! He never admitted it but I remember I walked in to tune up and the head came off. He just said, 'It wasn't me' and I said, 'Well who the fuck else was it?' So, I didn't have a Les Paul. Thinking back, I think it was during the recording of *Johnny The Fox* he broke it, which is the reason the solo on 'Don't Believe A Word' was played using a hired Stratocaster. Because I wanted a Les Paul, The Who's roadies phoned Pete [Townshend] up and asked if they could borrow some guitars for me. He had something like a three tonne truck full of guitars, so I took them all out and there was actually broken Les Pauls all over the place, bits and pieces everywhere. On the ones that were fine the strings were like telegraph cable so I ended up using the Strat until we got my Les Paul fixed. It was recently stolen in Sweden and it's the guitar I had since I started with Lizzy – not good."

On hearing that Robbo used a Stratocaster, engineer Will Reid Dick was taken aback: "I'm very surprised at that, 'cos I know for a fact that John Alcock didn't like Strats. Another band we worked with afterwards were using Strats and John used to refer to the Strat as 'a nasty sounding stick'.

"There's a bit on 'Don't Believe A Word' – I was actually listening to it the other day – which annoys me intensely, which is Robbo's bit of voice box guitar. You can only just about hear it 'cos Phil didn't want it up too loud. There's a sort of space particularly right at the end, after the vocals are finished and there's the riff and it goes around maybe four times or something. It would have filled that space beautifully. He played it throughout the song I think, or played it at various parts of the song and I think little things like that could have made it that much better a song. It was annoying and it always annoys me to this day, and every time I hear it.

"Fool's Gold" closes Side 1 in confident fashion, and features a memorable emerald-tinged riff. The spoken introduction by Lynott, in full Irish verbal regalia, is an added bonus, and incidentally led to Lynott's participation on Jeff Wayne's *War Of The Worlds* album. Using his own accent in song was something Lynott had tried on the *Nightlife* album, specifically on the track "Philomena". He later confessed to Harry Doherty in an *NME* interview that producer Ron Nevison "Had no inkling of what I was tryin' to do", which resulted in the song "sounding really empty".

Alcock had his reservations about the song. As it was developed from the initial demo, verses were rearranged to ensure the storytelling flowed smoothly and the story made sense. The final verse is a lyrical highlight of the entire album. On the demo, the spoken introduction is absent and Lynott is clawing around trying to find the right sequence for the lyrics.

"Phil had problems with the lyrics to this song; more the finer details, as the vocals evolved in the way he was again and again trying to come up with something different to what had gone before," says Alcock. "Each time I hear the song there are a couple of lines that stand out which I know I wasn't overly happy with, and I know that Phil wasn't entirely sure about either. In the end, he just couldn't come up with anything that he felt was better and so ran with them. Also, I have to emphasise, he was pleased with the final vocal – but I just felt a bit uncomfortable, mainly to do with the phrasing."

The album begins to unravel on Side 2 as soon as the needle hit the vinyl. "Johnny The Fox Meets Jimmy The Weed" kicks in, pushing the album towards uncharted waters. Credited to Gorham, Downey and Lynott, it's a brave and uncharacteristic venture for the band. Churning out the same stylised songs wasn't quite where the band was headed, and likely climaxed during the classic years with the release of "Dancing In The Moonlight" the following year. Had there been enough time to develop some of the band's ideas it's quite possible that "Dancing In The Moonlight" might have made an appearance on the *Johnny The Fox* album.

"Johnny The Fox Meets Jimmy The Weed", though a lyrical and musical triumph of sorts, is also a worrying indicator. It showed the band couldn't be contained in their striving for evolution, but also highlighted a disparity in the collective sound of the band. It's so wildly off course with what had been established on the *Jailbreak* album that its oddity value soars, and perhaps did more damage than good as it failed to build on the previous formula established by the band.

The Lynott-penned "Old Flame" follows the funky side-opener, and is again so far removed from the expectations set by the previous Lizzy album that it disrupts rather than contributes. The band had already thrown in the left of field "Johnny The Fox Meets Jimmy The Weed" as a sidestep for the listener, and "Old Flame" is a misstep of sorts. It vaguely recalls the adventures of Randolph, he of "Randolph's Tango" fame from the Decca years of Lizzy but in more advanced years; sat on the porch instead of the range, raindrops representing individual memories as he reminisces about the dying embers of failed relationships. As nobody specific is mentioned in the lyric it's open to interpretation as to who Lynott is singing to, or given his reputation, the many he may be singing to.

The band soon come back to familiar ground on "Massacre". Lynott's initial inspiration for the song was drawn from television footage he witnessed while convalescing in Manchester following his hepatitis, which showed scenes of war-torn zones in the world. With the overstated Americanisms evident across the lyrics on the album, most notably on the "Johnny the Fox Meets Jimmy The Weed" track, he considered one event in America's history, the Battle of the Little Big Horn, where Custer fell.

He developed the idea of bloodied battles, and later augmented this with an experience he had of a protestant clergyman who visited his bedside. Lynott himself was Catholic and he later admitted to slightly dismissing the clergyman's enquiries. Questioning God's existence given the moral failings in the world, Lynott's spiritual nature was beginning to surface in his musical output. A highlight on the song is Downey's anarchic drumming and Lynott's relentless grooving on the bass.

Lynott later admitted to Chris Salewicz in an interview with the *New Musical Express* on how contracting hepatitis affected his outlook:

114

It does hit you after a while that the night life is maybe a bit of a wild life. You're chasing the wrong things. That was the idea behind "Fool's Gold". I wouldn't have written either that or "Massacre" without having been ill. (10 Sept 1977, *NME*)

Gorham's "Sweet Marie" follows the triumphant and telling message of "Massacre" but again falls short. An ode to his then girlfriend, its laid-back coolness and even dreamy feel isn't quite enough to get it over the line. Side 2 of the album hiccups along at a sedate pace, much too sedate for the expected rough and tumble of a *Jailbreak* sequel. It's admirable to see and hear a band take the chances so apparent on this album and also interesting to note that never again were so many chances taken on any album that followed.

Of course, it all falls down to not really having the right kind of material written by the time the recording sessions started. If more time had been allowed for the band to develop and write new material, it's a certainty that at least a third of this album would feature different songs.

"I liked 'Borderline'; different, but it still fitted. 'Sweet Marie' and 'Old Flame', less so," states Alcock. "I personally would have preferred Lizzy to stick with their tougher side, with occasional forays into more hooky songs like 'The Boys Are Back In Town' and 'Don't Believe A Word'. But some of the songs (on *Johnny The Fox*) I'm less fond of is more to do with Phil's poetic, softer side, which looking back might have been better suited to his solo records."

It is apt that "Sweet Marie" found a home on a Lizzy album, as the lyrical content reflected Scott Gorham's personal life. So many of the lyrics in the band were handled by Lynott, looking at the world from his points of view, that it was a relief of sorts to allow other members' emotions to be allowed to be brought to the boil. Robbo had his confessional on "Borderline", Lynott likewise on "Old Flame" and then Gorham on "Sweet Marie". The telling sign here is a group of emotionally fragile people and, in such a pressurised environment as a recording studio, gaskets being blown were only a misinterpreted glance away.

The friction throughout recording between Robbo and Lynott in particular was a worrying sign. Robbo's personal life was in disarray, which he allowed to flow over into his professional life as the recording progressed. In such a highly charged environment it was ultimately left to Alcock to try to diffuse any tense moments that could have brought the sessions to a halt.

"John was very good at making everyone feel at ease; that was one of his strong points I think, and he could give everyone an air of confidence," states Reid Dick. "John was quite a jovial character and he never made you feel like there was any pressure because he'd be quite happy to talk about something else other than recording."

The dynamic in the band's relationship certainly changed as the recording of *Johnny The Fox* progressed, as all were probably mindful of the fact that the material wasn't representative of a band at their peak – though in all fairness there are highlights on the album that easily match some of their best work.

Alcock is keen to put the *contretemps* between band members in perspective between the production of both *Jailbreak* and *Johnny The Fox*: "On *Jailbreak* there was clashing, but certainly not that bad; in fact no worse than any other band I've worked with, and there is always going to be clashing. See it like this: if a band is good at what they do, have separate personalities and ideas, then creative differences invariably come into play. That kind of clashing can be good. People find compromise, and subsequently the end result becomes better.

"But then clashing can be taken to another level – that's when it gets dangerous, destructive, and when things don't end up getting done. On *Johnny The Fox*, hours and hours would go by if you added them up: Robbo would tune his guitar and play something, and Phil would be in the control room and say 'go back – you're out of tune'. Robbo would adjust his strings and play it again, again Phil would say: 'I can hear it and it's not in tune'. Robbo would take another slug from the bottle and play it back again and Phil would say the same thing again.

"Now, half of the time I couldn't make out what Phil was talking about, but he was the leader, I can't say, 'Phil, you're deaf!' If I do, the argument gets worse. This kind of thing happened a lot on *Johnny The Fox*. Now, if you really wanted to get down into the psychology of it, this type of interaction represented the disintegration of their relationship, and had little or nothing whatsoever to do with tuning a guitar."

The album closed on the bewildering inclusion of "Boogie Woogie Dance". If the band had sufficient material then this track would without doubt have taken pride of place on the outtakes reel. It's certainly Lynott at his laziest lyrically, but then, given the music, it's hard to suppose what alternatives he could have turned out. The band could easily have resurrected "Blues Boy" or "Brian's Song" to try to fill the hole, but given that Side 2 was awash with ballads it's conceivable they wanted the album to play out on an uptempo number.

It had its fans, as Will Reid Dick recalls: "Big Charlie [MacLennan] loved 'Boogie Woogie Dance'. Towards the end of the day after having a couple of beers down the pub and if anyone came down to the studio he had to play them 'Boogie Woogie Dance', very loud. Charlie was a character on his own, he was a lovely guy, really liked him. He was like a big brother, or even a younger brother, to Phil in a way. I've heard the story of how they met and it is slightly bizarre. I think they met at a Lizzy gig in Glasgow and he [Charlie] sort of arrived and never left. He kind of presented himself to the band and pretty much carried on from there.

"Charlie was someone that could be relied on, he had that air of 'I have everything under control' even if he didn't know what the fuck he was doing. He was one of those kind of characters, he sort of breezed along as if everything was fine, and I can't even remember exactly what his job was. I got along with him very well and we struck up a good understanding, and I saw him a fair bit outside of Lizzy as well."

The new Lizzy album was titled *Johnny The Fox* and released on 16 October 1976, just seven months after *Jailbreak*. It peaked at No. 11 on the British chart listings and, just as importantly, the band had their third consecutive hit when "Don't Believe A Word" made No. 12 on the singles charts. Alcock muses on the only UK single to be taken from the album: "It was the one song that everyone knew throughout the sessions was ideal for a single. The lyrics always resonate well with me; it's a very simple lyric, not really poetic – the relationship with the girl, the guy messes up, he says he doesn't understand their relationship or why he messed it up but he for some reason wants to still be in the relationship."

The band shot three promotional videos, namely "Rocky", "Johnny The Fox Meets Jimmy The Weed" and "Don't Believe A Word" at the Hammersmith Odeon in London, which was intercut with live footage taken of the band. The latter song was the only UK single issued whilst the others were used for different territories.

The band subsequently undertook a sold out nationwide tour before plans were in place to fly to America to fulfil the dates cancelled earlier in the year due to Phil's hepatitis. They say lightning doesn't strike twice in the same place, but with Lizzy it did when it came to jinxed American tours. The night before the band were to fly to America, Brian Robertson was involved in an incident at the Speakeasy Club in London with his friend Frankie Miller. With a cracked bottle on its way to meeting Miller's skull due to some argy-bargy in the Speakeasy, Robertson held out his hand to shield him and felt the blunt force of the cracked bottle slice through the tendons in his hand.

Unable to play guitar, the tour had to be cancelled, but all was not lost. The band attended the launch of Queen's new album *A Day At The Races* at London's Advision Studios. Soon after, an informal agreement was reached whereby Lizzy were to be Special Guests for Queen's three-month slog across the States, beginning in January 1977. Gary Moore agreed to participate in place of Robertson, who was to all intents and purposes history, for now. Prior to touring with Queen, the band reviewed recently shot footage taken at Hammersmith on 14 November. Rehearsals and the show on the 14th were filmed for a potential commercial release, though the only footage to date used was short snapshots for the "Rocky" promotional video.

To finish this chapter, Tony Platt comments on the band's appetite for self-destruction around this time: "In terms of the misfortune that befell the band, most of those, you'd have to say, were largely self-inflicted. The drug use really led to the problems that Phil had. Brian's injury was probably more due to him not being capable than, say, a pure accident. I guess they really were a rock 'n' roll band almost in the same way as a band like The Doors, that were right on the edge of everything... the image of Thin Lizzy you know, 'The Boys Are Back In Town'... it's an outlaw image, let's face it. I think the whole thing went together. I think it's entirely possible the band could have been quite massive rather than just really, really big."

9
BAD REPUTATION

Once the band returned from their American tour courtesy of Mr Mercury and company, they enjoyed a short break before much of April was spent developing some of the new material in rehearsals. Prior to their US visit, Lizzy's management team of Chris O'Donnell and Chris Morrison had approached producer Tony Visconti about the idea of working with the band on their next project. Visconti had met Lynott a year or so earlier where they casually discussed the possibility of working together, though nothing more came of it at the time. A major hook for Lynott was Visconti's association with Bowie and T-Rex.

A further meeting took place at Visconti's home where Gorham and Lynott showed up inebriated. Charming and drunk, the pair convinced the producer they could make a great team. Having been impressed by the "The Boys Are Back In Town", Visconti was sold on the idea, and plans were put in place to try again at recording abroad for the tax incentives it created. However, a repeat of the Munich sessions was not on the cards. Of the experience on *Bad Reputation*, Gorham comments "Tony Visconti was great. It was just the three of us that did it. Brian was just fired by the time it came to recording and the rest of us wrote the material, arranged it and played it".

New material was coming together in rehearsals quite well, songs such as "Southbound", "Dancing In The Moonlight" and "Opium Trail" being more complete than other fragments the band had. Robbo was still out of the picture when the band were rehearsing, though he had recovered from his hand injury. Negotiations were on ongoing as to whether or not he would be participating on the new recording sessions. Lynott confided to *Sounds* writer Pete Makowski on how much of the album was in shape prior to the commencement of recording:

About half of it. We had all the arrangements worked out but I hadn't got all of the lyrics. (*Sounds*, 27 Aug 1977)

By early May, Gorham, Lynott and Downey arrived in Toronto, specifically to record at a facility made famous by Rush; Toronto Sound Studios. Gorham, a reluctant lead guitarist at the best of times, was unsure if he could pull off recording both rhythm and lead parts for the album. A few weeks into the process it was at his urging that Lynott relented and allowed the door open for Robbo to come back into the fold. Prior to Robbo flying out to Toronto, Visconti was quick to note that "Band morale was low" while the first week of sessions were unproductive, as recreational pursuits made all too frequent appearances during their attempts to get the backing tracks down.

Though Lizzy had a reputation as a wild bunch, their use of drugs was generally limited to coke and smoke, washed down with copious quantities of alcohol. It seldom really interfered with their studio life up until the recording of *Bad Reputation*. Now they had bigger budgets for making their albums. They were generating large amounts of money for their record label and with that combination came a more lax approach to work in the studio.

John Alcock, who began to spend more time working in America after *Johnny The Fox*, comments: "Phil struck me as a man who knew perfectly well what was going on around him, but sometimes he chose a path that was easier to deal with rather than make changes he knew had to be made if he was to become hugely successful."

Thin Lizzy were also a band of their time, and pursuing highs through those untaxed drugs was a pursuit that differed little from their heroes and contemporaries. They not only pushed the envelope, they opened it and emptied it of its contents. However, their drug *de jour* tended to be in the form of downers, such as the perennial favourite Quaaludes.

Such was their hunger for recreational pursuit, Visconti was forced into the position of calling a halt to sessions after the first week, demanding the band's management address the drugs issue before the recording reconvened. Phone calls were placed by O'Donnell and Morrison, and the band were reasoned with before the second burst of sessions commenced.

The album was recorded at two different studios in Toronto. The main bulk of work was done at Toronto Sound, while a lot of the vocals and overdubs were done at Sound Interchange. Visconti was assisted by engineer Ken Morris and Jon Bojic at Toronto Sound while Ed Stone assisted at Sound Interchange.

Morris recalls his introduction to the Lizzies: "The band was on the studio floor setting up, and a staff member went on the talkback and announced 'We have a young lad, Ken, from Dublin working here in the control room, boys'. 'Oh really' replied Phil, 'Where did you go to school, Ken?' I went on the mike and said 'Mountjoy School on the Malahide Road in Clontarf'. Without missing a beat Phil immediately responded 'Pack up the gear lads, there's a fucking Protestant in the control room'. I still laugh about that to this day."

Morris was a musician himself, playing the Dublin scene in the late 1960s before emigrating to Canada in 1970 to play the Southern Ontario club circuit, and only began in Toronto Sound as a tape operator six months before *Bad Reputation* was started.

"Lizzy had sent an advance party to check out Toronto Sound and discovered that it closely resembled a studio they were fond of in England," says Morris. "Robbo was not there for the first few weeks of the sessions. I remember hearing from Brian Downey that he'd hurt himself in a scrap before I met him, so the lion's share of the backing tracks were done without Robbo."

Although some arrangements were worked out prior to starting work at Toronto Sound, there was a slew of jamming sessions reviewed by the band to see what could be filtered and developed further. For example, a riff from an untitled instrumental jam lasting a little over three minutes was burgled and bundled together for the introduction to what became "Dear Lord". The song existed without the choir voices on its own terms as a very lightweight acoustic number to begin with. Featuring an acoustic guitar, Lynott's near whispered vocal and some very subtle rhythm guitar noodling by Gorham, it needed something more if it was going to work. That something more was to arrive in the shape of Visconti's then wife Mary Hopkin. The early lyrics of the song reflected a pleading for friendship rather than the spiritual guidance and redemptive pleading it progressed to.

Another song, with the provisional title of "Rattlesnake Shake", was also worked on, but it too sounds unfinished. Running to a little over three minutes in length, it's a throwaway number in the style of "Baby Drives Me Crazy". Indeed it was probably a contender to replace that song for some live set fun, but it never quite upended it and is probably best left to the archives or a box set release as a curiosity piece.

"Soldier Of Fortune" is the album opener, and signals solid intent by the band. An alternative version exists in the band's archive, with different lyrics and a longer running time. The initial working title of the song was "Ireland" but Lynott was persuaded to change the lyrics by Downey and Gorham who, Lynott confessed, considered the early lyrics corny. Given that he had already attempted to glorify Ireland on previous albums with "Dublin" and "Eire", it was a cute move to give the song a more international flavour to further its appeal.

The change in sound from the previous album is immediate, as the band's use of a real gong and keyboards on the introductory track indicate. The song replaced *Jailbreak* as a live set opener on their next tour but was a short-lived change. It was an audacious album opener with its intricate and well-paced guitar work. Downey's pipe band drumming apprenticeship in his youth was used to great effect.

Lynott later discussed the song in *Sounds*:

> I started writing the song to put down mercenaries, saying how disgusting it was going off and becoming a trained killer, then as I started to write the lyrics I began to realise that everybody has a little bit of mercenary blood in them. Y'know, like sometimes I'm real brutal with chicks, just go after them, get what you want and "see you later". Everything I do and say is to get what I want. (*Sounds*, Pete Makowski, 27 Aug 1977)

The title track follows, with Downey's taut drumming at the forefront. It's also one of John Alcock's favourite tracks in which he didn't participate. The overcast shadow and slightly gloomy nature of the song was present from its precarious demo form to the finished article. The band had put serious time into earning a bad reputation with their rock 'n' roll lifestyle, and celebrated those shenanigans in the song's title.

"Opium Trail" originated with Gorham, though eventually credited to Downey and Lynott as well, as it was developed significantly beyond the riff Gorham created. A close relation of "Warriors" from the *Jailbreak* album in terms of theme, in its demo form the song clocks in at just over three minutes. Multiple versions exist in the band archive, while Lynott's initial lyrics have no relevance to the ominous "Opium Trail" he eventually refers to.

The luxuriant "Southbound" closes Side 1 with its inescapable mid-tempo magic, a counter balance to the intensity of the preceding track. Rumours exist as to the origins of the song beginning with Gary Moore. "To my knowledge, Gary didn't have anything to do with the song," remembers Robbo. "Lynott brought in the 'Southbound' idea, played it on an acoustic guitar and had some lyrics, but the guitar parts were worked out by Scott and me. I think we thought about releasing it as a single because it's going in the right direction; an obvious choice to consider. It wasn't as good in the studio – it worked much better live, a lot better."

In demo form, the keyboard is placed much higher in the mix, due to the absence of Robertson's contribution, but this is a demo after all. The main differences on the demo are the lead guitar solo and the backing vocals which feature other band members. These were later removed allowing for Lynott to continue his enjoyment of singing across all tracks. The one mainstay from demo to finished article is the existence of the chorus, which remained unchanged.

As the sessions progressed, Gorham continued to niggle Lynott about bringing Robbo back on board, particularly as Lizzy couldn't tour as a three-piece. But it was about much more than that. As a four-piece they had broken through, and when things were going well they were an unbeatable combination. It made sense for the Prodigal Son to return.

Robbo's passage to Canada wasn't without interruption however. "On the way to Toronto I got stopped going through customs," he recalls. "They ripped through my luggage, my clothes and stuck a glove up my ass looking for drugs, because I'd been a mate of Keith Richards. He had been busted recently in Canada. Don't ask me why they linked us up but they did, so again things didn't start all that well."

In Robbo's absence, Lynott conceived the idea of getting a variety of guitarists to come in as session musicians to play his parts. Both Gary Moore and Brian May were mentioned as possibilities, but this was only a fleeting and somewhat unrealistic thought. In any case, the recording schedule didn't really allow for this kind of indulgence.

"Basically I was called up and asked to go out to do some overdubs in Toronto, which I thought was a bit of a weird place for the band to record," says Robbo. "Actually, I did the work as a session because as far as I was concerned I wasn't back in the band. I had already started Wild Horses before the recording began and I didn't wanna let Jimmy [Bain] down; I should've done but I didn't want to. It was kind of a weird one to walk into; strange studio, but it was a place where Rush had worked before, and they were old friends. It was quite quaint, a really good studio. I hadn't worked with Visconti before, but had met him at other recording sessions."

During Robbo's enforced downtime due to the hand injury, he started sharing a flat with bass player Jimmy Bain in Pimlico, London. Unsure of his status within the band, the pair started outlining a project they named Wild Horses and, though they started writing material and rehearsing, it never came to anything until the following year due to Robbo re-establishing himself within Lizzy.

"Dancing In The Moonlight" opens the batting on Side 2 and, though one of the band's biggest hits, it sticks out like a sore thumb in the band's catalogue. Various demos exist, which feature the acoustic guitar as a prominent instrument and also use completely different lead solos. Lynott's embellishment of youthful adventures in the cinemas back home in Dublin are evident from the onset, and the song can't easily be ignored for its terrific tale-telling, no matter if there isn't an ounce of truth in the story of the hand jobs he enjoyed in the back row seats while watching his heroes on the silver screen.

Ken Morris recalls the external input which has contributed to the song's mainstay status on radio today: "The sax solo was a spur of the moment thing, and not as the result of dissatisfaction with 'only' a guitar solo. I seem to recall that Scott Gorham's brother-in-law was the drummer in Supertramp, and Phil had been raving to them about the 'full Irish' fry-ups that I made for the band when they came to work hungover and dishevelled each day. They just came to visit and have some beer and authentic greasy UK-style food, and John [Helliwell] ended up doing the sax solo."

Helliwell just happened to be in Toronto when Lizzy were recording. Supertramp did two gigs in the city, after which they enjoyed some downtime. On the evening of 3 June, John Helliwell arrived at Toronto Sound to unleash a sweetener that time refuses to forget.

"The first time I ever met Phil was in the studio in Toronto; I can't say I recall the name of the studio, but when I arrived Scott, Phil and Tony [Visconti] were there along with a very attractive girl, Mary Hopkin," recalls Helliwell. "There was a nice atmosphere when I arrived and it quickly became apparent that these guys knew what they wanted to do in the studio, and were very adept at achieving their collective aims for the recording process.

"As I recall, when I was working on 'Dancing In The Moonlight', the song seemed to be complete with fully fledged vocals as opposed to any guide vocals. As the guitar solos were in place it was decided to use this as the guideline for what became the sax solo on the track. We may have double tracked it as well. After [the sessions] I remember Scott saying that I should really go on the road with them for a while, but it was always going to be a stretch as it wasn't really economical to bring me on the road and guest on one song."

Lyrically, though, is where it had its strengths, a masterful storytelling feat by Lynott but, as with any variation from the established status quo, also had its detractors. Will Reid Dick: "I never liked 'Dancing In The Moonlight', it was just too poppy. It never did it for me at all, not sour grapes or anything like that either."

"Killer Without A Cause" follows next. It was a Lynott/Gorham composition that featured what sounds remarkably like a middle eight from an older number, "King's Vengeance". Unlike *Jailbreak's* cool and precise pulp noir lyrics on "Angel From The Coast", here the Americanisms don't quite hold together as well. Lynott's lyrical obsession with underworld figures and operations were starting to rival fellow Irishman Rory Gallagher, whose obsessive lyrics frequently contained stories of international espionage and intrigue.

The sordid activities as outlined in the verses don't quite align with the poppy and alliteration ridden chorus; in fact they seem to be at complete odds. The killer of the title is coming in to settle up scores; the transparency in the conceit of the song works well but when it comes time to collect and settle the scores, the lyric unhinges with Lynott trying to be too clever, and the killer comes off looking more like a frolicking nymph. More time may have been needed to work out another lyric, as Lynott bombarding alliteration at the listener does the song a disservice. The demos of the song vary little musically from the eventual final cut, though lyrically there were many changes made.

"Downtown Sundown", credited to Lynott alone, is an open letter to female fans, written as the antithesis of the previous album's hit single "Don't Believe A Word". It's also a simple and straightforward love song, much like "Don't Believe A Word" but just with different concerns. The primary instrument audible on the demo is an acoustic guitar, featuring a riff which was eventually worked out for Lynott's bass guitar track on the final version. The slightly different arrangement and vocal-less demo makes for intriguing listening.

John Helliwell makes his second and final contribution to the album as he recalls: "On 'Downtown Sundown' I played some clarinet; not that you could tell as it seems to be well down in the mix. I might have just been noodling on that and they decided to keep it in. It was a very relaxed experience in the studio with them. Phil and Tony in the control were ever present, and Phil seemed to have a really tight grip on where he wanted to take the material for this album. Tony was a very professional guy, not at all in a cold way either; he was really on the ball for the duration I was there.

"Of course, having Mary Hopkin in the background was also nice. It was just one of those friendly things that you do, I may even have got paid for the work that night. Mostly, it was just something that was done. Like Scott came and worked on our album as a favour. I don't look at myself as a session player and I can say I didn't really view it as a job, it was just me helping out, and if it didn't work and none of what I did was used, then that was OK too. Turns out they kept it and ended up with a hit single which was great for them."

"That Woman's Gonna Break Your Heart" breezes into sight next featuring some thunderous interplay between the rhythm section of Lynott and Downey. The initial demos, of which there are many, feature the song's working title as "That Woman". The demo relies heavily on Lynott's bass riff to drive the song forward. In fact the early versions feature little contribution beyond bass, drums and acoustic guitar.

Downey's traditional Irish background playing style is again utilised. It's one of the lesser numbers on the album, but again features some clever lyrics from Lynott as he sends out the warning signs of gambling with your heart. The implication is that the deck is loaded, even stacked against romance. Just as Lynott tried to infuse a change in his outlook, from a public point of view of love and romance on "Downtown Sundown", he quickly changes things up and displays further reticence here.

Lynott continued to refuse to be pegged, bagged and boxed with his lyrics as is evinced on the album's closer "Dear Lord". To give the song extra oomph, they settled on giving it a choir-like introduction, saving the listener from the initial version of the song which was supremely lightweight. Ironically the choir, faked using multiple overdubs of producer Visconti's then wife, Mary Hopkin, lends the song the gravity it needed. She, after all, had experienced greater chart success than Lizzy with her 1968 No.1 hit "Those Were The Days".

Lynott's vocals just didn't work, and it isn't known if his rendition of the vocal choir still exists. Lynott did handle the choir-like parts on "Warriors" so the task wasn't beyond him. It happened to be that Hopkin was visiting her husband in Toronto and willingly contributed to the sessions. Gorham later remarked to the late Harry Doherty "I swear to God, I expected the hands of God to come down and touch me. It was beautiful." It certainly stood as one of the more atmospheric tracks on the album and, given the band chose to release "Dancing In The Moonlight" as the lead single, with a little pause for thought they might have considered this as a follow-up. It's very poppy flavour added another toe-tapper to the Lizzy repertoire.

Though credited on just three tracks on the album Robbo himself played on much more than was made known, as friend and manager Sören Lindberg testifies: "Phil and the management were still upset with the fact that he fucked up the American Tour after his accident at the Speakeasy. Phil's plans to have either Gary Moore or Brian May to be the second guitar player on the album didn't work out, but Robbo was prepared to do it if his new writing partner Jimmy Bain was taken care of by the management back in London during the recordings. Robbo ended up playing a lot more than the three songs he's credited for, and he basically plays on the whole album, mostly rhythm guitar and keyboards."

Once the band concluded work at Toronto Sound, they moved onto Sounds Interchange. At the new studio, where vocals and overdubs were completed, Ed Stone took on the role previously taken care of by Jon Bojic and Ken Morris. "Toronto Sound had a few very minor technical shortcomings, and I believe the combination of that plus the desire to hear everything in a fresh environment caused Lizzy to move to the much 'posher' Sounds Interchange. Because the album was sweetened and mixed entirely at Sounds Interchange I didn't retain as much a sense of the overall project as I would, had I been present for the entire thing."

On his experience of working with Visconti, who was probably the hottest producer in the UK around this time, Morris reflects: "Tony was, at the time, a very 'hands on the console' producer. He didn't try to make the Lizzies something they weren't. I remember him as being someone who encouraged experimentation and then had this wonderful ability to identify the gems amongst a myriad of takes and tries. He didn't musically deconstruct individual parts as much as some musicians/producers do. Watching Tony's unique ability to identify magic in the midst of excess had a huge influence on me. He was patient, confident and showed great control in a discreet way. He spent his breaks practising Bruce Lee's martial art of Wing Chun out in our adjacent warehouse."

The band spent less than three weeks at Sounds Interchange and, suitably refreshed to be in a new studio, they were met by Ed Stone. The studio was designed by Tom Hidley and was fitted out with all the latest Studer and Neve gear with a huge array of microphones and all the latest in outboard gear. It housed a huge recording room with a separate glassed-in drum room with a slate floor.

"This was the room where Phil did a lot of his vocals, and I remember thinking how loud his boots sounded on the stone floor through the microphone," recalls Ed Stone. "They were all there at the studio and during the mixing. Brian Robertson, I recall, as seeming to be enjoying himself. Brian Downey and Scott were both extremely nice guys and Phil was such a down to earth fun loving guy. So the atmosphere was a fun, relaxed one. Tony was also very understanding of my being a relative rookie, but he liked my attitude and really gave me a lot of great advice. Lizzy gained a new fan in me after that and to this day."

During the recording sessions, Lynott contacted Fitzpatrick with a few rough ideas of what he was looking to do for the sleeve. Fitzpatrick completed some rough outlines, but it got a little fuzzy and he felt he didn't really have a brief to work to. The calamity continued when Lynott got lost *en route* to meet Fitzpatrick who was by now living in the USA.

"I've told this story so many times but it's a funny one," smiles Fitzpatrick. "He was meant to visit me to discuss the album cover. Frank [Murray] would be on the phone saying 'We're on the East Wharf Road and we can't see any houses'. I said, 'Look behind you, it's all houses'. So Frank asked a policeman passing by, and he came to the phone and asked for my address again. I said 'East Wharf Road, Madison, Connecticut' and Frank said, 'Ah fuck we're in Madison, Wisconsin'. They were leaving two or three days later so there was no time to do anything.

"I did some roughs for it but there just wasn't time. There wasn't any concept for the album when Philip first talked to me about it, but the roughs I did were fucking crazy. One was a dinosaur with a spaceship coming by. Because there was no title for the album when I was doing the roughs I wanted to do something wild. But there was no way that was going to work even if I had finished it as it just wouldn't have fit in with the album."

Pressed for time, Lizzy had to look elsewhere for a cover. With Fitzpatrick sidelined, the band turned to a company named Sutton Cooper. They had, earlier in the year, provided assistance on the promotion of the hit single "Don't Believe A Word", which was the first ever graphic they produced for the band. A cover sleeve for an album was an altogether different kettle of fish. Sutton Cooper were provided with three portraits: Downey, Gorham and Lynott. The artwork was copied onto line film giving a much grittier black and white image which accounted for the slightly mirrored effect on the final sleeve. The lettering was stencil, and chosen so as to make it look like a Wanted poster – a small visual pun on the album title *Bad Reputation*.

"The bag artwork had photographs of all four of the band and also photographs from the 1972 print folio *The Incredible Case Of The Stack O'Wheet Murders* by Les Rims, which Phil had seen in New York," remembers Linda Sutton. "The original choice of images, including the bound body of a dead woman, caused problems when the artwork went into Phonogram. With conversations between Chris O'Donnell and the top brass, some editing was done. I think the playing card motifs came from the *Fighting* album, with the spade representing Phil Lynott, the heart Scott Gorham, the club Brian Downey and the diamond Brian Robertson. We used these motifs again on *Live And Dangerous*."

The band filmed three promotional videos for the songs "Dancing In The Moonlight", "Bad Reputation" and "That Woman's Gonna Break Your Heart", of which two were utilised. "Dancing In The Moonlight" and "Bad Reputation" were released as a double A-side in July 1977, as a taster for the album which followed on 2 September. The latter received little airplay, as "Dancing In The Moonlight" caught the attention of radio playlists for the remainder of that summer. The song peaked at No. 14 on the UK charts as the band made multiple appearances on *Top Of The Pops* in promotion of it.

A famous show from the Bad Reputation tour was held at Dalymount Park in Dublin, the day after Lynott's 28th birthday on 21 August. Many old friends were invited to a party which was held in Celbridge House. Michael O'Flanagan, who had first met Lynott during the Black Eagles period when the Lizzy front man was still a teenager, brought along a slew of old photos, videos and slides while reminiscing about the early days of struggling in Dublin. "I remained friends with Philip over the years. He always invited me backstage whenever he had a concert in Dublin," recalls O'Flanagan, who is also the man responsible for a variety of film footage showing Lynott and others at various stages of their early career.

A trip to do some filming in the Dublin mountains remains a story worthy of recall. "None of us had a car so we all climbed onto a

Dublin bus," remembers O'Flanagan. "As the bus reached a rural area we noticed that there was a crane on the back of a truck in front of the bus. The bus was gradually getting closer and closer to the truck. Suddenly the truck in front stopped but the bus kept going. The crane came in through the front window of the upper floor of the double-decker bus. Myself and Philip were in the front seat. Although we both ducked down, we both got a shower of glass into our hair. After a few minutes another bus came along and we continued on up the mountain to complete our filming. I got a very memorable shot of Gary Moore smoking in the open air. The rest of the film is of the lads picking blackberries from the ditches along the mountain road."

The band took in a couple of German dates in early September, alongside Rory Gallagher and Santana, before commencing another American foray for the remainder of the month. They returned to the UK in November to tour in support of the album, which took them through until Christmas. Pete Holidai of The Radiators From Space recalls the opportunity provided by Lizzy when they were offered the supporting slot on the UK leg of the tour.

He enthuses: "I think Philip saw the shift and recognised the benefits of that alignment in the longer term; smartly he aligned with the Irish contingent of the punk movement – initially to reinforce his local hero status (which was totally earned). He wasn't the only one, they all did it, Marc Bolan in particular. However, I do feel Philip was genuinely into and liked the attitude and rawness of the punk movement. Lizzy were most definitely at the TOP of their game at this point in their career. The songs were supremely crafted for the intended target, and unlike others had a broad canvas of emotions. The Gorham/Robertson twin guitar axis was a 15-year-old's wet dream."

One particular thing to note is the quartet of Downey, Gorham, Lynott and Robbo had managed to complete a US tour in what was the period where they were unequivocally, at the peak of their power as a unit. *Bad Reputation* scaled as high as No. 4 on the UK album charts, giving the band their highest position to date. It was an album that met with much critical success even with all its pop music pretensions, with engineer Will Reid Dick considering that as an album it was "a step in the wrong direction."

On the US leg of the tour the band were supported by Graham Parker And The Rumour, who struck up a solid friendship with the Lizzies and, on more than one occasion, gave the headline act a run for their money. "Thin Lizzy were an anomaly," reflects Parker. "On the surface, their music was hard rock, almost heavy metal and their image also suggested this but they were much more soul than that type of stuff. They had a groove to their music which most bands of their ilk did not have. I think Phil was an original with his own unique vision which he steadfastly followed, a unique vision that always informed his music and made it his own, despite the apparent bombast of the style it was often couched in. I remember Phil as a lonely guy in the spotlight, drenched in sweat half way through the first number, living his rock 'n' roll dream to the maximum, surrounded by glorious pounding music, entirely alone."

Bad Reputation also represents the only full album recorded and mixed outside of the UK by Thin Lizzy.

10

LIVE AND DANGEROUS

Good Earth Studio was to play a major part in the recording and release of Thin Lizzy's and Phil Lynott's solo material over the next three years. Prior to that, it was known as Zodiac, and the chief engineer at the time was Colin Thurston, now sadly deceased. Zodiac was owned by a middle-aged Indian guy called Koki Thakur who was rumoured to have won the studio in a game of backgammon, which was his all consuming passion.

Thakur's deal with Thurston was that he wouldn't pay him anything other than subsistence money but he could use the studio for his own sessions if it wasn't booked by a paying client. Around this time, percussionist Andy Duncan started working in the studio as an assistant to Thurston and, given the free studio time, the pair were in there morning, noon and night, quickly growing to resent any interruptions.

A few months later, the pair were advised that some big-time American producer had booked the studio for three weeks, and that he engineered his own sessions, at which point Thurston bailed out on holiday. This left Duncan to assist said big-time producer in any capacity needed. During the three week period Duncan became friendly with the big-time American producer, A.K.A. Tony Visconti, who booked Duncan for session work when required.

It appears that Mr Thakur's skill at backgammon wasn't indicative of his business acumen. One night, as Duncan and Thurston were working at the studio, a bunch of henchmen turned up with a three-tonner, put a massive set of wire-cutters through the cabling connected to the console and basically did a runner with it and anything else that wasn't nailed down. The bailiffs arrived the following day to discover nothing more than empty beer cans and a few broken music stands.

Realising that the studio space would become available, Duncan and Thurston put in a call to Visconti, who purchased Zodiac, tore it asunder and renamed it Good Earth Studios. Visconti installed a Kiwi named Graham Myhre as studio manager while Thurston became his chief engineer. Visconti didn't offer Duncan a studio position, feeling that his calling was to be a musician. In effect, Duncan became the house rhythm guy.

Myhre was Visconti's go-to guy; a fantastic carpenter and a whizz with electronics. As an engineer, he was also taught by Visconti. Good Earth Studio was originally located in Melrose Terrace in Hammersmith, on the ground floor of a large terraced house owned by Visconti. When Visconti took over Zodiac, Graham Myhre, assisted by Kit Woolven, rebuilt it based on Myhre's design.

Woolven recalls: "The way the Good Earth control room was laid out was a three-tier level. There was the original floor which had all the machines. It then came up a level which had the desk on it and most of the effects. Then it came up another level behind that, which was the sofa area where the band could look out over the top of us out through the observational glass and into the studio."

Located on Soho's Dean Street, the atmosphere was intimate and relaxed, in a cool part of London. Some of the first sessions at Good Earth were done in the spring of 1977. Thin Lizzy first started recording at Good Earth in January 1978, and it was here that their crowning album *Live And Dangerous* received an additional polish under producer Tony Visconti's eye, ably assisted by Kit Woolven on his first Lizzy project. The original plan in the early weeks of 1978 wasn't initially geared toward assembling a live album, though the thoughts of putting one together had been a topic of discussion over the last couple of years.

Since their inception as a four-piece, the band were recording more and more live shows. From 14-16 November 1976, the band played three consecutive nights at London's Hammersmith Odeon, all of which were recorded by Will Reid Dick. The first night's performance was filmed with a view to releasing it as a live special for television but nothing came of the plan and the footage remains unreleased.

Reid Dick remembers: "I loved the way they had 'Johnny' segue into 'It's Only Money' in their live set. Those gigs at Hammersmith in late 1976: all I did was take the tapes into Ramport one morning and did it over a couple of days. It must have been around Christmas as it wasn't very busy. I did a quick mix for Phil, as he asked me. I recorded the three nights; I think we had the Maison Rouge mobile outside for the gigs. Phil would come in and listen to some of it after the show and he seemed quite pleased with certain bits of it. He asked for a rough mix onto cassette of all three nights so he could listen to them and see what he wanted to use. So, I just nicked some time at Ramport and went in to do it.

"So, I had the 24-tracks and went in shortly afterwards, when I could get some free time, and ran off the three nights. In actual fact, I only ran off two nights because I think we decided the first night wasn't very good or something. I mixed it onto cassette for him and ran a ¼" at the same time, which I kept and still have here. After doing that, it was the last I ever heard of it as it was all out of my hands. But I don't think there was an intention to start working on a live album at that time, because there was some other stuff later, that Rainbow thing. I remember going to the TV studio to work on it."

The two nights mixed by Reid Dick present a slightly different set list to the live album that emerged 18 months later, but it's the untouched sound and mistakes that make it a real treasure. In effect, it was *Live And Dangerous* Mk 1, but that's as far as it went. Opening with "Jailbreak" before slipping into "Massacre" then "Emerald", there is no let up as the band unleash fervid versions of "Johnny" and "It's Only Money". "The Cowboy Song" is missing in action, but no matter as "The Boys Are Back In Town" causes the faithful to raise the Odeon roof. The band finally slow it down with "Still In Love With You". Lynott's confident delivery is further pulsed by his ad-libbing of some vocals toward the climax, before ultimately dedicating the song to his "cailín [girl] in the land of green".

The roughly 80 minute set bears a strong resemblance to the finished article under Visconti's watch, in both sequence and energy. The charming appeal of Reid Dick's early attempt at assembling a live album for Lizzy is the fact that no overdubbing took place and he simply mixed what was recorded on the given nights. It's ultimately unfortunate that the band saw fit to choose a different route when playing their hand with a live album release, as the musicianship is top notch here. Lynott is in great voice and as a collective it proves just how powerful the band were onstage without any studio gimmicks or embellishment.

The early part of 1978 wasn't spent assembling a live album, though this was soon to change. Thin Lizzy were at work on new material such as "Black Rose", "A Night In The Life Of A Blues Singer", "Rockula" and "Fanatical Fascists" at Ramport Studio. Other songs emerged in February such as "Are You Ready", "Hate" and "Cold Black Night". The band were hopping between Good Earth and Ramport during the first two months of the year, and it was at the former studio where Lynott worked out another new idea called "Jamaican Rum".

With various sessions completed, the band didn't really have enough material to flesh out a new studio album, nor did producer Visconti have the time to record one, as he was already committed to working with David Bowie. According to Visconti's autobiography, the choice was his: he could start on a new studio album with Lizzy and work for a month before breaking to complete his commitment to Bowie and then reconvene with Lizzy. The second option was to work on mixing a live album for the band which they envisioned could be assembled within a two to three week period: he opted for the live album, but spent nearly two months working on it.

Given that this idea had been on the band's radar for some time, a live album would also keep the group in the public eye, while also allowing time for them to develop new material. The band had wisely waited and got together another studio album in *Bad Reputation*, from which they could draw material if a live album was in the offing.

Many ingredients were required to make the project work: the title, the sleeve, the songs for inclusion and their sequence, and all had to align perfectly to reflect the approximate experience of Thin Lizzy Live, the working title of the album.

Photographer Chalkie Davies had accumulated an extensive archive of life on the road and on stage of the band over the previous

18 months. He felt that a live album was always in the works when he was out in America with the band during autumn 1977. Davies had first seen Lizzy perform in 1973 and again in 1975, and by 1976 he was photographing the band on stage and off. Some of these pictures accompanied features in the *NME*, Davies' employer at the time. Welshman Davies had also accompanied the band on their last US tour, taking a slew of pictures in all manner of locations.

"When I was taking pictures it was a bit more than a possibility that they were going to be used for the album sleeve," says Davies. "I had put quite a few months into doing it, like going to America a couple of times to different places, to get the right place to stand in order to get some of those pictures. You only get one go per night and it takes a while to even figure out the exposure. But, there are certain venues that were good: Cardiff [Capitol] was good, Southampton [Gaumont], San Antonio [Municipal Auditorium], there's a few places."

While the band and Visconti chose the recorded concerts to draw from to build the album, Davies continued to work on the sleeve art. Under the guise of the album's working title "Thin Lizzy Live", Davies tried to work out a shot featuring the band's logo, which was planned to feature on the front cover. Not having an appropriate shot from the series of gigs he documented the previous year meant experimenting in the studio, much like the band were soon to do with Visconti.

"The only problem was the cover, which initially was supposed to be the mirrored logo as if it was at a gig," says Davies. "We tried doing that but it was very, very difficult to do. We even rented a soundstage off The Who and filled it full of smoke, and it just didn't work. Trying to get the shot of the Lizzy logo would have taken days and days of work and it didn't really work in a small room. I could do it now, having been a still life photographer for over 25 years. To make it work you'd have had to have done it at a venue and not on a soundstage. Although that did stay as the concept for quite a while; probably until we got back and looked at the second or third set of pictures."

Once the complete set of pictures, as taken by Davies on the tour in the USA, were reviewed it was hard to pass up what was in evidence. One shot in particular stood out, which was as a result of Davies staying out on tour longer than anticipated.

137

"What happened was that I was in LA with Frankie Murray and due to go back home," explains Davies. "The band had too much other stuff to do in LA to give me the time I needed to do something properly. So, Frank Murray and Chris O'Donnell suggested that I stayed on the road for three shows, which would have gotten us to Phoenix and that I could go home after Phoenix. But I didn't know if they could do that, if the *NME* would let me get away for 11 days, so I told them [Murray and O'Donnell] to tell *NME* that they had kidnapped me. So, if they could do that then I would use that as an excuse and stay as long as was necessary. So, I stayed a little bit longer to do more shows and then once I did that show in San Antonio, as far as I was concerned we had a front cover, although that decision wasn't taken until the very end. Then I started to work on the inside sleeve."

Back in Good Earth Studio, Visconti, Woolven and the band got down to the task at hand, detailing and logging in the region of 40+ multi-tracks of shows recorded in America and across Europe. It was a time-consuming process. Woolven was essentially the tape operator for the project, as he explains: "On the final album, there are at least three different gigs out of 40 odd tapes, which was a nightmare. It was certainly a baptism by fire for me and I was thinking: 'this isn't what it's like for every session is it?' Answer, 'no', but I didn't know that back then. Trying to keep a log on what songs were on which reels... because suddenly there might be a question from the band asking, 'What was that really good take that we liked a few days ago... aahh I think it was reel 17, third track in...' that type of thing. I got to do some transfer work at another studio. I was transferring stuff to make all of the tape compatible."

Transferring the tapes was all about how the engineer that was recording the show liked to record. As the live gigs recorded were done on separate tours, different engineers had been at the desk on given nights. One engineer might record the bass drum on track one, snare drum on track two etc., while a different recording engineer might do it completely in reverse, so if the band was using a 24-track recording set up sometimes the drums might be coming down from track 24 to 14.

"In itself it doesn't cause a huge amount of problems, because you go into the studio, you bring it up on the desk and you find out where the tracks are," says Woolven matter of factly. "The thing is, should you want to try editing these, you can run into problems. Editing like this you would think is almost impossible, because all of the sounds are going to be different, but in fact we did do it on some of them."

Other obstacles were detailed in Visconti's autobiography, *Tony Visconti: The Autobiography: Bowie, Bolan And The Brooklyn Boy*, such as the formats: "The difficulties started when I found the tape formats were different: some were recorded at the new fashionable 30 ips and the rest at 15 ips. Some used Dolby A system, some didn't: some with the AES frequency curve and some with the European CCIR curve."

Visconti continues to maintain that a large portion of re-recording took place, and the album is barely live at all. Both Gorham and Robertson vehemently deny any major guitar overhauls, as does drummer Brian Downey. Certainly an official release of Will Reid Dick's recording from Hammersmith in November 1976 would give weight to the skill and strength of the band in live performance during this period.

"Robbo's solos were great, and I don't think we re-did any of Scott's solos either," Woolven recalls. "Because of the live situation, you get a lot of spill from instruments on different mikes. You could beef up the rhythm guitars for instance, because all you're going to be doing is getting Scott or Brian to play what they played live. If you're trying to get someone to better a solo you're still going to have the old solo leaking across the drum mikes, down vocal mikes and the audience mikes as we were always trying to put a lot of ambience into the tracks as well. So you couldn't really re-record solos, and that was one of the criteria in putting the songs together: 'That's the best solo there, we'll use that', the actual live solo and in that respect Robbo and Scott didn't re-do those parts. Downey didn't have to do anything in post-production.

"With the bass and Phil, he was having to sing, be the frontman and play bass and the band might have a great drum track, great overall 'feel' track and Phil might have played the wrong note. So, he'd say

'I coulda hit the right note there if I'd put my mind to it': So in post-production we made sure he did."

So, apart from the well-stretched tale of how much of the album was embellished in the studio, one way to reach your own conclusion is to look at, and hear, the project through co-manager Chris O'Donnell's widely reported comments, which was that the album was meant to represent "an approximation of what Lizzy sounded like on a good night". The album certainly delivers tremendously in this objective. However, the word "approximation" carries with it negative connotations and so is wide open to interpretation and, more obviously, misinterpretation.

The most astonishing thing that the technical team found when listening back to the different tapes was Brian Downey. "We didn't have click tracks in those days, and his ability to be playing at exactly the same tempo every single night wherever they played was amazing", recalls Woolven. "Each song had its own tempo and he was on the button every single time. What a fantastic drummer." The different tape formats, along with how the recordings were done in terms of which tracks were used for which instruments, cost the band time and money. Getting Woolven to transfer all said tapes was also another time consuming issue which led post-production to run considerably longer than first anticipated. It certainly wasn't going to be completed within the initially expected two to three week period.

Aside from studio-recorded additions, there was also the issue of the set list and what songs would make the album. The band certainly had a serious quantity to choose from; so serious, in fact, that tracks such as "It's Only Money", "Johnny", "Opium Trail" and "Soldier of Fortune" never made the cut, amongst many others. Material of that standard left on the cutting room floor is an indicator of just how far the band had developed. Visconti had his say in how the songs were sequenced, but the final word was really all Lynott's.

"Any major decisions like that were always made by Phil, because he was, at the end of the day, a megalomaniac," laughs Woolven. "Lizzy was a democracy as long as you did exactly what Phil wanted, that's the way it worked! I can't quite remember as to who said yay or nay as to which tracks went on, but it would become apparent. At some stage, they would have been putting together a set list, a retrospective set list. That would have in some ways helped them decide in terms of what song naturally flowed nicely into the next and so on. I don't personally know why certain songs were dropped, such as 'Johnny' or 'It's Only Money'."

The album's contents are largely hewn from the band's recent three hits, *Jailbreak*, *Johnny The Fox* and *Bad Reputation*, with a sprinkling of other highlights such as the recently recorded "Are You Ready", which came together on the most recent tour of America. The album also featured the non-album track "Baby Drives Me Crazy". It's one of the few songs in the band's canon that never received any degree of work in a recording studio. All overdubs were completed at Good Earth Studios in London. While the band was hard at work completing the final mixes, photographer Chalkie Davies was facing a battle of his own.

"Philip was very concerned that the whole group should be on the front cover and it shouldn't be [just] him," says Davies. "Chris O'Donnell and I agreed it needed to be the picture that you know. Independently of each other, both Chris and I showed the sleeve to people at the record company. He showed it to his lot and I showed it to my lot, which made the whole record company know what the record cover was. Then it was just a case of convincing Philip not to worry about it, because three out of four of them were on it, just. Brian Downey didn't mind when I asked him: I said we have these other great group shots but we don't have anything quite this dynamic and I asked him how he felt about it... and he said 'It's OK, it's OK'. We did it, but there was a reluctance from Philip to be featured to that degree, and I don't know if people realise that."

The shot of Lynott that eventually featured on the cover was taken on the evening of 11 October 1977 at the Municipal Auditorium in San Antonio, Texas. Davies had been very meticulous in his note-taking when at venues on tour, selecting which theatres to take pictures in while also writing down which parts of which songs contained things worth photographing. "It was the second to last day I took the shot that became the cover for *Live And Dangerous*. San Antonio was a hall that had an orchestra pit which was perfectly sized for the stage. It allowed Philip to move towards me and just drop to his knees. I think I got about five frames. That was pretty much the only time he ever did that. He incorporated it into his act at a later stage but differently."

The additional recordings made with Visconti were completed by the third week of April, and now came time to get the artwork together, approve the selected shots and give them over to Sutton Cooper, the design team responsible for the *Bad Reputation* album.

"Who wouldn't have chosen the cover image of Phil Lynott in skin tight leather trousers for a live double album? I don't think any other image was seriously considered," says Roger Cooper emphatically. "Chalkie Davies had been taking photographs at a number of venues on both the *Johnny The Fox* and *Bad Reputation* tours during 1976 and 1977, and we got a huge parcel of 35mm and 2¼" transparencies to work with. We met Chalkie a couple of times but he wasn't part of the design work of the band."

With offices located a short stroll from Dean Street in Soho and Good Earth Studio, both Linda Sutton and Roger Cooper met with Lynott during the period of working with Visconti, as Sutton affirms: "Phil was indeed our main contact in the band, Scott Gorham was interested too, but the others not. It was intriguing being briefed by Phil in Good Earth Studios. You had to realise that he often thought he had been having a conversation with you before, and to get the detail right you had to take him back a bit. Our job was to listen to his thoughts and try to interpret them. Briefs were often hazy, but we knew that Lizzy fans always reacted well to lots of action shots of the band."

Once all the elements fell into place, the promotional gears kicked in. Lynott was convinced that the chosen cover sleeve worked best; Sutton Cooper spent just under one month preparing the artwork before sending it to Phonogram who then spent about another three weeks getting it in order before it was sent to the printers.

As part of the promotion for the album, manager Chris O'Donnell intuitively suggested the band produce a live performance video of the *Live And Dangerous* set which could then be sold for broadcast as a one hour TV Special. The slight problem involved here was what songs would make the final cut for broadcast and best complement the upcoming live release, which was now slated as a double album. A one-off show was booked for the Rainbow Theatre in London for 29 March, while the band put in extensive rehearsals beforehand, during which they filmed a promotional video for the single they were soon to release in April, "Rosalie".

Will Reid Dick was present for the recordings completed on 28 and 29 March before convening with the band on 23 and 24 May to complete the film dub. Over two days, Reid Dick worked with the band in setting the tracks to the visuals and audience levels with overdubs. However, work was only completed on the songs chosen for broadcast on the special. Various clips have appeared on YouTube over the years featuring alternative footage of the band with some of the songs that didn't make the broadcast cut, though unfortunately no further official release has been forthcoming.

"Rosalie", the lead single chosen to promote the album, peaked at No. 20 in the UK, giving the band another sizeable hit and the public a taster of the album that was to follow.

The first days of April 1978 saw Lizzy holed up at a variety of studios prior to a planned working holiday in the Bahamas. During the day of 12 April they recorded at Island Studios with Will Reid Dick before finishing up at Ramport later that evening. They returned to Island Studios the following day before again ensconcing themselves at Ramport on 14 and 16 April. Further work was completed between 18 and 21 April at Good Earth Studios before Lynott and posse flew out to Nassau. On 23 April, Lynott began recording sessions at Compass Point Studio in Nassau and continued working there through until 3 May. Engineer Will Reid Dick oversaw the sessions for the duration of their stay.

"I went out there just the once," recalls the engineer. "I just got a call from someone, from Chris Morrison probably. The trip was primarily getting away to somewhere warm, maybe a tax-related thing also. We were in the studio from around six until about 10 at night and then we'd go to the Playboy Club, have a drink and do a bit of gambling.

The days were spent on the beach just hanging around. Compass Point was a pretty decent studio. A West Indian guy called Ben, who was my assistant on the sessions, took some photos of us on the streets, with Phil messing around with the locals and the local police force. Later on I showed them to Caroline [Lynott's wife], who asked for them; I gave her some and they were later used for press related stuff."

"Phil brought some of the Lizzy stuff with him, some bits of his own, and also worked on Brush Shiels' songs," remembers Reid Dick. "It was very laid back... there were four of us who flew out; myself, Scott, Phil and Mick who was in the road crew, a tall guy. He was keeping everything together and organising things when we got to the studio.

"Then Huey [Lewis] arrived later. Huey was probably the only one who wanted to do any work out there [laughs]... I seem to remember there was a lot of Valium around so it was fairly easy going. Phil was into taking it easy around this time. Basically we just worked on stuff that was already recorded. That stuff that I gave Universal (for the recent deluxe releases) was pretty much everything we had from the sessions. I think I did a rough mix of all the stuff on the last day. Third World were doing an album, and as they were coming out we were going in; they were fairly serious about their recording. I remember Phil chatted away with them and one of them put down some percussion, but on what songs I have no idea."

Listening to the work produced in Nassau confirms Lewis' attempts to emblazon every track with harmonica, which in some cases works quite well; particularly on a work in progress called "Black And Blue". Several of the songs worked on would later turn up on the next Lizzy album. Songs worked on at Compass Point include: "Got To Give It Up", "Tattoo", "With Love", "Black Rose", "Blues Boy", "Cold Black Night", "Christmas Song", "Parisienne Walkways", "Jamaican Rum" and the aforementioned "Black And Blue", along with four others by Brush Shiels, all of which received a mix by Reid Dick.

Robbo was previously unaware that Lynott had taken certain material out to Nassau and offers the following opinion: "I had recorded the stuff in England which Phil then took out to Nassau to work on. He actually liked 'Blues Boy' but I don't know why he took the song out there; short on songs maybe. I know they had a little bit of a time out there, so to speak, and didn't do enough work. I think it was a bit more about lying by the pool. He must have thought 'I'm going to Nassau, let's have a good time.'"

Released on 2 June 1978, *Live And Dangerous* proved to be an immense success, peaking at No. 2 on the UK charts and setting a new standard for the presentation and execution of a live album release. It was to be a pinnacle that the band were unable to sustain for much longer though, as the tour the band undertook to promote the album after its release was plagued with further Lizzy mishaps. The band completed some dates across Europe before taking in shows in England and Spain, all in preparation for a major tour in the US, slated for August.

In early July, Robbo left Thin Lizzy for the final time, just four weeks before the commencement of the US Tour. Once the US leg of the promotional tour was completed there were also dates in New Zealand and Australia to fulfill. Based on loggings and dates in the band's archive it appears Robbo's final sessions on demos took place in early July 1978 while his final appearance as a full time member of the band was on 6 July.

Robbo had been disgruntled for some time, and of his exit from the band his friend and business partner Sören Lindberg shared this sentiment: "It was for the best that Robbo and Phil parted ways, as they had serious problems working together towards the end." Gorham's view on Robbo's departure is that, "Phil and Brian bumped heads again and that was it: Brian was out. I said 'Fine, fuck it, it's over' and that was it."

Worse was to follow when Brian Downey quit the band, leaving just Gorham and Lynott as the two members involved in assembling the *Live And Dangerous* album. Gary Moore had been on the Lizzy subs bench for a long time and his comeback was mutually beneficial, particularly with touring commitments ahead. For the American tour, Mark Nauseef [ex-Ian Gillan Band and Elf amongst others] was on drums and, as Downey still wasn't in the right frame of mind to return to the band, Nauseef continued on tour, where he was part of the line up that played outside the Sydney Opera House in Australia. The event was filmed and an edited version of Lizzy's set was later released on video and DVD, though the full 80 minute performance remains unreleased.

The line up changes for the tour certainly didn't aid the band's attempt at progress outside of Europe, particularly in the US. The loss of Robbo from the band is something they never quite managed to overcome. John Alcock recalls: "None of the other guitar players could hold a candle to Brian, in my opinion. Gary Moore was a great player, but Brian brought an attitude, emotion and fire to Lizzy that in my opinion was unmatched. I also think that Brian's loss was sorely missed by Lizzy and was the beginning of the end, so to speak."

Another to lament Lizzy's revolving door policy to personnel is David Jensen: "A lot of the changes that happened with their line ups no doubt hampered their progression, particularly after Robbo left. I think it did matter in those days as well, because fans tended to have their favourite member, so if one leaves and is replaced it changes things from the perspective of the fans, and I think in the end it affected the band negatively. What heightened this was the reporting of the time in the music papers. The level of hype back then was significant enough to impact the band as well."

11

BLACK ROSE (A ROCK LEGEND)

Lynott's fist met the contact sheet in front of him with a heavy smash, much to the chagrin of sleeve designer Andrew Prewett. He had been tasked by Phonogram with getting the finished artwork for *Black Rose* approved and ready for release, so as not to cost the record company thousands of pounds and nullifying the already in-process marketing. Prewett had invited Lynott to see the first proofs where the band was ghosted through the rose on the back cover.

"He hit the roof when he saw them," recalls Prewett. "Swearing and cussing me for not getting his flesh tone right. Now I had a problem: he was threatening in his dizzy state to tear up his contract but, because of all his procrastinations in getting the final design done, we were running late and in real danger of missing the release date."

To placate Lynott, Prewett invited him to the printers on the south coast of England where adjustments could be made to the colour of the print run. They agreed to meet up the following day to make the journey.

Prewett had to indulge in a little subterfuge: "What I did not tell Phil was that I had already approved the print run because we were so late. Thousands of sleeves were done and ready. The flesh tones were perfect, but seemingly not to his eyes. I called the printers and had them set up all the flat sheets in a pile, so that when Phil came through the factory with me he would see a man guillotining them for waste, allowing me time to explain to him that we were not happy with the colour either. Phil, late as usual, came through the factory. He appreciated seeing the operator cutting up the sleeves. It all looked very impressive to him."

Having adjusted the colour to his satisfaction, Lynott duly signed off the running sheet and both he and Prewett left the factory. Just before leaving, Prewett pushed the button for another 5,000 sleeves to be made and these to be kept aside for later. "Meanwhile in another part of the factory Phil was unaware that all of the thousands of flats I had signed off were being made up into finished product. This was deceptive work but it made Phil happy."

Black Rose (A Rock Legend) was the first and only studio release from the band to feature Gary Moore as a full time member. It's also significant to note that a large portion of the album was demoed while Robbo was still a member so, for as much as it can looked on as Gary Moore's only full album with the band, it is equally a lost Robbo Lizzy album.

The record was over a year in the making, with demo sessions taking place during January and February 1978. These demo sessions continued intermittently until October, after which the band left for France with producer Tony Visconti and engineer Kit Woolven. It would be Visconti's final time working with Lizzy on a full album, which was largely due to the band's increasing alcohol and drug abuse. The emotional baggage of the Lynott/Moore mutual animosity society was also a lingering burden on all who participated on the album.

The band's archive suggests that there was also some demo work done in the final weeks of 1977; such is the first documentation of what was to become the title track, then known as "Black Rose", with no mention of the subtitle "A Rock Legend". There was also a home demo by Lynott with a working title of "Waiting For The Man To Come" which clocked in at less than two minutes.

Of the first batch of songs to emerge during January and February, a large portion didn't surface on Lizzy's next studio album, instead finding a home in Thin Lizzy splinter groups. With Robbo's exit came the gallop of Wild Horses and the use of some of the material recorded during his period still in the band, such as "Blackmail" and "Flyaway". "Wild Horses was a safety net for me at the time," recalls Robbo. "I was still young at that point. I had a friend in Jimmy Bain and thought we could get something going. I paid every penny I had for that band. It cost me a fortune while the management didn't pay a thing."

There was also an even slightly older tune called "Dealer" which Robbo had worked on with Gorham, as he recalls: "That song 'Dealer' would never have suited Lizzy and is even one of the weaker songs on the first [Wild Horses] album," says Robbo. "I don't think that was ever considered by Lizzy, or even asked to be considered. I never thought that song would've worked in that format, but there are other songs on the first Wild Horses album that Lizzy did try out, such as "Blackmail" and "Flyaway". "Flyaway" was tried on Phil's solo album but we ended up doing "Girls" instead. I've still got the demo of "Girls" somewhere with me playing drums, a rockier version. It was written on piano and drums. It was a Bain/Robertson song, and Phil changed a few lyrics so he could get some of the publishing. I wasn't happy about that."

Work on the new material was halted to allow time for *Live And Dangerous* to be assembled but, once this was completed, the band returned to a routine of documenting the new ideas. "Are You Ready", though played live by the band, until now hadn't received the studio treatment. It was worked on and finished while Robbo was still in the band. Multiple versions exist in the band's archive, some bluesier than others while, staggeringly, a version recorded at Odyssey Studios saw them try the song using a sax solo instead of a guitar break.

While songs such as "Rockula", "Fanatical Fascists", "Black Rose" and "A Night In The Life Of A Blues Singer" all received attention during January, early the following month fresh material was developed. "Parisienne Walkways", "Blackmail" and "Waiting For An Alibi" surfaced. Lizzy's tape log suggests the first complete demo of "Waiting For An Alibi" was done at Good Earth Studios on 1 February 1978 and produced by Lynott in the absence of Tony Visconti. In fact, the majority of the demo sessions were handled without Visconti's assistance as he was busy on other projects, though he had committed to working with the band on recording sessions planned for later in the year.

Meanwhile, Decca also re-released "Whiskey In The Jar" to ride off the back of Lizzy's new-found success. Guitarist Scott Gorham discussed the Lizzy plan for the forthcoming studio sessions with writer Candy Magaw:

Phil and Brian thought it was a good idea for Decca to re-release it. Since it's been out, the single has gone silver. I think we'll be going into the studio sometime in September for a new album. The work had already been started on it though, I've got three or four songs written, Phil's got at least that many and Brian has a few.

In early June, more work followed on with Colin Thurston. He engineered sessions containing most of the same material worked on by Reid Dick, but a new song was amongst them: "Get Out Of Here", an idea Lynott initiated with Midge Ure. The song appears to have been initially worked on in Lynott's then home in Cricklewood, where Ure hung out frequently during this period.

Aside from being assisted on demo sessions by Colin Thurston, Will Reid Dick and Kit Woolven, the band also worked with Graham Myhre at the desk. On one demo session, Woolven found himself to be the only person available, though at this stage he had yet to engineer a recording session on his own.

"How I became involved on a permanent basis was Tony was away somewhere and Graham Myhre was also away," remembers Woolven. "I think Graham may have gone to New Zealand to visit his folks. Jan Nicholas, who was the manageress at the studio, said to me one day: 'You've got a Thin Lizzy session tomorrow starting at such and such a time' and I said 'What do you mean I've got a Thin Lizzy session tomorrow?' So she said 'They're coming in and recording tomorrow' but I said: 'I can't do that'. I had never done that sized session before. I was OK assisting on this and that. 'Anyway,' she said, 'there's nobody else here to do it.'

"I had been involved in a lot of sessions where Graham was engineering but Graham and Phil didn't really get along too well, to be honest. Phil could be very demanding in the studio and might say 'Give us another three tracks'. And if we were running out of tracks Graham might reply, 'What, you want me to magic them out of my ass' and it didn't go down well with Phil. If he said he wanted three more tracks, you gave him three more tracks and you didn't sort of question it; even if they weren't there you made sure you found them somewhere."

The night before the session, Woolven took home a bunch of manuals and read up on parts of the studio that he felt uncertain about, terrified that he might blow the whole session. Having got so worked up about it, and frustrated that he had been put in a position he felt was unfair, by the time that morning arrived he adopted a new demeanour. "By the time the session started I thought: 'This is absolutely stupid, and I should never have been put in this position'. Even if I wiped what they had recorded I got it into my head that it wasn't going to be my fault because it was absolutely ridiculous. I went into the session with that attitude in mind. Just totally quite relaxed, like just get on with it and if it all goes wrong, that's it! But it didn't go wrong, it went really, really well. We had a fantastic time, really good session and we all really enjoyed ourselves. I got on very well with everybody and at the end of the session Phil turned to me and said, 'Right, I want you on every session we do.' and I thought 'Oh shit'."

Once the band got off the road they enjoyed a short break, dabbled with some of the new material in the studio and prepared themselves for the recording of the new studio album, with Tony Visconti returning to the producer's chair to try to follow up the platinum success of *Live And Dangerous*. Unlike the last album, this time the band did actually travel to France to work, settling in at Pathé Marconi Recording Studios in Boulogne-Billancourt near Paris. Kit Woolven flew out ahead of the main crew to get everything set up for the band's arrival.

"Tony was working on something else, maybe another Bowie thing," says Woolven. "When it came to going to Pathé Marconi Studios, Tony said to me: 'Right, you go, get the band set up, start recording and I'll see you in a week'. So I went out there and met up with the band in the studio and of course Phil went 'Where's Tony?' So I told him he's coming in a week's time and he wanted me to come out and set everything up. That didn't go down well."

Visconti's relationship with the band, and specifically Lynott, was by now very strained. Under Woolven's watch the recording went well. His relationship with the band was solid, as trust was building.

Woolven pursued a more open, live feel to how he recorded the band. During the first week, the band got through a few backing tracks and vocals and by the beginning of the second week Visconti arrived. After doing a few days' work, Visconti was unhappy with the studio. Lizzy were in Studio B as Studio A was occupied by Cliff Richard, but when he finished work Lizzy took over the bigger studio and started recording from scratch. Wiping the work completed by Woolven was another move that didn't go down well with the band, but no doubt Visconti was keen to make his own mark on the material.

The album opens with a Lynott composition, "Do Anything You Want To", the second of four songs to be issued as a single from the album. The introductory kettle drum drama, alongside Lynott's shuddering bass line, exacts the big production sound the band always aimed for on their studio output. Soon a flurry of guitar harmonics eases the listener into the established Lizzy sound and style. Given the recent line up change with Robbo's exit and Moore's renewal of his Lizzy vows, it was a very specific kind of song that was required to open the new album, and "Do Anything You Want To" was perfectly suited to fans' expectations.

Its high energy and punk-esque aggression was reflective of Lynott's continued flirtation with the punk movement, and without the experience of The Greedy Bastards (Lynott's side project with two Sex Pistols), the song may not have been in Lynott's canon. He spent hours upon hours re-working the lyric in the studio much to the frustration of the control room as he measured the impact of each rhyming couplet.

"I think Phil pulled a lot of ideas from the Sammy Cahn *Rhyming Dictionary*, which he'd walk around with frequently around this period," says Woolven. Released as the second single from the album for the UK market on 16 June 1979, the sleeve was worked on by the partnership of Sutton Cooper.

A promotional video was made with David Mallet in the director's chair, while the song peaked at No. 14 on the British charts. Mallet remembers: "Phil liked the work I had done and rang me up to know

Top: Phil at Odyssey Studios in 1981.
He fancied himself as a producer. (*Popperfoto*)
Above: "You hum it, I'll play it". Phil with Darren Wharton in 1982.
(*Magnus Rouden*)

Left: Lynott on rhythm guitar during a solo outing in 1982. (*Magnus Rouden*)
Right: Guitar genius Snowy White with Thin Lizzy at the
Hammersmith Odeon in November 1981. (*Mark Hurley*)

Top: It's not all glamour being a rock musician. Snowy White stealing
a bite when he can. (*Jan Koch*)
Above: On the other hand, there is glamour sometimes as White's replacement
John Sykes, and Scott Gorham prove by rocking out at the
Manchester Apollo in 1983. (*Howard Potts*)

Top left and top right: Lynott, Gorham, Wharton and White soundchecking in 1982.
Above: Darren Wharton not quite believing he's in Thin Lizzy.
Facing page: Gorham and Lynott. (*All photos by Jan Koch*)

Top left: No book on Thin Lizzy would be complete without a picture of
Gary Moore, taken in 1983. (*Howard Potts*)
Top right: Lizzy supporter Jalle Savquist with Phil outside his house in Richmond
in early Sept 1985. (*Jalle Savquist*)
Above left: Lizzy supporter Darren Loy backstage with Lynott. (*Kieron Loy*)
Above right: Phil at home in Richmond the day Jalle Savquist visited. (*Jalle Savquist*)

Wish you were there? Two superb action shots from Sweden in 1982 and 1983.
Mike Mesbur subbing for an injured Brian Downey in '82. (*Magnus Rouden*)

Top: Lynott solo tour of Sweden in 1983. Flanked by John Sykes and Doish Nagle. (*Jalle Savquist*)
Above: This shot is significant as it is the last ever live Lizzy performance in the Lynott era. Taken on 4 September 1983 at The Monsters Of Rock Festival, Nuremberg. (*Wolfgang Gürster*)

if I would like to work with the band on a few video promos. I agreed instantly. 'Do Anything You Want To' was shot at Molinare Studios [London] and probably cost in the region of 12 to 15 grand. Most of the shoots I did with Lizzy back then only lasted a day, again maybe eight or 10 hours' worth of footage. It was just leading up to the time when big budget videos started appearing."

Photographer Chalkie Davies was on set for the shoot, documenting the production behind the scenes: "I did that, but the point about that is that it's not your picture, it's the director's picture. It's merely documenting something someone else has done. I didn't see any of what I did as being my picture. I just did that one video because Philip specifically asked, because I think they needed pictures for a reason. I had done Elvis Costello's *Trust* sleeve, and that's shot from the video while it was being made. That's different, because that's where I'm involved at all levels. On those [Lizzy] videos they knocked out, it's a formula thing and it's not mine."

A Gorham/Lynott/Moore collaboration follows, "Toughest Street In Town" and, given the album opener, it could easily be construed as Lizzy's attempt at a fully-fledged punk album, with Moore effortlessly affecting the aggression so evident previously in Robbo's playing. But he was no Robbo, and while Robbo was no more within Lizzy, it's interesting to note that the template established by him when he was in the band is little deviated from by Moore.

When the song was finished and presented to the record company, they initially found the lyrical content far too nasty and made overtures toward Lynott to re-write it, which he did, though changing very little. It's a tale of social decay, wrapped in Lynott's lyrical loneliness while portraying the austere underbelly of urban life, a theme he returned to on another song, called "Hey You", on the next Thin Lizzy album. Under Lynott's wing, as he gazes down upon the disconnection and decay, there's little hope from start to climax. One of his most telling social commentary songs.

A couple of weeks into the recording sessions, Lynott asked Woolven and Visconti to put up a song that was written by Moore, as he wanted to record a vocal for it. "The tape happened to be there," recalls Woolven. The song was put up and Lynott put down his vocal, after which Moore decided that he wanted to add some guitar. A guitar solo was recorded and no more was thought about it. "It was 'Parisienne Walkways'. A few months later, of course, it gets released and becomes a hit, and it's produced by Chris Tsangarides", says Woolven laughing. "I remember Tony turned to me one day and said, 'I could've sworn blind we recorded that in Paris'. So there would be stuff going on, and you'd have to ask, 'Is this part of what we're doing?'."

Brian Downey's only songwriting credit on the album is a collaboration with Lynott on the salacious "S&M", originally demoed as "Black And Blue" before being taken out to Nassau earlier in the year. The initial demo made, then added to by Huey Lewis in Nassau, retained a lot of the initial work and lyric, though Lewis' contributions were entirely omitted from the album version. On a later demo worked on with Colin Thurston, the tempo was upped and provides a thrilling though incomplete taste of how the song might have been realised, featuring blistering guitar work from Robbo. Its final incarnation lacks some of the raucous and riotous playing. It's nevertheless a contender for Lynott's most sexual lyric, and touches on themes which he admitted to the press was something he considered the public expected from him.

During a playback at the studio near Paris, a watershed moment occurred when Lynott was sat in the control room. "Phil actually said to me that he wanted me to co-produce the next album," Woolven states. "He said this to me while music was playing quite loudly in the control room, but I did have Tony sitting on my left hand side while Phil was on the right, so I had to whisper into Phil's ear: 'Well let's get this one finished first'. It put me in a very embarrassing situation, because I was employed by Tony and I've got one of his artists saying he wanted me to do the next album. I had already started doing a lot of recording of Phil's solo tracks by this time as well."

The album's lead single follows: "Waiting For An Alibi", solely credited to Lynott. It was originated from a home demo titled "Waiting For The Man to Come" that featured keyboards, acoustic guitar and a drum machine. The band had been playing versions of the song in their live set for nearly six months prior to recording with Visconti, while carefully gauging audience reaction. The slower original take of the song was improved greatly over the long period of gestation. Loosely inspired by the gambling adventures of a friend, Joe Leach, the song features some jaw-dropping guitar work by Moore. Multiple demo versions exist in the band's archive with completely different lyrics, though the adventurous vibe of the song doesn't change hugely from the original demo to the finished mix.

A video promo was filmed, again at Molinare Studios, with David Mallet at the helm, and shows just how the band had evolved in their ambition for the format. A variety of different edits of the song exist, with the band in some cases bordering on acting; a thin line in these early days of promotional video-making which many artists unfortunately crossed. Various staged scenes are intercut with the band performing the song, though Lynott's constant gazes off-camera are comically hard to ignore.

Chalkie Davies comments on the battles that ensue on set for a band like Lizzy: "The only thing more boring than making a record is making a film. The time delays can be enormous, plus you know, they're musicians. They're not built to make pop videos or have their picture taken. They're built to play music. On one of the Lizzy [fan] websites there is a picture of Philip bare chested, and he hated doing that. It was very difficult to get him to do that. He was a very reserved person. Also, if you can imagine being Scott, who doesn't really like a camera at the best of times, having to get there and throw shapes in front of a camera and do stupid things with girls... back then they would have wanted to be filmed performing live. A lot of the bands I did just didn't like having their picture taken, which is why I did them."

For the first time in three years, the boys were back in the Top 10 of the singles charts in Britain when "Waiting For An Alibi" peaked at No. 9 shortly after its release on 3 March. Linda Sutton of Sutton Cooper drew up a number of Thin Lizzy "handwritten" logos, one of which was chosen for the sleeve of the single.

Many of the shots used were derived from a photo session in Paris done under Chalkie Davies' supervision. "We rented a studio in Paris for all of the *Black Rose* stuff," says Davies. "Sometimes studios are built backstage, studios can be built anywhere: you can build one in a bathroom, a corridor, anywhere really, and create the illusion of a studio. Doing a band picture was as bad for me as doing videos was for Lizzy, because you've got to realise that these people really don't like doing this.

"I've talked to Chris Thomas and Tony Visconti about it, with them getting a drum sound is not dissimilar from lighting a complicated shoot. Then you take these people and you have to coax a performance of some kind. There are various ways to do it. For example, if you've got them in a studio you don't play them songs... you play them music: because if you play them songs and they hear the words, they'll think; and if they think, their eyes will change and it doesn't look right. So you play them instrumental music. Or, you play them their own music. If you play them their own music then you can get facial reactions and everything else that they do without realising it, by reflex."

The unexpected "Sarah" closes Side 1, a perfect antidote to the toils conveyed by Lynott on "Waiting For An Alibi". Written with Gary Moore, and recorded separately to the album sessions in France, it featured contributions from Mark Nauseef and Huey Lewis. The song itself was recorded at Morgan Studios and it was never intended to be included on a Lizzy release.

The early demo of "Sarah" was worked on by engineer/producer Chris Tsangarides, who would soon become a key collaborator in the Lizzy story. The same night that "Sarah" was recorded, Nauseef, Lewis and Lynott also worked on a discarded track originally done during the *Bad Reputation* sessions in Toronto; the song was called "Talking" before it evolved to "Talk In '79" and appeared on Lynott's debut solo album *Solo In Soho*, released in 1980.

"Sarah" was written for Lynott's recently born first daughter and also became the third and final single issued from the album for the UK market on 5 October. It peaked at No. 24 and enjoyed a longer stay on the charts than the other songs culled for single release.

The cutesy lullaby became a surprise chart success, revealing another unexpected side to the band. Ian Cooper, a cutting engineer on many Lizzy records, recalls a phone call from Lynott while he was in Ireland, "asking me to etch the date of her birth on the record". David Mallet directed the promotional video for the song, this time shot at Hewitt Studios in London. The highlight of the richly saccharine shoot is a hilarious closing cameo from Scott Gorham, which looked unrehearsed based on Lynott's response. Given the sentiment of the song Mallet also included some shots of his labrador. Here Mallet comments on his working relationship with the band: "I also edited all of the videos that I did for the band. Philip was rarely, if ever, involved in this aspect as he trusted my judgement and felt I would do as good a job as anyone when doing it. It's good to have that trust among people you work with."

"I always found making videos a pain in the ass," Gorham affirms vehemently. "I'm not an actor, and to have a camera shoved in your face and doing the play back thing, acting this way and that way, I never liked it. On the other hand, Phil loved it and always loved being in front of the camera; doing his Errol Flynn thing, that was his element. But he was good at it, the camera loved him, the clothes always fitted him perfectly, he loved acting the part. I, on the other hand, only went along with it because it was part of the gig, and he would drag me along to do all these things with him. The band always had a lot of input into how the storyboard of a shoot would take shape. As we were picking the singles I think Phil always had an inkling of what he wanted to do with them. Back then it was pretty early technology and they always came out looking very cheesy. I could never get too excited about that stuff."

For the single sleeve, the band continued their association with Sutton Cooper, who produced three different sleeves for the "Sarah" single. Linda Sutton says: "The lettering 'Sarah' and 'Got To Give It Up' used on the back was drawn in the same style as Thin Lizzy. Three versions were made with the heart containing Phil Lynott, Scott Gorham and Brian Downey, with the hope that real Thin Lizzy fans would buy all three – I have no idea whether you were offered a choice in the record shops. Gary Moore was not included as he had already left the band."

The solemn "Got To Give It Up" opens proceedings on Side 2; as with many other tracks on the album it too underwent many developmental changes with each engineer who handled the song. On Reid Dick's watch, the song was a slow tempo monument to those struggling with addiction. It's the earliest and most direct admission by Lynott of a peek behind the mask that adorned his writing in this period. Downey's prominent bongo playing on the demos perfectly pitches the "monkey on your back" vibe of the song. Many of the lyrics on the early demos were filtered through to the final version, though in time Downey's bongo addition was removed. In much the same way as "Don't Believe A Word" started out as a slow blues number, the same could be said for "Got To Give It Up". It remained as a slow tempo number until a session much later in the year, though once the band rocked it up with Woolven at the desk it really became the song we have come to know today.

It was under Woolven's mindful eye that the crooning introduction appears, before later being further developed by Visconti. It was chosen for a single release in the USA, though it's unknown if a promotional video was filmed to abet its chart assault. The recording of the song in Paris was also a key moment in the unravelling relationship between Visconti and Lynott.

"When we were doing 'Got to Give it Up' from *Black Rose* Phil was out there singing the vocals 'got to give it up' with a joint in his hand and a bottle of brandy alongside lines of coke," says Woolven. "I'm sitting next to Visconti and he's muttering 'this guy's a fucking hypocrite'. So Visconti's on one side saying 'I can't work like this anymore'. Also, I couldn't turn around to the band because of the egos and say, 'Well it's OK that you don't want to work with Tony because he doesn't want to work with you any longer'. So, like I said, they turned to me and said 'We'd like to continue working with you'. I was in an awkward position. Luckily Tony said to me 'You know, you keep working with them and I'll keep being busy'. It worked out OK in the end."

"Get Out Of Here" follows the sordid depths as described by Lynott on "Got To Give It Up". A co-write with Midge Ure, the breezy pop-rock of the song was inviting, and the clever vocal delivery featuring Lynott's conversational technique with himself highlights an almost jovial paranoia.

One time he was strumming away and said, "Help me do this song". We had the chord sequence going and the chorus – "Get Out Of Here" – but when he played the verse he was singing the lyrics to a completely different song – "Randolph's Tango" – over the top of it. It fitted, because Phil ended up writing the same song over and over, recreating what he already had. (Midge Ure autobiography, *If I Was*)

As with "Sarah", "With Love" was recorded at entirely separate sessions to the main batch completed with Visconti in France. In fact, Lynott never actually played bass on the track, leaving that task for Jimmy Bain, his sometime writing collaborator. The song borrowed a riff from a different track recorded earlier in the year called "Fanatical Fascists", which Lynott donated to Gary Moore for his debut solo album, *Back On The Streets*, which was to appear later in the year. Chris Tsangarides was the producer on that album, where he oversaw the recording of "Parisienne Walkways" along with a series of unreleased sessions that Lynott recorded with Sex Pistols Paul Cook and Steve Jones. "When You Fall In Love With Love" is a track amongst this unpublished stash.

On "With Love", Lynott unshackles some great lyrical couplets from previously unreleased Lizzy material such as "Leaving Town", but most directly he had sung a variation of the same lyrics used on "With Love" in live versions of "Still In Love With You". Like most of the album it was worked on by a multitude of engineers before eventually being completed at Good Earth Studios, and not originally intended to be part of the *Black Rose* album. A promotional video was also made for the song, on the same set as "Waiting For An Alibi", though mysteriously it was never issued as a single. It's a stirring number that never made the band's live set but remains one of Lynott's lesser known paeans to lost love. Jimmy Bain says, "I played bass on the track and Phil said he liked it, so it stayed on the recording. It was done for one of the solo records, but because Lizzy were short of one song for *Black Rose* it went on. Lucky for me, as I could say I played on a Thin Lizzy album!"

The title track, "Róisín Dubh (Black Rose): A Rock Legend" is the album closer, and credited to Moore and Lynott. Coming in at just over seven minutes in length it represents Lynott's final epic tribute to Ireland, while also being his weakest salute in many ways to the Emerald. Interestingly, as a song, it contains elements that Lynott in particular wanted to get away from after the success of "Whiskey In The Jar".

The inclusion of a rocked-up version of "Danny Boy" didn't quite hit the mark. As a song it's also far removed in spirit and tone from the rest of the album. The raw and punkish energy of "Do Anything You Want To" and "Toughest Street In Town" are at complete odds

159

with the overblown and borderline pompous "Black Rose". Though superbly executed musically, there are audible jerks of cliché in the lyrics which were considered unforgivable by the late Phil Chevron (Radiators from Space & The Pogues).

"At his best, Philip was a terrific writer, a wonderful craftsman," remembered Chevron. "His best work tapped into an Irish romantic-heroic tradition which could now visualise Cuchulain and Ferdia slugging it out at the OK Corral. He was born into a pre-television Ireland when dreams and notions were fashioned from Saturday morning cowboy pictures and schoolyard yarns. His genius was to offer this as an alternative reality in his songs. In an Irish context, this had more meaning, more substance, than the pipe-dreams coming out of San Francisco by the mid-sixties. As almost the only black kid in Ireland, he was always going to view the world from an idealised angle. But he also understood it was a worldview that others could share and celebrate. And ultimately, when the heavy riffs, played mainly on the bass and on the lower strings of the guitars, turned out to have the soul of ancient Irish music printed in their DNA, Philip forged a song-world that was as timeless as really great music must be.

"However, it cannot be denied that he later became a master of self-parody too. The dire puns of 'Black Rose' spring to mind, the lyrics of a man no longer in command of his wit. He had, I believe, bought into The Rocker to such an extent that he sometimes had trouble connecting with The Poet. There weren't enough people in Philip's life to remind him that even John Wayne went home, unsaddled the horse, kicked off his boots and watched *The Lucy Show*. He definitely came to believe he was living the mythology he had created and, at that point, he was no longer the master of his own gifts."

Material left over from the *Black Rose (A Rock Legend)* album remains varied. A recurring theme in how Lizzy conducted their studio lives was how many different types of songs with unknown destinations were put to tape. This particular method of recording ultimately resulted in everything falling apart. Producers and engineers never knew if they were working on a Thin Lizzy song or a Phil solo song.

That eventually trickled down to the members of Lizzy, who in turn complained to Lynott about using Lizzy recording time for his own pet projects. "Just The Two Of Us", a Lynott song and utterly disposable, was recorded at Good Earth in London after the sessions in France. It was utilised as the B-side for the "Do Anything You Want To" single.

"I always had doubts about that track to be honest with you," says Woolven. "A Night In The Life Of A Blues Singer" was repeatedly revisited and added to over the years but ultimately never appeared on any Lizzy album. Once the sessions in France were completed, the recordings were taken back to London and the album was mixed at Good Earth. Once Visconti finished his work it was then brought to Ian Cooper, who was largely the cutting engineer on their albums and singles for the remainder of their career.

The band returned once more to Jim Fitzpatrick for the cover artwork for the first time since *Johnny The Fox*. "This was one of the few albums where Philip had a fairly clear idea of what he wanted for the sleeve," remembers Fitzpatrick. "No matter the time constraints in place when trying to work out a cover, the purpose of the artist is to inspire as well. I was happy to be working on a new sleeve and it was very nice to have a title to work with."

Once Fitzpatrick had completed his work, the images were supplied to Sutton Cooper, who incidentally had no contact with Fitzpatrick directly. "Jim Fitzpatrick most probably drew up the *Black Rose* lettering but he had little interest in the more conventional use of type," says Cooper. "Thin Lizzy is in Optima, a typeface we used in a privately printed book of Phil Lynott's lyrics. This is another Sans Serif typeface, but with a softer, more romantic look reflecting the more folksy music."

In the final weeks before the release of the album sleeve, the put-upon designer Andrew Prewett approved the extra 5,000 sleeves based on Lynott's preferred proofs and they were finally made up. Again, subterfuge played a part. "I asked the sales department to have these records and sleeves placed into retail outlets anywhere round Phil's home and favourite haunts," remembers Prewett. "It was the same with all the fly-posting done at this time. Phil was fine and never mentioned it again. The record did well so he had no problems with the tens of thousands that were circulating in the rest of the country. But, most importantly, we met all the deadlines. He was at times, it seemed to me, insecure, almost shy. He had a low personal perception of himself. I liked him, he was a brilliant performer, but you had to tread lightly as he could flare up quickly."

Lynott and Moore's relationship was soon to boil over. Even before the release of the album matters were coming to a head. Given they had known each other for a long period of time meant that each knew what drove the other crazy, and both played on such familiarities.

"Gary could often be sarcastic toward Phil, and Phil wouldn't take sarcasm from anybody," observes Woolven. "Gary knew this and would constantly be sarcastic towards Phil because he knew that Phil needed him. That was the difference with Gary: Phil really needed Gary at that point and so Gary would play on that. There was a constant friction there... constant might be overstating it, but it was there and did exist. Gary wouldn't take any shit either."

Percussionist Andy Duncan, who was in the vicinity through the time that the band were preparing material for *Black Rose (A Rock Legend)* at Good Earth, had this to offer, giving a keen insider eye on the evolution of the band and its members: "Handling Brian Downey was easy for Tony. Brian was (is) a great drummer. Solid, consistent, reliable and musically creative. He knew what he was doing, so Tony would just let him get on with it, making sure that his kit sounded great on tape and in his headphones. Although Scott Gorham was a loud and gregarious American, Tony used his 'fellow American' angle to relax Scott and direct his playing.

"Gary Moore was obviously more of a handful, but a wonderful player, and here I think we assume that Tony's existing reputation helped to counteract Gary's more fiery and impulsive nature and calm him down. Tony also realised that keeping Gary and Phil apart when one or the other was working would probably save everyone from any potential tension or physical injury. Brian Robertson was easy as long as he was sober. In many ways an absolute pussycat, and a talented musician. But his various neuroses combined to make him nervous and desperate to impress, which was usually hidden behind a double whammy of Glaswegian bravado and alcohol-induced aggression. Tony managed to counteract this tendency with his arm around the shoulder technique of nurturing and encouragement. This, combined with determined efforts to hide the brandy."

Thin Lizzy's ninth studio album was released on 13 April 1979 to resounding commercial success, peaking at No. 2 in the British album charts and housing three Top 30 singles to boot. Reviews of the album were generally positive with *Words* magazine suggesting "quality of melody and lyrics make this the kind of rock album that wins gold records, and on this creative showing Thin Lizzy will doubtless go on in strength for years to come". *Sounds* writer Phil Silverton struggled to be overly impressed by the band's latest offering, though: "An album which promises much, gives you quite a bit, but still falls slightly into the trap of the band's own mythology".

Black Rose (A Rock Legend) was the band's second successive No. 2 hit album within 12 months, and a peak they were not to maintain for the remainder of their career. Engineer Will Reid Dick says of the album on whose songs he worked when they were initially demoed over 12 months earlier, "I really liked some of the songs on there, stuff like 'Waiting For An Alibi', it's a very listenable album."

Another visit to Compass Point Studio was pencilled in for early June, where some new material was recorded as well as rehearsal time for the upcoming US tour to promote *Black Rose*. The excessive behaviour during the recording of *Black Rose* was typical of the band and had been building since the success of *Jailbreak*.

"I wasn't really aware of the substance abuse during the *Black Rose* period," admits Woolven. "I mean, there was a lot of coke, dope and alcohol, but I never personally saw any smack going on, but I've been told since then that there was a fair bit of that going on too. A few times, Phil didn't turn up at the studio, just stayed at the hotel all day." The trip to Compass Point in June 1979 was Woolven's first visit to the Bahamas with the band. He was assisted by a tape operator.

"Benji was a tape op who was very, very funny," recalls Woolven fondly. "He used to insist on running the tape machine. It had a very loose atmosphere out there. Part of the Bahamas thing was that if a foreign company set up a business there you had to employ 80% local staff. That meant at the recording studio, which Chris Blackwell owned, for every two Europeans out there he had to have eight locals, and he had to find them all jobs. Every time you added another person he had another bunch of people to stick on the payroll.

"Anyway, Benji was the tape op in 1979 and we were using an MCI 24-track recording [machine]. On a lot of the recording machines back then you had to press play and record together to get it to go into record but on an MCI machine the record button has a shield round the outside of it so you can hit it. But you had to hit it bang on the middle and you only have to hit that button. You don't need to press play and record.

"Benji used to dance all the time when the band would play, and if you have a 'drop in' coming up and you just need to do this overdub, and when you need to drop something in at, say, Bar 38, I'd usually grab the remote for the tape machine, but Benji would say 'No mon no mon, this is my job'. So while he was dancing away he'd rush up to the tape machine and hit the button to drop in the overdub, be it a guitar piece or vocal, and he missed the fucking button every single time. It looked great with him dancing in the studio but was totally ineffectual."

The upping of the ante in terms of substance abuse is generally associated with the recording of the *Black Rose (A Rock Legend)* album in France, but for the most part the band members had been indulging for many years before. Certainly the heavier stuff made more frequent appearances, though Downey confirms: "Phil never went looking for heroin, he was never interested by it. Sometimes you find these things being thrown in front of you and eventually you end up trying it. But I can say, heroin was never something he went looking for."

Robbo confirms the unravelling he witnessed as an outsider from the band around this period. "Mark (Nauseef) was a very good player. I don't think Brian Downey even wanted to go out to Nassau for recording because of what was happening. There was a few things happening, he wasn't into it... like, Brian is one of these guys who'll take so much and then he'll go 'Nah'. I think he'd had enough to be honest. Brian's been like that a few times throughout the band. So, then, if you give him a little time to himself he'll come round. He needs that room and a break from the boys. I think the music suffered when he wasn't there. That's not to say that when Mark was there he didn't do a good job, Mark just didn't have an awful lot to work with, like personnel, like Phil. I mean there was nobody like Alcock there to give guidance."

Black Rose (A Rock Legend) was supported by a national and international tour. In March, the band toured America before returning to tour Britain in April and May. Selected dates across Europe followed before the band returned to the USA again to tour in June, July and August.

Midway through the second US tour of the year, guitarist Gary Moore walked out of the band, leaving them high and dry in the middle of promoting their latest album. Lynott recruited Midge Ure to fly across the Atlantic to help the band finish the tour. One last tour of the year took place during September when the band visited Japan for the first time. For the tour, Lizzy retained the services of Ure and also brought in Dave Flett on guitar to help them through the gigs. Flett had about a week's rehearsal with the band prior to flying to Japan. After hearing that Lizzy were looking for a new guitarist to cover the tour, Flett went away to learn their material. His preparation paid off and he landed the gig. Their paths had crossed the previous year when Flett was doing *Top Of The Pops* with Manfred Mann while Lizzy were promoting the "Rosalie" single.

Ure switched from keyboards to guitar for some numbers, so the band had, at times, a three-guitar attack. The experience of having a keyboard player would later pave the way for a full time one in the shape of Darren Wharton.

"I've thought about Phil quite a lot," says Flett. "To me he was the consummate rock 'n' roller. I often hear Lizzy on the radio and the old memories roll back. It seems the name of Thin Lizzy or Phil Lynott really clicks with people. It makes you realise that they are still making an impact on people who discover their music. Phil wrote through simplicity, he could get all that he needed to get into that three or four minutes. He could keep it simple, make his point and make it mean something to someone. That was the magic of his songwriting."

Once the tour dates were fulfilled the band were once more on the lookout for a new foil for mainstay guitarist Gorham. Lynott even found time to close out the year guesting with Dire Straits a few days before Christmas as David Knopfler recalls: "I knew Phil initially because we were on the same label, Phonogram, in the seventies. He made some generous comments to me about my playing which was very characteristic of him... enormous generosity of spirit. Then I heard a demo he'd made of 'King's Call' which I'd very much liked, and so was able to return compliments back. He guested on a Dire Straits concert, at the Rainbow I think, where he was terrific, despite being fortified with enough cocaine to kill most mortals. As I recall it he laid out five lines – we all politely declined, so he was delighted to take five lines himself. I think Phil would probably have liked the William Blake quote 'The road to excess leads to the palace of wisdom'."

One final word on the *Black Rose (A Rock Legend)* album from Andy Duncan: "I liked the *Black Rose* album and felt that Gary's involvement offered an extra dimension that justified the undoubted grief that he and Phil suffered. The history of rock is littered with examples of bands whose fiery interpersonal relationships benefitted the music and still managed to last more than five minutes. The Daltrey/Townshend axis in the Who being an obvious example. So, on a personal level, I'm sorry that they couldn't make it work. However, I do accept that a scrap between Gary and Phil might have been more potentially lethal than, say, a dust-up between the likes of Noel & Liam [Gallagher], so I suppose it was for the best that they went their separate ways."

12
CHINATOWN

Lizzy began the new decade a musician short given that Flett was gone and Ure would soon follow. The band were tight-lipped on who exactly was in line to fill Gary Moore's shoes. The band started recording new material at Good Earth Studio on 12 January 1980 while Lynott was also putting the finishing touches to his debut solo album. Kit Woolven officially took over from Tony Visconti for the production of the album. Woolven's diary is riddled with Lizzy sessions up until, but not including, 4 February. He spent the 4th and 5th of February at Utopia Studio with cutting engineer Ian Cooper working on "Dear Miss Lonely Hearts". "I think the band didn't think it was strong enough to be a Lizzy song, and Phil didn't want to throw it away", recalls Woolven. "On the other hand, I didn't think it was really right for the solo album because it sounded so much like Lizzy. It was one of those ones that got through."

Unknown to the public at large was that, at the time the group commenced recording in January, the new foil for Gorham had already been chosen. The band found him at Shepperton Studios prior to Christmas where they were auditioning guitarists, though the guitarist they chose was playing with someone else. Guitarist Kirby Gregory also met up with the band having got a call from their publicist, the late Tony Brainsby, who asked if he was still thin and had his own hair. Gregory met the band at John Henry's rehearsal facilities. "When I confirmed to Brainsby that I hadn't let myself go he invited me down", says Gregory. "I was aware that they were in need of a guitarist but I didn't know if it was a permanent gig or just to cover a tour. I was still with Stretch at this point, but I don't think we were doing much at the time so it was an attractive proposition to me. I never got any feedback from the band after that."

Lizzy jammed on the Stretch hit "Why Did You Do It" amongst others, though whether or not the rehearsals were recorded (as Lynott had a tendency to record auditions) is unknown as nothing has ever surfaced. Soon after 1979 gave way to 1980, Thin Lizzy announced Snowy White as their new guitarist. Both Lynott and Gorham had briefly met White in New York a couple of years previously when White was playing with Pink Floyd.

"Phil and I were at this gig and I remember this guy taking a solo and myself and Phil turned to each other saying 'Who the hell is that guy?'," remembers Gorham. "So we headed backstage and met up with him. But it wasn't until we were holding auditions for the next tour at Shepperton Studios when I got really bored by the whole thing, so I took a break and started wandering around to the different sound stages. I walked into the studio where Cliff Richard was playing, and who is on stage with him but Snowy White? So we got talking, and I told him about the auditions and then inquired if he wanted to come down and have a blow with us. So at this point I hadn't even thought about asking him to join the Lizzy set up, it was just something to do to ease the boredom. We all got along great and played some of the new material and it sounded great; and that's where Snowy got in."

White says:

> So the next day Scott phoned up and asked if I'd like to come over and have a blow and that was it. Then it came up that I had to finish the Pink Floyd thing, and Philip said he was willing to wait until I finished, which was great. (Ronnie Gurr interview, 1980)

It wasn't just White that was a new face in the band. Darren Wharton, a keyboard player from Failsworth, Greater Manchester, England, was also on the radar. Given the experience of having Midge Ure in the band while on tour and while Flett was handling guitar Lynott became convinced that adding a keyboard player for the gigs would help add texture and depth to their live sound. At this stage, there wasn't any talk of keyboards becoming a permanent addition. Once White had joined the band it was a new decade, with ever-changing trends at the musical turnstiles. Could Lizzy adapt and grow with the new decade and the changes that threatened their future?

"I don't remember any specific conversations about musical direction," says Snowy White. "The fans just wanted to hear Thin Lizzy sounding like Thin Lizzy, and that's very understandable, so I just learned all the existing twin lead parts. It's difficult to change a successful format. Phil decided he wanted to use keyboards, and he drafted Darren in. I was never sure that keyboards fitted the Thin Lizzy image or music, but I was the new boy and I didn't really have a lot of input at the time. I liked what Darren did though, I thought he added some nice touches."

The band continued to record and rehearse throughout March, before abandoning sessions to fulfil an Irish tour in April. Some of the new material came together quite quickly, particularly once White was in the studio with the band. One of the works in progress when he joined was a song with the working title "Lady Killer On The Loose", the demo of which differs little from the final version other than a slightly different guitar solo and of course "Lady" being removed from the title. Lynott refined the lyric and it became a much more focused affair.

There was so much going on during this March, April and May period, particularly with Lynott's debut solo album clogging up the Lizzy chutes. He even asked his fellow band members to appear in the promotional video for his debut single "Dear Miss Lonely Hearts", adding further confusion. The first product of the new decade offered by Lynott was a solo song which featured the new Lizzy guitar player along with Gorham and Downey. Jumping, as he did, between tracks in the studio caused much frustration when destinations were undetermined for the material. The lack of communication from Lynott was an eye-opener for White, and this work ethic of Lynott's continued for the next couple of years.

"I had just returned from doing the Pink Floyd *Wall* shows in the US and was in the studio the next day to work on the new Thin Lizzy album," recalls White. "I certainly had no inclination to appear on anybody's solo albums, but Phil was doing one and getting it a bit mixed up with our Thin Lizzy recording sessions. Later on it became a bit of a problem, because occasionally we didn't know if the particular track we were working on was for a Thin Lizzy album or Phil's solo. Scott said at the time that he wanted to know which songs were for Thin Lizzy and which were for Phil because he felt that it shouldn't come under our Thin Lizzy money, it should have been a separate thing, and we needed to know how much expensive studio time was being devoted to which project. I don't think that was ever resolved."

With recording sessions on the new album brought to a halt so the band could complete the Irish tour in April, plans were also in place to record some of the live shows. It was certainly a brazen move by the band to start recording live shows so quickly after the additions to the line up. This was achieved by using the Maison Rouge mobile recording truck. As ever, Ireland was used as a testing ground for some of the new material. As early as April, the new album had a title: *Chinatown*. The title track as well as another new song called "The Sacred Sweetheart" were debuted on the tour. The largely low-key tour was an uneventful spectacle apart from the penultimate date in Tralee, Co. Kerry at St. John's CYMS Hall. Woolven flew to Ireland on 12 April and travelled on to Tralee for the recording. The engineer that came with the mobile recording unit was Tony Taverner.

Woolven recalls the date as being chaotic: "The Tralee gig was a nightmare but it was so funny. We were using the Maison Rouge mobile and we parked up outside this Church Hall sort of place in Tralee, and it was a nice little town but I was thinking 'where are all the punters going to come from?' So we got the place all wired up and went into this pristine building that looked like it was used for choir practice and things like that. There was a decent-sized stage and we got it all sorted out, and then coming toward gig time the crowd started building up but the doors weren't opening.

"The kids were lined up and down the road, and then a load of them thought it would be a good idea to try to tip over the recording truck. So, I'm inside the truck with two Maison Rouge guys (Tony Taverner was one) and the thing gradually starts rocking back and forwards. I'm radioing through to backstage: 'Somebody open the bloody doors, they're trying to turn the mobile recording studio over out here'. Soon the doors duly opened and the crowd went in and we recorded the gig. I couldn't see what was happening [inside the gig] as we didn't have video links, but having seen the place beforehand where it was pristine, shiny and clean, then the gig ended... and the ambulances started arriving to take some of the people home and to hospital. Literally people exited with broken arms and it deteriorated into a massive punch up.

"We went inside after and there was blood, beer, piss and God knows what all over the floor. I went backstage and Phil was just sitting there with his head in his hands and he looked up and said: 'Fuck me, I've never seen anything like it. They came out of the hills'. It was like an almighty Saturday night punch up. The thing with the Tralee gig is that you couldn't really see where the people were going to be coming from. It looked like a very sweet village or town but as Phil said 'they came out of the hills'."

The tour concluded with a relatively civilised gig at Cork City Hall whereupon the band had another break before departing for a few dates in Scandinavia. Once the Irish tour was completed Midge Ure departed for good, and, on 17 April, the band started reviewing the live recordings back at Good Earth. Not long after, the band were at Rak Studios when they couldn't secure time at Good Earth.

At Rak the band met Darren Wharton, as Woolven recalls: "Some friends of Phil's from Manchester had told him about this kid that was a great keyboard player who was about 16 or 17 and just playing local bars. Phil was thinking about bringing in a keyboard player for live gigs, for thickening the sound up. Darren came down one weekend from Manchester and came into the studio at Rak. He was sitting around all afternoon, and eventually Phil said 'I'm really sorry but we're busy'. Thinking back, it might be the 'Chinatown' single that we had to get finished. Phil's idea was to have a jam at Rak studios to see if Darren fitted in. There just wasn't time and Phil was very apologetic toward Darren and then asked him if he knew any Lizzy songs.

"So Phil told him to go home and learn a couple of songs and come back next week and we'll have a jam. So Darren went home but came back again the next week and this time they were definitely having a jam. So Phil asked him if he had learned a couple of songs. Darren said he did and Phil asked which ones. Darren quickly replied... 'all of em'.

Phil thought he meant all of one album or something like that. So Phil asked him to name a song he wanted to jam on but Darren said 'you name one and I'll play it'. This was a 16-year-old kid. And he bloody had learned them all. We just sat back thinking 'flipping hell he's a bit good isn't he'."

A couple of weeks later, Wharton made his live debut with the band. Around this time, Lizzy also filmed two promotional videos: one for "Chinatown" which was due for release in May and another promo was made for "Killer On The Loose" which was planned for release closer to the time of the album. In surviving audio footage of the Irish Tour, Lynott regularly announces the "Chinatown" song as the title track of their "Soon to be released" album. There was much fumbling to be had over the coming months when by the end of summer it still hadn't appeared.

Around this time, things started to become confused and musical direction was a real problem. The recording sessions for the new album were brought to a halt to facilitate a tour instead of finishing the new Thin Lizzy album and then orchestrating a tour to promote it. Instead, the band were out on the road at the time that Lynott's debut solo album was released, even incorporating his debut solo single into their set list. Soon after the tour began, the band issued the title track of their new album, "Chinatown", as a single, which peaked at No. 21 on the UK listings. It wouldn't survive in the band's live set beyond the tour.

In fact, little of what appeared on the album was carried over in subsequent live set lists. Also, numerous concerts were recorded for a planned new live album preliminarily titled *Lizzy Killers*. While the band were on the road, the live recordings were returned to the studio where engineers Kit Woolven and Gordon Fordyce mixed them, in preparation for the band's return to the studio to review the material and take a view as to the suitability of releasing it. The planned live album, though worked on to the degree of receiving some clean-up work in the studio, was never released – though some of the material did emerge as bonus material over the coming 18 months, mainly as B-sides to singles.

Guitarist Kirby Gregory met up with the band again at a gig on the UK Tour at Bingley Hall in Stafford: "I was around at the soundcheck and went to say hello to Phil and the band. He said, 'Hey it's Kirby, the guy who was nearly our guitarist'. This was news to me. It's interesting that of the two times I played with them, they were without a guitarist and they seemed a bit subdued. However, I guess that they were going through a time of change and upheaval." By the middle of June 1980 this incarnation of the band came off the road and were soon shacked up in Good Earth Studios, where they would record their first and only complete studio album, *Chinatown*. Though the studio had been used for a variety of demo sessions and other recordings, this was the only album fully recorded at the studio with Kit Woolven on board as co-producer.

A handful of songs from earlier in the year did much to shape the direction of the album though some of the newer ideas were startlingly wide of the mark. A new song called "The Act" submitted to the band by Lynott didn't pass muster, and though a demo of it was recorded it was ultimately rejected by the band. An instrumental of the song exists in the band's archive clocking in at just under four minutes whilst another slightly shorter version complete with Lynott's vocal also exists, though the song appears to be re-titled "It's Going Wrong". The song was later stripped back and re-recorded for Lynott's second solo album and again re-titled as "Don't Talk About Me Baby", losing much of the original charm in the process.

"Turn Around", a song which the band had been playing with in soundchecks throughout the UK tour was also re-worked during this period. The changes weren't huge, nor were the lyrics developed much beyond what initially stood. The available soundcheck recordings do spotlight White's searing solo ability revealing much promise in his contributions for the forthcoming album. It never made the album cut and would have remained in musical purgatory until it was used as a B-side, paired particularly well with the album's second and final UK single (from *Chinatown*), "Killer On The Loose".

This Lynott/Gorham collaboration was unfortunate to be overlooked given what did eventually appear on the album, though if it falls down anywhere it's on the lack of lyrical development. Another off-centre song, again originating with Lynott, came under the working title "The Story Of My Life". In the band's tape archive it's listed as being a consideration for inclusion on the album, dated 12

July. In fact by mid-July 1980, the album looked altogether different from what eventually emerged. To Woolven's recollection "The Story Of My Life" was never finished.

In the band's archive of this time they had enough songs to fill out a new album but the material wasn't quite there yet. By July, a rough running order was compiled, which shows Side 1 opening with "Chinatown", soon followed by "We Will Be Strong", "Didn't I", "Turn Around" and closing with "Killer On The Loose". Side 2 opens with "Hey You", followed by "Having A Good Time", "Sweetheart", "The Act", "The Story Of My Life" before closing up shop with "Sugar Blues". So by the end of July it was an altogether different type of album that the band had on their hands, with much of it being more suitable to Lynott's solo adventures. The aforementioned track listing within their archive is also reflective of how the band went about their work.

Here Woolven clarifies the existence of an alternative *Chinatown* album: "What we used to do at the end of every day, or if we were working on any given song, before we would take that reel off and start work on something else we would do a monitor mix. Because of the nature of the way we worked, you wouldn't just sit there and start to record one song and keep going until the end and then mix it. You might do a load of different backing tracks at different times and then keep adding to songs as they progressed and built. So as we'd work through an album we'd do monitor mixes of the songs we had and these would then be put onto a monitor mix reel so at any time we could listen to any one of the songs in its given state. It was sometimes very useful for sticking the 2-track up before you put the multi-track up just to see how you left it the last time you worked on it.

"These days in my home studio I bring everything up, my desk is completely computerised, the song will sound exactly as it did the last time I put it up. Back then in those days it didn't, because we didn't have recall and all those sorts of things. So you put the 2-track up, listen to how you left the song the last time and then do a monitor mix and re-create it, which is no big deal. It was just what you did. As part of creating an album, Phil might ask to hear the monitor mix reel, so when you're listening to the monitor mix reel sometimes he might say: 'We'll stick that song in front of that one because that song sounds weird coming after the other one. Let's move it somewhere else, 'cos we know that it doesn't work'. It might be the key change, or the tempo of the song might not feel right, so you move the songs around. So you just try to find somewhere it did feel right. That's how you gradually work out what songs work together.

"You'd end up towards the end of an album with having some tracks on your monitor mix reel which were pretty close to the finished mix. So these monitor mixes were like your work in progress album. At some stage you'd end up with a compilation of songs that would almost be the finished running order, in various stages of completion. In fact, some could be completed and others could just be drums, bass, maybe a guitar and a few guide vocals."

So, by July 1980, this alternative *Chinatown* isn't necessarily an album, but an album in progress. The disparity of the material was largely the result of Lynott's *modus operandi*. That's not to say that when he was in the studio he wasn't focused on what he was doing, but with so many ideas being put to tape and many left half-finished, while others were finished and banished to the shelf never to surface again, it's no wonder frustrations were peaking across the board from studio engineers right up to the band's management.

Lynott, by this stage, had taken to making his own decisions as to band direction, and was consistently accepting less and less input from Chris Morrison and Chris O'Donnell. Once the band reviewed this rough draft of the album, they realised additional material was required and subsequently regrouped at Good Earth Studio during August to re-work the album. One additional song was added to the list during this period, "Genocide (The Killing Of The Buffalo)" and instead of writing new and more appropriate material the band decided to whittle back the amount of tracks planned for inclusion. Thus, they had a new album, *Chinatown*.

Lizzy's 10th studio album opens with the jubilant "We Will Be Strong". In much the same way as the band announced a new guitarist in Gary Moore for the opening track of *Black Rose (A Rock Legend)*, on *Chinatown* the band use a similar ploy. Cynics might suggest a formulaic mould had set in, but the symphonic guitar harmony qualities shine through leaving the listener in no doubt that the old Lizzy still remain, still sounding fresh, no matter the new faces on board. It was a surprisingly overlooked choice for single release in the UK, given its melodic commercial attributes.

It did receive a release as a single in the USA, though no records appear to exist on how it performed. Nor is there any known promotional video in existence. There are multiple alternative versions of "We Will Be Strong" in the band's archive, and each runs slightly longer than the album version. There are minor differences to the lyrics while the guitar cacophony remains rigorous as both players frantically interplay on the fret board. Lynott's vocal harmonies lend an air of romance and reassurance as the song serves both the intent of the band and his recent commitment to his wife Caroline.

On the choice of single chosen for release, Snowy White says: "We all discussed the singles aspect, but I think in the end it was a decision made between the band and the management and the record company. To be honest, I wasn't really interested very much in the singles, I enjoyed doing the albums. I just wanted to get some more bluesy things going on some of the album tracks."

The title track follows, a relentless workout for Downey on drums. Its snappy guitar riff is unfortunately let down by Lynott's uninspired lyric. The demo of the song is a much more explosive guitar event with its climatic fervour awash with Lynott's oddly entrancing vocal delivery. The lyric, however, is less than top drawer, but he does deliver the song slightly differently vocally, in a more conversational context. All of this experimentation was abandoned on the eventual album version. It was also telling just how Lynott had fallen in his commitment to his lyrics, with a huge quantity of the work in progress lyric eventually kept over and streamlined for the eventual recording.

"I brought the idea of the opening riff, and a few chord progressions, and the guys liked it and, if I remember rightly, everyone put a few ideas into it," remembers White. "Phil always wrote the lyrics, although we sometimes chipped in with the odd word or two."

"Sweetheart" is the first of a few wayward wanderings on the album, credited solely to Lynott and initially starting life as "The Sacred Sweetheart". It was randomly tested in the band's live set during the Irish tour in April but never really surfaced beyond this period. Under Woolven's guidance, it worked as a poppy, twee type of track and, for all its commercial leanings, it's let down once more by a lazy and meaningless Lynott lyric. The demo of the track, again featuring very similar lyrics to the finished version, is delivered by Lynott in a quick-fire and clipped manner, almost making fun of his ability to previously bend and annunciate words in a way which held the rhyme and context of a song.

Here, on "Sweetheart", its title mercifully changed, this delivery doesn't work and sounds more like a drunken afterthought than a serious way in which to deliver a vocal. The heavy keyboard finish on the song, courtesy of Darren Wharton, is also a key indicator as to the path the band were due to take, whether or not anyone of them knew it at the time.

"Sugar Blues" follows the lyrical sacrilege of "Sweetheart", and again stalls the album with its coy and undemanding appeal. With the recruitment of White, Lizzy were marooned between a rock and Lynott's crotch. It was a band collaboration and, given the title of the album and the subsequent theme offered as per the album's two introductory songs, "Sugar Blues" is a curious oddity for inclusion. "Turn Around" or, as it eventually came to be known, "Don't Play Around", may have been a healthier and altogether more digestible blues number that offered White another "in". His input on the title track was admirable and also showed his willingness to adapt to the band's style. For all its shortcomings, "Don't Play Around" offered White more scope, and it's unfortunate that the throwaway "Sugar Blues" made the final cut.

While taking nothing away from the workout nature of the song and its purpose in helping the band come together, it's simply too much Snowy and not enough Lizzy. Its narrow girth pushes the album to veer and wobble. It's Thin Lizzy displaying vulnerability as they grasp for direction on their material. So far, *Chinatown* rings in the recollection of the *Johnny The Fox* album where some wayward tunes define the album and where the stronger numbers aren't fierce enough to forgive the lesser numbers.

Side 1 exits with the second single issued for the UK market, "Killer On The Loose", the most controversial track on the album. Written around the time that the "Yorkshire Ripper" was at large, the song drew heavy criticism in the press. Interpreted in some quarters as glorifying rape, Lynott was careful in his responses to the press after the backlash.

The success of the song when it was released as a single, reaching No. 10, was coloured by the ire it drew, but the popularity of the song by the record buying public was not anticipated by the record label. "I remember distinctly Chris Morrison and Philip telling me the record company completely fucked up because they hadn't pressed enough copies and they underestimated that it would go straight into the charts, and they had no second supply stream," says Jim Fitzpatrick. "In other words, once it went into the shops it sold out and they couldn't get more stock for a week or two. By that stage the impetus had gone."

Both the "Killer On The Loose" and "Chinatown" video promos were directed by David Mallet and represent his final collaborations with the band. Both are a notch up again in production values from their previous work together on the *Black Rose (A Rock Legend)* single promos.

These were also shot at Hewitt Studios in London, as Mallet recalls: "Out of all the work I have done with them my favourite one was 'Killer On The Loose'. It caused uproar when it first came out because of the similarity with what was happening with the Yorkshire Ripper, but we didn't take much notice of that, a video for the song was what it was. We were making state of the art videos of that time and that's as far as it went." Mallet's recollections of collaborating with the band remain warm, but with a hint of sadness: "One of my biggest regrets is not having directed them live in concert."

Side 2 opens with the insignificant "Having A Good Time", an unnecessary nag from the Lynott/White stable. It thankfully guffaws its way to a speedy conclusion. It offers the album little in terms of direction and is at best a consideration for a B-side. The demo of the song, as in the case of much of the material on the album, differed only slightly. Most notably the lyric, once more, had little or no advancement from the demo stage through until the final cut that made the album.

"Genocide (The Killing Of The Buffalo)" follows it and finds Lynott, the sole writer of the song, harking back to American history. It never quite reaches the peak it might have; while the subject material is political – and Lynott had written of such topics in the past – here it sounds unfinished or perhaps he had bitten off more than he could chew.

"I had a huge input into that song so I was totally disappointed when it went nowhere," laments Jim Fitzpatrick. "I thought Phil's heart was in the right place on that one. Some of the wording I found a bit clumsy, but there you go. At that point some of his words were getting very clunky. He needed to get off drink and drugs and write properly, he had great ideas. Now I don't mean that I was writing lyrics for him, I would correct what I felt were historical inaccuracies and try and rephrase them. I did it on 'Black Rose', quite a bit in reference to stuff about Cuchulain."

The delectable "Didn't I" is the album's penultimate offering, complete with contributions from Tim Hinkley on keyboards with an additional sweetening provided by Fiachra Trench, his first time back on a Lizzy album since 1976's *Johnny The Fox*. Trench had been spending less time with Lizzy and more with Lynott on his solo projects. In the band's archive an extended version exists, running to just over six minutes, with the complete orchestration of Trench's strings intact, though this version is without the guitar solo. The lyrics differ slightly from the final version but do reveal Lynott and Downey's intense rhythmic sensibilities.

"Whether I was working on a Thin Lizzy track or a Phil solo track, I always came in toward the end of the process," says Trench. "I'd listen to what they or he wanted in terms of strings or brass, and then the sweetening began. I was never really there from the ground up when it came to working on the tracks. So, essentially, the tracks already existed by the time I got involved, unlike my work with Van Morrison, being there from the inception and playing piano on some rhythm tracks.

Tim Hinkley had gotten friendly with Lynott during and after the making of the *Jailbreak* album, and was only too happy to offer input on the *Chinatown* sessions while always remaining impressed by Lynott's ability.

"His bass playing style was fairly unique, using a plectrum when it's more usual to finger pick," observes Hinkley. "If his style is reminiscent of anyone, to me it's Entwistle from The Who. It's always a compromise when you're playing and singing at the same time, especially bass guitar as you are trying to hold a perfect rhythmic and harmonic balance. His focus when playing was obviously the bottom end of things, but then at the opposite end of the spectrum he had to deliver the vocal, so he had to cover the top end with his vocals: that is a very unique talent to be able to maintain."

The final slice of *Chinatown* is more in line with the expected annual Lizzy offering. "Hey You, You Got It Made", as it was originally titled before being reduced to "Hey You", is easily one of the album highlights. It was a songwriting collaboration between Lynott and Downey. With its dense dialogue and its picturesque pandering to social isolation, together with Lynott's growling delivery, with occasional piano to help perfectly punctuate the piece, it rightfully received release as a single in foreign territories. On the demo, Lynott's delivery is even more chilling, and it's interesting to note the changes as the song was developed. There's some warmth even in the coldest of Lynott's lyrics, knowing he knew and acknowledged in song what anyone else in everyday life felt, such was his connection with the street. It's quite simply one of a few Lizzy classics from this era.

The *Chinatown* album was eventually released on 10 October 1980, five months after the release of the first single shorn from it. It peaked at No. 7 on the UK album charts but didn't outstay its welcome and, given no further singles were released in the UK following its arrival, the band were, by and large, without any promotional materials to create awareness for it. At the time of its release, the band was on the road, where they completed an Australian and American tour in promotion of the album. This was to be Lizzy's final tour of America with Lynott leading the charge.

Discussing the album's strengths, Snowy White says: "Difficult for me to answer that. I guess overall I thought it was a pretty strong album, but needed a little more work maybe. Plenty of good ideas and some decent playing. I discovered that there was a lot of time wasted in the studio, and that frustrated me a bit. I'd be there at 11 a.m. and Phil sometimes wouldn't turn up until 8 p.m. a bit the worse for wear and not really able to make the most of the session. He'd often bring 'friends' down, and they would sit drinking and talking instead of working. One day, while I was waiting, I put some guitar ideas down so as to not waste time sitting around doing nothing, and Phil didn't even listen to them, just told the engineer to wipe the tracks as he needed them for vocals. Not my idea of how you should treat a fellow band member. A pity, because he was a great frontman, he wrote some great songs, and he could have been much more successful if he'd had a little more understanding of the way to go about these things."

As Woolven continued working with the band while Visconti kept on "being busy", plans were in place to spend some time abroad to record some new ideas that Lynott had developed while on tour in the States. Woolven was also relieved at Visconti's stance on him working with the band, as he was still an employee of Visconti's and though the Lynott/Visconti relationship had fizzled out and the band were still using Good Earth quite frequently, it could have made for an uncomfortable environment in which to create.

"I don't think this is in retrospect but I think I thought the *Chinatown* album might have been a bit more rock 'n' roll," reflects Woolven. "It needed a Robbo or someone like that in there. It needed that sort of rock 'n' roll guitar instead of a bluesy guitar. In no way is that meant as a slight against Snowy. I don't think it was the best chemistry, that particular line up. The substance abuse was definitely going up too, and it was making life more and more difficult."

13

RENEGADE

The somewhat chaotic style in which 1980's *Chinatown* was recorded continued on the next Thin Lizzy studio album. The disorganisation peaked around this period for the band, with Lynott keenly pursuing the recording of solo material across allocated Thin Lizzy studio time. Members of the band commenced recording in Compass Point Studios on 4 January 1981 accompanied by Kit Woolven. Huey Lewis again flew in to provide harmonica to some songs.

It wasn't just a new Lizzy album that was on the horizon, however, as Lynott had triggered a clause in his record contract which made money available to be able to record ideas for his second solo album. Four songs received work over the week-long period spent in the Bahamas: "Cathleen", "In The Delta", "A Little Bit Of Water" and "It's Getting Dangerous", with only the latter surfacing later in the year on the new Lizzy album. "Cathleen" and "Little Bit Of Water" featured on *The Philip Lynott Album*.

On the multiple trips that Lynott made out to Nassau, though work was completed, it was a generally loose affair. The average working day was to get up for breakfast mid-morning and thereafter meet by the pool. Pretty soon the Goombay Smashes [rum-based cocktails] were wheeled out. Suitably tanked, the posse would head for the beach and then grab an early evening meal before meeting around 7 p.m. The drive from the hotel to Compass Point Studios took under an hour and, when possible, recording would go on until 2 or 3 a.m. By the time Lizzy started working there during the first week of 1981, the new Studio B in Compass Point wasn't fully operational. Before the first sessions commenced, Woolven was hard at work getting the mikes sorted, when he noticed his assistant, the late Harold Dorsett, was looking a little nonplussed.

"The patch bay at the end of the desk is where you would link up mikes to channels and any effects you wanted to plug in," says Woolven. "All patch bays are different in every studio, so it's ideal to have someone that knows what they're doing. I had been setting everything up for the recording session and the assistant there didn't seem to be doing very much really, and I turned around to him and asked 'You are fully aware of what we're doing here aren't you, and what's going on here?' but he just turned around and said in his Bahamas accent 'No mon, it all looks like a fucking spaceship to me'. It was so funny but... good times."

By 11 January, the band had four songs in the can, worked up to varying degrees, complete with guide vocals. Lizzy regrouped to complete another touring schedule which took them through to the end of February. As per the band's archive, it appears that after a short break, Lynott decided to switch his attention almost entirely to recording material for his next solo album. There then appears to be a change of tack and, even though by May Lynott had enough material to flesh out a solo album, work on it stopped and he resumed with Thin Lizzy, this time in Odyssey Studios. Between the final tour date on 22 February and Lizzy beginning to record again in May, the band also used some time in the studio. For example, in early March they worked with engineer Steve Prestage at Townhouse Studios putting together work on a half dozen tracks.

"In The Delta" received additional work since its original recording just two months earlier. "Someone Else's Dream" was recorded, "The Act" was resurrected and again abandoned, while three brand new songs received attention, all with working titles: "Kill (Gotta Get A Gun)", "Wham Bam", an idea that Gorham came up with, and "Fats", a song which originated with guitarist Snowy White.

During April, the *Killers Live* EP emerged. There are variations to the release with extra songs contained on the 12" edition. The lead single "Are You Ready" was backed up by "Dear Miss Lonely Hearts" and "Bad Reputation". Again, mixing solo and Lizzy material was ultimately a poor decision. However, the release is notable as it was the last time the band featured in the Top 20 singles chart in the UK, the EP scraping in at No. 19 shortly after its release.

It was becoming apparent that time spent in the studio was increasing, whilst recorded output was falling. Ideas were demoed and frequently forgotten about, older ideas were added to and never finished. "Phil would try to write a lot of the lyrics 'on the spot' instead of doing some homework on them, which meant hours of hanging around while he tried out different ideas," recalls White. "On the *Renegade* album I think he was still writing lyrics when the deadline passed for delivery to the record company, so some of them [songs] were never really 'finished'."

On 2 May, with Kit Woolven overseeing production duties at Odyssey Studios, the band worked on some new material, while once more work was completed on "The Act". The shift from Good Earth Studio had begun, but was more as a result of the studio not being available than anything else.

"If Tony was in [Good Earth] doing something and Lizzy wanted to work, Tony [still] had Chris Porter and Gordon Fordyce [to assist] which freed me up to continue working with Lizzy, says Woolven. "Eventually, myself and Tony did part ways as I had started working less and less at Good Earth. The funny thing was, once I left [Visconti] I started working at Good Earth quite a lot after. Odyssey was big, a double studio complex. It was a purpose built studio. Wayne Bickerton owned it – he went on to become president of PRS. He was a big songwriter himself. Odyssey had matching MCI desks in both control rooms, more toys than you can imagine. It was a really nice studio."

However, the material that was worked on was so diverse that it's conceivable it was intended for Lynott's solo album. A demo of a song titled "Mexican Girl" was put down with just an acoustic guitar, bass and drum machine and shows Lynott feeling his way through the lyric, almost sussing out the plot of the story he was trying to convey. This interesting demo runs to eight minutes with the riff for the main part staying constant until the lyrics were refined, and the song re-titled in later sessions as "Mexican Blood". The song for the most part starts off like a tale of civil war, before the lyrics are honed, and it became a somewhat traditional love story set against the landscape of 1880s Mexico.

During the early May sessions another new song reveals itself: "Darren's Tune", soon to become known as "For Always". A lush ballad with a 1980s feel, the initial demo features a repetitive keyboard riff which grinds the listener's ear. Multiple takes exist in the band's archive with alternative vocals and arrangements, whilst some versions see the keyboard lead replaced by guitars, again all tried at different tempos. It's hard to pinpoint a destination for the track. On some takes, the trademark dual Lizzy leads exist, but it takes too long to get going. Lynott's crass lyric does little to elevate the song the way it could have done with lesser material in the past. In some cases, the demos run anywhere from seven to 10 minutes in length, while the final version complete with string arrangement from Fiachra Trench comes in at just over six minutes. It's no surprise the song remains in the archive, as it falls between the split in Lizzy and Lynott's solo work.

The roots of "For Always" lie with Wharton. "It was written and recorded sometime before the *Thunder And Lightning* sessions," he says. "It was a melancholy number but Phil really liked it. It's a pity it never found a home on any album, but it's still hanging around somewhere." "For Always" was actually written during the band's 1981 *Renegade* recording sessions and was Fiachra Trench's last contribution to a Thin Lizzy recording session.

"'For Always' as I recall – when I put strings to it – was done during what I would call a Lizzy session, but it was one of those songs that could've been interchangeable [Lizzy or Phil solo]," says Trench. "Lizzy might not have used it. It was done around the same time as "Old Town" and "Cathleen". I think we did it at Advision Studios. I'd really like to hear it again, but I wonder if it'll ever see the light of day. It's no great surprise to me that there are many embryonic songs that Phil wrote, some demoed, and even tracks that were completed but never released. Think of Hendrix dropping into studios everywhere, and he may not have intended on the recordings going any further, but they've helped his legacy since his passing. The same could apply to Phil if the record company/estate approves their release."

The band re-grouped during the third week of May at Odyssey Studios, putting down work on three new songs between the 22nd and 25th, again with Kit Woolven at the desk. "Banging My Head Against The Wall", "I'm Gonna Leave This Town" and "Only Woman" received various degrees of work, the latter featuring Snowy White on lead vocal. There is no record to suggest Lynott ever sang lead on the track in the band's archive. In all, these works in progress would have their lyrics rewritten and the arrangements of the songs changed in many ways. For example, by the middle of July "Banging My Head Against The Wall" received a lyrical overall and was retitled "Down On Your Luck". It was then reworked further, and once again re-titled "Hollywood (Down On Your Luck)". The first demos of the song are very rough lyrically, with Lynott loosely referring to hard times on the street. As the song was developed the hook was changed, and it's one of the few songs on the album which shows a serious amount of development.

Another new song, "Moving Away From Here", was written by Snowy White. It was recorded with White singing the lead vocal. A hard rocking number, it features a great riff and, given the circumstances within the band, its title and lyric are telling. It's unknown whether or not Lynott recorded a vocal for the song, but the Lizzy archive indicates no further work was done on the song after this time. White's trademark bluesy rock stamp is all over the song and, with a little work, it could have been an interesting addition to the new album.

"I think I was just kicking around ideas that might have been OK for Thin Lizzy to use," says White. "I certainly wasn't doing them for me. For a start, I was no singer, and the vocals were just rough ideas for Phil to maybe work on and take further. Lots of ideas fell by the wayside, that's the normal way it works."

The band continued recording throughout June at Odyssey Studios and by the 12th they had recorded "Trouble Boys" and "Memory Pain". A third song, "Sweet Samantha" was worked on when Jimmy Bain arrived into the studio on the 10th. It doesn't appear to have been worked on by the band. It was written for Bain's daughter, to whom Lynott was Godfather. As it stands, it's a demo in the truest sense of the word and features just an acoustic guitar and Lynott's trusted drum machine, astride his chorused bass sound. There is a complete vocal, though this is without doubt meant as a guide.

Lynott would have intended to return to it but it's unknown if he ever did. In its demo form it runs to nearly six minutes in length, and a suitable home was never likely to be a Lizzy album. Further work appears to have been completed in July on "Kill (Gotta Get A Gun)" and also "Mexican Blood", complete with the minor title change. By the end of July the barrel of songs that the band had been gathering was eclectic to say the very least.

Lynott harangued the band and record label into releasing "Trouble Boys" as a single, which was a cover of a Billy Bremner song. Rockpile guitarist Bremner was also present in the studio when the song was recorded. In a rather bizarre twist, the record label agreed and the song was issued as a single on 31 July 1981, backed with another cover song, "Memory Pain", written by the late Percy Mayfield. It failed to breach the Top 40 in the charts, though the band promoted the song widely on a variety of television shows. No video promo was specifically filmed for its release and it exists as an oddity in the band's catalogue of released singles, with guitarist Snowy White saying simply, "Phil wanted to do it."

It may also have been in the back of Lynott's mind that releasing a single prior to a few key outdoor festivals the band was booked to play was a good thing. As the new album was in no condition for release, having a single out would generate some buzz, and it's altogether unfortunate that the "Trouble Boys" song was the chosen one.

By this time, Lynott simply had too much power and his abuse of it led to the slow disintegration of the band. *Trouble Boys* was also the working title of the new Lizzy album for a time, after the original working title was thrown out, that being *Living Out Somebody Else's Dream*. The "Trouble Boys" single found its way into the public domain and failed to breach the Top 50. Fitzpatrick contributed the artwork for the single sleeve and this represents one of his last contributions to the band. "Memory Pain", the B-side of "Trouble Boys", was a perfect vehicle for White's playing style and featured prominently in the band's live set list later in the year. It was not, however, a vehicle Lizzy ever should have buckled up in.

By July, the band's recordings included: "I'm Gonna Leave This Town", "Hollywood (Down On Your Luck)", "Fats", "Mexican Blood", "It's Getting Dangerous", "Trouble Boys", "Moving Away From Here", "Only Woman", "Memory Pain", "Kill (Gotta Get A Gun)", "Bad Is Bad", "If You Save Souls" and "For Always". There were a series of other fragments and ideas but at this stage these were untitled. Several of these fragments were later reworked, but as it stood in July the band really didn't have an album's worth of material. Nor did the material that they had in the can resemble anything which could be fashioned into a Thin Lizzy album: the songs just weren't there. In fact, much of the new material was more akin to a solo record rather than anything appropriate for a Lizzy release.

Before the band took on some festival dates in August another new song began to emerge, with a working title of "Disaster"; apt given that this was exactly what the band were facing after the summer sessions for the new album. This new song was premiered at a filmed performance in Rockpalast, Loreley, Germany in late August. Featuring Lynott's early lyrics it was at the very least something that offered a little more depth. The band also played another unreleased song, "Hollywood", which was extremely close to the final version that later appeared on the album.

The band also took time out to perform at the inaugural Slane Festival, Ireland, during August 1981 before returning once more to the recording studio during September and October. Their live set was again peppered with some new material, but the available recordings show the band were not quite on the money that day.

With the festival dates out of the way, the band resumed work at Odyssey, and also Morgan Studios where various overdubs were being done. It was at Morgan Studios when the change came that saw Kit Woolven cease his role as producer of the album.

"At some point we were up at Morgan Studios, which turned into Battery Studios, and we were all in the bar waiting for the studio to clear, for us to go in," remembers Woolven. "I was having a few personal problems at the time and Phil was saying to me, 'Buck your ideas up'. I just said I wished we could stick to one project and stop hopping around. It was around the tail end of the *Renegade* sessions. Chris Tsangarides worked out of Morgan Studios and had worked with the band before. He had done a lot of stuff with Gary Moore, and that's when we did the changeover. We had about a week or ten days and I passed over to Chris. So Chris took the album on from me. I had virtually finished everything at that time."

Woolven's frustration was borne from not knowing which album he was going to be working on from day to day, and felt that his message to Lynott was misunderstood when they were in the bar at Morgan Studios. "Sometimes, Phil would say 'there's a tape with an idea and I've got an idea I want to add'," says Woolven. "So you go with the flow, but it did become irritating because you ended up not knowing what project you were working on. Snowy White complained about it. I remember he couldn't figure out if he was working on a *Chinatown* song or a Phil solo song. Tony [Visconti] felt the same during the *Black Rose* period and I started to feel like that particularly by the time we got to *Renegade*. That's probably part of our falling out.

"I asked him, 'Can we just work on one thing or another: Lizzy or solo?'. I just asked one or the other but Phil read what I was saying differently to what I meant. He then asked 'What do you wanna do? Solo stuff or Lizzy stuff?' So I said the solo stuff. It ended up being that he wasn't allowing me to do both when all I really wanted to know in advance was some clarity on what we were going to be working on from day to day. If we went into the studio and he said 'This is a solo day', then that would've been great. Or 'today is going to be all Lizzy'. But if you go in and you're working on Lizzy and then Phil says 'let's put such and such a song up for my solo jobbie'. So you had to get your other hat on. We were doing this and now we're off doing that – it was just very, very confusing. It did get to be frustrating for everyone, as you might lose the flow. I wasn't particularly keen on the way *Renegade* was going. It didn't do it for me. I stuck with the solo stuff as it was more interesting. We were doing brass, orchestras and it was more diverse."

So, Tsangarides met the band and reviewed the material and announced his worry about the focus of the material recorded. Some material, entirely unsuited to a Lizzy album, was discarded, and the band set about recording new material to add to some which was recorded earlier in the year. The material being reviewed, however, was largely only ever intended for Lynott's second solo album. "Trouble Boys" was out, though if it had been a hit it may have swung a place on the new album. Another song, "Beat Of The Drum", recorded during July, was also dismissed, though in all likelihood this was only ever suitable for a solo-related release by Lynott. One of the fragments initially started by the band with Woolven was resurrected under Tsangarides' guidance. Its working title was "If You Save Souls". Once more holed up in Odyssey Studios, with engineer Andrew Warwick assisting Tsangarides, work was done on the song on 18 September.

Lynott sang "If You Save Souls" across an otherwise lyric free chorus, until a chance encounter from afar while on a break from the recording studio. He had seen a biker with the Thin Lizzy logo on his jacket and written alongside it was the word *Renegade*. Consequently, the direction of the song was resolved, the title "If You Save Souls" was dropped and the band had a new song in the form of what was to become the title track of the album, "Renegade". By this stage in September the band were still shy on material deemed appropriate for inclusion and so set about writing additional material. What came out of this late recording stage was "The Pressure Will Blow" and "No One Told Him", a revamped version of "Disaster" which soon became known as "Angel Of Death".

The band were scheduled to tour the UK in November and December to coincide with the release of the new album. However, aside from the one-off "Trouble Boys" single back in July, a new single to help promote the new album never appeared. *Renegade*, Lizzy's 11th studio album, was released on 15 November 1981 and featured some of their most diverse offerings to date. On its initial release, the album was a commercial failure, reaching no higher than No. 38 on the UK charts.

190

The album opens with keyboard player Darren Wharton's first writing credit on a Lizzy album, a collaborative effort with Lynott on "Angel Of Death". The lyric was inspired by Lynott seeing *The Man Who Saw Tomorrow*, recounting the prophecies of Nostradamus. The album opens with Wharton's menacing keyboard tones before Lynott utters a single line alluding to "millions of them", presumably dead bodies strewn across the land post the deathly arc of said Angel. The six-minute-plus epic is an emphatic introduction to the album with the heavy swooping guitar dual riffs acting as fluttering wings of the Angel of Death. Wharton's strong keyboard bedding on the rhythm track is for once perfectly attuned with the song. As he was present and co-wrote the song his keyboard playing is less an intrusion and more an essential ingredient.

Another six-minute-plus epic follows by way of the title track "Renegade". On it, Lynott revisits the theme of the outsider, a role he is consistently identified with. The melancholic riff, originated by White, is afforded sparse but standout lyrics: less was more or, at least, enough. Unlike the band's last epic, "Black Rose (A Rock Legend)", "Renegade" was very different. This was a new type of classic that the band committed to vinyl. The sadness of the melody almost languishes on the perimeter of its own poignancy, and is an affecting and mature lyrical musing on being the outsider.

It's a tough strike from the band and could easily be construed as a metaphor of their failed efforts to break on through to higher divisions of musical success. Co-writer of the song Snowy White says: "I think I came up with most of that song, except the middle section, and I think I wrote and played most of the lead guitar parts on it. But I had no idea what the lyrics should be, so Phil came up with those, and also the *Renegade* idea for the album title. I don't remember the 'If You Save Souls' bit, but it was probably Phil just kicking around ideas." Tsangarides also recalls White's input on the title track: "That was mainly all Snowy on the 'Renegade' song, the whole style of the song was really him. This was also the song that needed the most work by the time I came to work on the album."

"The Pressure Will Blow" follows, a Gorham/Lynott collaboration, and one of just three developed and polished by Tsangarides during the September and October sessions. It was also recorded with Woolven, though to what degree is unknown as no demos are listed in their archive. It carries over minor military themes reminiscent of "Soldier Of Fortune", but Lynott carefully weaves in a sub-plot to the story as revealed in the lyrics; a love triangle in some ways. Lynott's consistent questions on trust, deception and departure complete with his rasping vocal delivery, again in line with "Soldier Of Fortune", were becoming more and more frequent.

At least two demos of "I've Gotta Leave This Town" exist in the band archive. The first demo, running to just over four minutes, features Lynott mainly offering the song as a commentary rather than singing. Only when it comes to the chorus does he make any effort to deliver a vocal. A second demo running to just over four and a half minutes is closer to the album version musically, though it features completely different lyrics. Lynott's idea for how the lyric should unfold is in place, as he name checks various towns and cities. It's an amusing take and tale that could be considered autobiographical given his reputation with the opposite sex.

It's also an indicator of the parody that had unfortunately snuck its way up into Lynott's lyrics. Lynott discussed the influence of the song with Tommy Vance in a promotional radio segment:

> The minute I heard Scott play the riff I went "That's like ZZ Top"; immediately I sort of ripped off ZZ Top for all their worth. I mean I'd rip off anybody if I thought I could do it as well. If I can do it better, great. A couple of other ideas did come from that.

Side 2 of the album opens with "Hollywood (Down On Your Luck)", another Gorham/Lynott offering, soon to be the only single issued from the album in the UK. It features some clever lyrics from Lynott and a typically strong riff from Gorham. In a minor way, it's a commentary from Lynott on making it in the business, that very showy business.

"They did struggle to find a single on the album, and I struggled to see one, but I think we felt that 'Hollywood' was the closest, and even then I wasn't quite too sure how it might do," recalls Tsangarides.

"Without the promotional tool of a video promo, the band were forced to perform/mime the song on a variety of television shows. Getting the single to chart was also going to be a battle given that it wasn't issued until February 1982, three months after the album. It never stood a chance, and peaked at No. 53 on the UK charts, the same unenviable destination as the calamitous "Trouble Boys".

"No One Told Him" follows, one of just two songs on the album solely credited to Lynott. In hindsight, given the recording sessions earlier in the year afforded to his second solo album, it's little surprise that his input was slighter than on previous albums. Though he co-wrote much of the album it's interesting to note that the two songs he is solely credited for are un-Lizzy like numbers. "No One Told Him He Was Crazy", as it was introduced by Lynott at some live gigs prior to the release of the album, has its moments – unfortunately they're just not Lizzy moments. It's Lizzy pop, throwaway stuff; much like the next two numbers, "Fats", a Lynott/White collaboration, and "Mexican Blood".

"Fats", as experimental as any song Lizzy included on their last three albums, is a loose musical tribute to Fats Waller while also unveiling Lynott's worst lyric in years. Such is the departure on this song that it's hard to comprehend that this is the same band that could come up with "Emerald" and "The Boys Are Back In Town". But, in effect, this wasn't the same band that came up with those numbers. Different members have separate influences, and while "Fats" is a curiosity to hear, it's also a deafening indictment of a band running out of steam.

"When I hear the *Renegade* album now – I get it. It contains some very strong songs, but I think it was maybe ahead of its time," says Tsangarides. "It was just too diverse for people to accept when it was first released. If you listen to it you'll notice how no one song on there is like another."

Multiple versions of "Fats" exist in the Lizzy archive at various levels of development. On a visit home to Dublin, Lynott worked at Windmill Lane Studios with Kit Woolven where he recorded a version of "Fats", though it still lacked the piano solo that Wharton later married to it. Differing lyrics exist across the demos, with many of them appearing to show the influence of working and socialising in the Soho area of London. A later discarded sub-plot Lynott included on one of the demos refers to a character "Having the looks though he knew she hooks".

Lynott discussed the development of the track with Tommy Vance in a radio interview:

> I was gonna make up a great story to give the tale of the song, about when Sigmund Freud went to see Fats Waller and Fats Waller didn't wanna see him. But of course they never met, well not as far as I know... but I was gonna tell a lie. But the idea was a simple one, I just thought "Thin Lizzy play Fats", it's as corny as you can get. Then the idea... I wanted to try and sing almost like Satchmo, you can hear me trying to do that.

"Mexican Blood", Lynott's only other solo songwriting credit on the album, shows where his mind was focused. From the demo through until the finished work, Lynott put sufficient time and development into the lyric, but it was much more in tune with his solo work than Thin Lizzy. Lynott's explorations on the themes of love and violence are, as ever, evident on this song and also reveal details about his perspectives on the subjects. It's a terrible tale of loss, a theme Lynott would return to over and over from the start of his career until the end.

The album is redeemed by its closer, "It's Getting Dangerous", a loose idea that Lynott brought with him to Nassau earlier in the year. Co-written with Gorham, its message can easily be misconstrued. Lynott confessed that the tale of the song is all about the loss of friendships, about growing up and the sense of loss someone feels when they grow apart.

Of course, given the personal state of both Gorham and Lynott it's easy to interpret the message in the song as one of personal woe due to drug abuse. But this is where Lynott is at his most clever: his songs are wide open for interpretation, there is usually more than one angle and also space for the listener to interpret as they feel fit. Tsangarides confesses, "It's one of my favourite tracks that I still listen to, to this day."

Given the fairly disjointed nature of the sessions throughout 1981, the album content is reflective of this due to the inclusion of "Fats" and "Mexican Blood", in particular. The album may not have spawned a hit single in "Hollywood", unlike *Chinatown* which yielded two hit singles in the UK, but *Renegade* is a far superior album lyrically. When Lynott was on form, such as he was on "It's Getting Dangerous", "Angel Of Death" and the title track, the lyrical content on *Chinatown* can't hold a candle to these songs, and all this at a time when Lynott's laziness with his lyrics was coming to the fore. The feeling remains that the album could have been so much stronger, particularly if the time had been used more economically. If there had been more time with which to re-create the album after Woolven's handover to Tsangarides and the release delayed until the new year, it's highly possible the album could have been re-worked. In the meantime, Lynott's second solo album languished in the studio and didn't appear until later the following year.

The failure of *Renegade* commercially was a body blow for the band, and the perceived lack of record label support didn't help group morale. "Whether an album sells a lot or not is as much to do with the record company's input regarding money spent on promotion as the quality of the music," reflects White. "My impression was that the record company was not fully behind the project."

The band toured the album from February through until May 1982, culminating in two shows at the Dominion Theatre in London, which were filmed for a planned commercial release. Ultimately the footage remains in storage with no plans for distribution. Once the Lizzy touring commitments were completed, Lynott reverted to working with Kit Woolven on the second solo album. By August of 1982, Snowy White had left the band, just prior to recording what turned out to be their final studio offering, *Thunder And Lightning*.

"Any band has a natural life-span. There comes a time when you're just repeating yourself," comments White. "Maybe it was that time for Thin Lizzy, I don't really know. When you try to do something a bit different you risk losing all the old fans, so it's easy to get stuck in just repeating the formula. Phil was the leader and he had the image, and there was a lot resting on his shoulders. He did well considering all the pressure on him. In my opinion he was really great at what he was, which was being the frontman for Thin Lizzy, but ultimately he succumbed to trying to be a celebrity instead of a musician. Maybe that was part of the problem. I felt that he wasn't part of a band any more, he was trying to be a solo artist. Nothing wrong with that, but I didn't want to be involved in it."

Jim Fitzpatrick was called upon to produce some artwork for the album sleeve, though his efforts never went beyond the rough draft stage. By now Phonogram were ignoring Lynott's requests for bringing in outside artists for the artwork. The industry was changing. Budgets cuts sliced through any ambitions artists such as Lynott had for Lizzy record sleeves. The eventual sleeve that appeared was shot by photographer Graham Hughes, cousin of Roger Daltrey. The sleeve art that ended up on the cover was loosely inspired by Tsangarides' then cigarette habit.

"The cover concept of *Renegade* came from me, well sort of anyway," remembers Tsangarides. "At the time, I used to smoke Dunhill International cigarettes. I remember Phil pointing to the colour of the box at the console and immediately identifying with a concept in his head. Straight away he was on the phone to the director in the Art Department to get his idea across. So what you see, with the flag on the reverse side as well, is none other than my ciggie box. I always have a laugh when I think of that."

Fitzpatrick's idea, as previously mentioned, was never actually finished though it does make for fascinating reading given the concept established by the title track. Fitzpatrick: "I did roughs for that – a beautiful Wanted poster of Phil in the centre, all Wild West lettering. I remember seeing the final version (of what appeared on the album) and it was rubbish. The rough I did was a very sinister looking Phil lighting a fag and looking up, wearing a sombrero. He loved that whole thing. I haven't seen the Wanted poster of Phil in the sombrero since I did it - that vanished."

The Graham Hughes-shot front and back cover sleeve is a novelty in that it's one of very few Lynott-approved photos where his upper lip isn't housing the "In like Flynn" pencil thin moustache.

Fitzpatrick would again do some rough work on Lizzy's final studio offering, but again these were never finished due to the record label refusing to extend their budget. With the band on the brink of bankruptcy due to the failure of *Renegade*, they still had to deliver two more albums to Phonogram to fulfil their contract. Chris Tsangarides was retained as producer for what turned out to be Lynott's final studio album for Thin Lizzy.

14
THUNDER AND LIGHTNING

The *Renegade* project may have suffered as a result of Lynott's solo distractions, but at least he appeared to acknowledge the meanderings of the recent 18 months when Tsangarides insisted that the band use rehearsal rooms to develop new material, as well as studios in Ireland.

The salad days of booking expensive time in a recording studio to develop material for a new album were over. Again a guitar player short and contracted to deliver a new studio record, Lynott's eye fell upon a friend of producer Chris Tsangarides. His name was John Sykes, a relative newcomer on the scene, who had already contributed to a couple of albums by the Tygers Of Pan Tang before he ended up riding shotgun with Lizzy.

The summer of 1982 was largely spent in Ireland. Lynott toured with a solo band and also used Dublin studios to rehearse the *ad hoc* band. Recordings exist of their rehearsals, much of which was to feature on his second solo album. Meanwhile Tsangarides was also working in Dublin, where he helped Sykes meet a commitment by producing a single at Lombard Studios called "Please Don't Leave Me" on which Lynott was asked to guest as lead vocalist.

During the pre-production period on the album in Dublin, the band, along with Chris Tsangarides, used Lombard as their base prior to taking the ideas to England. Daire Winston, an engineer that worked out of the studio during this period recalls: "Phil was in the studio with Lizzy but he was also in with Auto De Fe [a band formed by Gay Woods and Trevor Knight of Steeleye Span fame] around this time. The Lizzy sessions were definitely demos with Chris Tsangarides. I remember them working out one of the guitar solos in the control room. They seemed to be dropping in something on every bar. I was pretty amazed at the way they constructed the guitar solo.

It was hard work in those days dropping in on a tape machine every couple of bars. Tsangarides would build the solos like this and he seemed to have a good idea at this stage so by the time they got to Eel Pie Studio he would have had a very clear idea of what the band were supposed to do."

In addition to White leaving the band, Lizzy's co-manager Chris O'Donnell had also thrown in the towel, frustrated at the direction (or lack of it) the band were going and the impossibility of trying to manage Lynott.

White was a blues aficionado, a Lizzy-lineage too stretching back to the Decca days, though seldom in an overwhelming way. As a co-lead with Gorham the blend wasn't quite right, the balance off kilter. Gorham needed a foil to play off, not be the foil to someone else. However, he possessed other qualities that the band needed, particularly at this time in their career.

"I think Scott's role in Lizzy was very important. He was a very likable bloke," remembers Woolven. "Always very amusing, would always create an air of calm about things. He was very affable and very chilled and relaxed. He was just what you needed when someone like Robbo was on the other side. I don't think Snowy was right for Lizzy, and in all honesty I wouldn't have thought that Snowy thought he was right for Lizzy. I think he did find it frustrating half of the time."

Losing White also meant losing a certain discipline. White was reliable, solid and committed to the Lizzy cause as long as he was also allowed some creative space. As time moved on, that space which he needed was becoming squeezed. The jump in terms of musical maturity between *Chinatown* and *Renegade* was very audible, and maybe even too sophisticated in some ways. Of all the guitarists that followed Robbo, White's playing style is the one that at the very least evolved the band's sound. The lack of commercial success of *Renegade* was really down to Lynott and his need to have an outlet as a solo artist. It was this dilemma that was the ultimate death knell for the band's future, along with his escalating drug use.

The space and scope for White to be able to introduce his own ideas never really got off the ground, but there were snapshots, in particular the "Renegade" song itself. Unfortunately, Lizzy were tied to the identifiable formula they established on 1976's *Jailbreak*. The band were shackled by the success of that album in many ways, and they could only deviate from the formula so far. By the start of the 1980s, the unravelling began within the band, but that's not to say they didn't go down fighting.

The pre-production work on the album was mainly carried out at Lombard Studios in Dublin where the band tried to get the new material in shape as best they could before traveling to England to record. The band arrived at Lombard with a big 18 wheeler. Tape operator Patrick Fenning assisted Tim Martin in the rehearsals and recalls the band arriving with "the whole back-line". "I remember setting up Scott Gorham's rig. He had guitar picks with his own name on them, I think I still have one. It was the first time I had ever seen such a set up. The same with Darren Wharton. They basically had their own PA system and all we had to do was stick a mic in front of it."

Fenning's introduction to Lynott's sense of humour didn't take long to surface as he recalls: "Phil was incredible to work with, he just had a manner that put you at ease immediately and it was impossible to dislike him. I remember someone had left a book in the studio and I started to read it. It wasn't very good but after a while I had invested enough time in it that I was determined to finish it. Anyway, in comes Phil into the control room and takes the book from me and goes straight to the last page and tells me who did it. All I could do was laugh and put down the book. I never did finish it but I did read the last page just to make sure he wasn't winding me up."

The new album was to be recorded at Eel Pie Studios in Twickenham, while producer Chris Tsangarides was tasked with bringing the album in within eight weeks, with the record label touting an early new year release followed by a nationwide tour. Tsangarides brought engineer Andrew Warwick with him, and found at the studio Chris Ludwinski, another engineer employed recently as a tape operator by Pete Townshend.

Ludwinski recalls the band being well organised when they came in as "they seemed to know what tracks they were doing. But there was also this thing with Sykes. When the band came in, Sykes was brought in basically as a session guitarist and then all of a sudden he was in the band, and Snowy White, who I never saw, was out of the band," says Ludwinski. "So there was a little bit of politics, just as they started the album, politics that I wasn't aware of."

"Every guitar player that played with Lizzy always contributed something, that was the deal really," reflects Gorham on the merry-go-round of axemen in the band. "It was Brian and myself that created the original sound and format that was to go on throughout Lizzy. I always look at Brian as a really great and creative guitar player at that point; he came up with some amazing stuff at just 18 years of age. At that point he was a much better guitar player, and I was happy to let him fly most of the time.

"Everyone else who came in had to go by the format but it was always expected that the new player would bring in his own style to the plate. We never tried to inhibit anybody in any way. Gary then came in for a while and then he was gone. Snowy was a blues guitar player being asked to play in a hard rock situation and I think he did really well. After Snowy, John came on board for the *Thunder And Lightning* album. John was great because he had a real hard rock edge to him, great attitude and was a very funny guy, though most importantly he was a great player."

Tsangarides was fairly concise in his vision for the album, as a series of songs, written after the band's touring commitments ceased in May, were soon put to tape. Thin Lizzy's financial position was also starting to become untenable. Commercial success in the UK for Thin Lizzy was the fulcrum on which their financial survival hung. If their records didn't sell in this market the financial ramifications could be fatal. The commercial failure of *Renegade*, in the UK in particular, ensured that the band travelled no further than Europe on the tour. Touring during this period was very expensive and, taking into account the reception afforded the *Renegade* album, it was a wise move not to sanction dates on other continents.

Prior to starting the recording sessions for the new album, rumours circulating in the press suggested that the band was on the verge of splitting up, owing to both the commercial failure of *Renegade* and also Snowy White's departure. However, due to the limited promotional tour of *Renegade* it did allow for more routine time to write new material. Any rumours of a split were denied and the matter of recording a new album was taking over. Gorham had spoken to Lynott prior to the recording sessions about quitting the band in order to get his health back on track. Lynott, ever the raconteur, deflected Gorham's initial request and quickly talked him into recording a new album and, following that, participating in a new tour to promote it.

For Tsangarides, the goal set for the new album had to be clear, so a repeat of the disjointed recording methods of recent years had to go. Thin Lizzy's final studio album, *Thunder And Lightning*, was also the first since *Bad Reputation* where the band could work uninterrupted without having to tour. Before the album was even finished an announcement was made to confirm that the band would be splitting up once their touring commitments for *Thunder And Lightning* were completed.

To most within the industry it came as no surprise. Old friend David Jensen says: "It was a natural progression for Lizzy to finish when they did, and it certainly wasn't earth shattering news when the announcement came that they were calling it a day."

"It wasn't a surprise that Lizzy ended," reflects Chalkie Davies, who has seen this happen so many times in his long and illustrious career. "There's a pattern that evolves with groups. You get 18 years to write your first record and 18 months to write the second. So, that sets you up for the third one which can be often bad, sometimes good, then come albums four and five. You can only go so far, or I thought you could only go so far, until either you had a drastic change or you disband. You're up against the fact that people who come and see you want two thirds of the show to be what you've previously done. So it's very difficult to introduce new material into a set."

To follow on from Davies' last point about fans not wanting to hear new material, unlike *Black Rose*, *Chinatown* and *Renegade*, none of the tracks included on *Thunder And Lightning* received any roadwork or early showing to the fans, simply because under taskmaster

Tsangarides the object at hand was to record everything to the highest possible standard, to ensure there was cohesion and direction and to make the record as accessible as possible.

"When I got to *Thunder And Lightning* we had to be focused, whether it was recording a ballad or a rock tune," says Tsangarides. "It also had to be in a certain direction, and melodic hard rock was what Thin Lizzy was all about. Even though this was Lizzy's last studio album, it wasn't meant to be the last. In my opinion it was a publicity stunt that went wrong and, because the press had picked up on the story and repeated it, to save face they had to split up."

Once the marker was put down and the theme of the album established under *Thunder And Lightning*, Tsangarides used numerous sound effects throughout the album to re-enforce this cohesion. Also, there was no resurrecting old and previously unused material under Tsangarides' watch, and little material was left over from the new sessions, excepting "Don't Let Him Slip Away".

On "Blue Parris", an unfinished number, Lynott used lyrics which would later surface on "The Sun Goes Down". Many of the lyrics sung on "Blue Parris" were later co-opted for another Lizzy track called "Don't Let Him Slip Away" though they are entirely different songs. The track features spoken word passages such as a female vocalist whispering, "I reject you, I reject you, I reject you" though the singer is not identified. The whirling harmonica sounds lend the track to a solo project rather than Lizzy. It isn't without its appeal and wouldn't require too much trickery to be completed.

Pat Fenning remembers his first experiences of working with Lizzy: "The first time was when Phil was putting *Thunder And Lightning* together, I didn't do too much on that except clean up after a bunch of rock stars, there were just too many people in the control room you couldn't get in. After that, though, he came in as a producer for a few bands, there was one from Howth I don't recall their name but I was really impressed; he took what I would have called an average if not very good trad. band and gave them a really great sound and showed them how to arrange and make their music present itself."

203

When Lizzy arrived into recently opened Eel Pie Studios, the main recording room also had a small stage at one end. There was a closed circuit TV set up in the control room as, when you were sitting in the control room, engineers and producers couldn't see the band perform. Featuring a mix between static cameras and ones you could operate to zoom in or out, it allowed the band to work without the big brother effect of both the engineers and producer gazing out at the band performing.

Downey's drums were placed on the small stage, while Lynott recorded his vocals in an isolated booth to ensure there wasn't too much spill over on the microphones. Lynott frequently sang a live vocal when the band were playing the songs in the studio prior to tracking, but one problem throughout sessions was Lynott's consistent delaying of recording his vocals; he simply hadn't developed the lyrics much beyond what was recorded on the demos in rehearsal in Dublin.

Another issue to contend with was the new relationship between Sykes and Gorham. By the time Sykes joined the band they were just about to start recording at Eel Pie, and so it left hardly any time for their styles to be married to each other. Gorham was fairly quiet throughout the sessions, somewhat despondent as he had wanted out to confront his drug problem. Having been roped in one more time by Lynott, his participation was limited and Sykes handled a large amount of the guitar on the album. However, given the short amount of time that both he and Sykes had in which to become familiar with each other, the album holds up musically; whether you're a fan of the content or not, the playing was impressive.

Gorham's traditional rock soloist leanings were at odds to the *arpeggio* solo style that Sykes was bringing to the table, and it's in evidence across the album. Keyboard player Darren Wharton also began to emerge from the shadows, securing writing credits on four of the album's eventual nine tracks. Nicknames abounded during the recording sessions, with Wharton appropriately saddled with "The Wart Man", producer Tsangarides was referred to as "Poontang" while engineer Ludwinski was referred to as "Spartacus", for reasons he still can't recall.

"Darren was fantastic, a great keyboard player," remembers Ludwinski. "For a few tracks we set him up in front of the mixing desk in the control room. Darren would say 'Give us a sound Chris, give us a sound' and what he meant was bring the keyboards up so he could hear them, and he would insist on turning it up louder and louder until it was blaring out of the speakers. We were in there thinking 'No way, I can't work like this'. So what we did was give him a pair of headphones to put on so he could have it as loud as he wanted but we didn't have to hear it blaring in the control room.

"He did all his keyboard overdubs like that, sat in the control room. It was quite funny, because as he was playing keyboard he's also making these strange sounds to himself as he's playing along. Of course he had the headphones on and couldn't hear himself making these really funny noises! He was a really great keyboard player and he was always, always, always working to improve every track as much as he could."

Tsangarides can also recall Wharton sitting alongside them in the control room working on his parts, and how his habit of eating crisps contributed to the way he played. "Well, what Darren would do is eat crisps quite a lot, and of course he'd have oily hands after the crisps, which he was then convinced helped him to play much faster," says Tsangarides, laughing. "I do recall him being in with us at the desk noodling away with the headphones on and it was killing us."

The album opens with a crunching Sherman Tank of a song in the form of the title track, "Thunder And Lightning". It was probably the heaviest song ever committed to vinyl by the band. Credited to Downey and Lynott its frantic pace and lyrical content was a 1980s update of "The Rocker". With Lynott throwing in every conceivable macho scenario, he saluted the stereotypes with which rock 'n' roll was riddled, almost welcoming them instead of trying to give them the wide berth they deserved.

Tsangarides asked Lynott to up the ante when it came to the delivery of the vocal: "I just told him to go out there and sing it as fast as he could with as much aggression as he could muster. He found this quite difficult to do but he got there in the end." As an asthmatic, who smoked heavily, delivering the vocal in such a way led to problems for Lynott. He was also by now in the grip of a heroin problem, along with Scott Gorham. In the vocal booth next to his microphone and music stand was a large old western type of ashtray which Lynott used as his spittoon. It was Ludwinski's job to empty and clean the spittoon before each session started. Lynott's coughing, not just that of a smokers' cough, had to be treated by a doctor who visited the studio on occasion during the recording.

A Lynott/Wharton number, "This Is The One", followed the robust title track, again laden with special effects. It's one of the album's better tracks, mildly annoying for the vocal overdub monopoly but it's a solid addition to the album. The litany of vocal harmonies and special effects do little to hide the true impact his lifestyle choices, plus the asthma, had on his voice. In some cases, once Lynott recorded his bass parts and the guitar parts were being laid down he wasn't present at the sessions, not like the old days when he was the last person to leave the studio with the producer – or even when he was sat next to the producer arguing with Robbo that his guitar was out of tune. As Lynott knew he was needed for vocals, and with the control room staff bearing down on him to deliver, sometimes they took to sending tapes to Lynott's house by courier. He in turn was meant to listen to them and try to expand on the lyrics already committed to tape on the demos.

The album's epic, in length alone, came via another Lynott/Wharton number with "The Sun Goes Down". Wharton's influence and his sneaking in of atmospheric textures climaxed on this, which eventually became the final Thin Lizzy single released in Lynott's lifetime. The idea seems solid but underdeveloped and essentially unfinished, lyrically at least. After the album was released, Lynott and the band were considering a final single release. Lynott travelled to Dublin in early May 1983 to meet with engineer Tim Martin, and the pair began work at Lombard Sound Studios to edit the track for a single release.

The pair then went to London and completed the remix and edit at Utopia Studios, where Martin was assisted by Chris Sheldon and Mark O'Donahugh on 9 May. "The Sun Goes Down" retains a lot of the features that were so prominent in Lynott's bass style: "That up and down stroke, it had great rhythm", recalls Tsangarides. Add to the mix his voice, which when used in the lower register still sounded strong and grounded.

"When we were cutting the tracks, Phil would always insist on doing a quick rough guide vocal, and when it then came to doing the real vocal you could tell that the lyrics or content hadn't changed all that much, if any at all", says Ludwinski. "If you listen to 'The Sun Goes Down' there's a lot of repeating of the same lyric, unlike when you go back to their earlier stuff. Now I know 'The Boys Are Back In Town' is a classic, but use that as an example; there's a verse and the verse is totally different to the chorus... but in the *Thunder And Lightning* songs a lot of the lyrics in the verses and chorus are quite similar, and therefore you haven't really got much of a storyline to the actual songs."

Side 1 closes with "The Holy War", originally titled "Chosen One" in rehearsals, the demo of which contains quite a lot of carry over. Credited solely to Lynott, it's an undervalued song. It features some great guitar work with the dual lead sound reappearing as per vintage Lizzy. Much of the template worked out by Gorham and Robbo back in the day on dual playing is absent on the album, with producer Tsangarides instead opting to harness the heavy and fast-paced Sykes as a foil to Gorham's steady rhythm playing. Lyrically, perhaps not one of Lynott's top tier offerings though it's a solid southpaw track and unlucky not to have been chosen as a single release. It was also one of seven tracks from the album that was played live at one stage during their farewell tour.

The lead single from the album, "Cold Sweat", opens Side 2, affording Sykes his only credit on the album, albeit co-written with Lynott. Before the *Thunder And Lightning* sessions the pair had also worked on "Why Don't You Call Me?", another idea destined for the unreleased rack. During development, the song was titled "Stone Cold Sweat", as is evinced on the chorus. The demo and final versions only differ marginally, with the verses being re-sequenced, though what is plainly evident is Lynott's vocal, stretching to reach certain notes; certain effects were used to cover up the charred remains of his vocal cords by Tsangarides when it came to mixing and the use of special effects.

The band went so far as to record a performance for *Top Of The Pops* when "Cold Sweat" charted and looked to be heading towards the Top 20. Ludwinski recalls being told the story of a disagreement at the *TOTP* studio: "Well what happened was they did a take and the stage manager says, 'Right, let's do another one', Phil replied, 'Yeah, give us about ten minutes'. Then there was an argument and they didn't do another take."

Tsangarides continues: "I was kind of surprised that 'Cold Sweat' was chosen as the lead single, it was a bit heavy, even for them. Some stupid argument at *Top Of The Pops* ensured they lost their spot on the show. It would have been great to have that song as a hit as it could have helped the album along."

On a break from recording some of the band headed out and, nearly three hours later, there was still no sign of them. Sykes and Gorham were left in the studio working out some guitar overdubs, knowing that in all likelihood the remaining band members had probably partaken of the cocktail selection at Crusts bar/restaurant in nearby Richmond, particularly 'The Brain Neutralizer', a heady concoction containing five different alcoholic shots and fruit juice. Around 2 a.m. the rest of the band returned to the studio with the entire restaurant staff in tow. The sessions came to a halt shortly after. Kit Woolven was no stranger to these types of shenanigans when he was in the studio with the band, going as far as to comment: "Thin Lizzy were sex, drugs and rock 'n' roll personified, quite possibly in that order."

"Someday She Is Going To Hit Back" is tucked in neatly after the album's lead single, a three way collaboration between Downey, Lynott and Wharton. Once more the special effects are wheeled out in force and, in truth, it's a piece owned by Wharton. His growing influence and confidence is best exemplified on this track. Downey's pulsating drumming is another highpoint, but not enough to save it. It's another song where the lyrics really needed further work. It's hard to conceive that the lyricist here is the same guy that came up with stories that adorn the melodies strewn across "Massacre" and "Waiting For An Alibi".

The Lynott-penned "Baby Please Don't Go" follows it and, while the musicianship of the piece is top notch, it again falls prey to a lack of development lyrically. It went on to feature prominently in the band's live set for the farewell tour. In some cases such as "Baby Please Don't Go", Lynott appears to be closing out any loose ends from characters in songs from past albums. It's not entirely inconceivable to suggest that the roving-eyed Romeo so apparent in "Don't Believe A Word" has received his comeuppance in the tales told on "Baby Please Don't Go". As with many Lynott songs, the listener could also interpret this track as a metaphor on Lynott's feelings about the band, his anchor.

"On *Thunder And Lightning* we were a gang, all of us in the studio and Phil was the leader," says Tsangarides. "They had to re-group at this time before they could take off again as they were running out of ideas. I got Sykes in and he geed everyone up. He was also closer to my age [Tsangarides was born in 1958, Sykes in 1959] and his youth really kicked them up the ass to get things moving in the right direction. *Thunder And Lightning* was proper rock."

Lynott had certainly taken on board the advice that Tsangarides wheeled out. On the *Renegade* album Lynott's solo writing credits are on "Mexican Blood" and "No One Told Him", unobtrusive and laid back numbers. On *Thunder And Lightning* he recovers his aggression well on "The Holy War" and "Baby Please Don't Go", no matter how forced it sometimes felt.

Though Lynott may have been the undisputed leader of the gang, timekeeping wasn't a strength of his, to put it mildly. The band normally convened for work before 2 p.m. in the afternoon, and more than once there was still no sign of Lynott by 11 p.m. that night. Phone calls were made to his home in Richmond to ask if he intended on coming down, only for Phil to advise he'd be down a little later. At one stage by 4 a.m. Lynott was still a no show so the engineers began taking the tapes off and putting them away. The roadies made their exit also, as Ludwinski recalls: "I put the last tape in the box and all of a sudden the door opened up and everybody came marching back in, followed by Phil who announced 'Alright so, let's put some tracks on'. Lynott may have been AWOL sometimes, but when he did show up, it was never hard to notice who was boss!"

209

Gorham's first appearance with a co-songwriting credit on the album is the penultimate track "Bad Habits". It's arguably the one with the most commercial appeal. Co-written with Lynott, its dual guitar playing is a return to the Lizzy of old, but once more wrapped up in a heavier lining, more in tune with the sound of the times. Gorham contributes a very addictive riff, though again Lynott falls short on affording it a sufficient lyric.

As pointed out by Ludwinski earlier, little development from the demo was achieved lyrically. The demo of "Bad Habits" runs nearly 30 seconds longer than the album version but features completely different lead solos. As with many of the tracks on the album, Tsangarides tempers the track with some subtle special effects, though what they are supposed to be is tricky to identify. It sounds like a gun battle of sorts, Alamo style, tucked away before breaking back into the guitar solo along with a cowbell.

Once the work had concluded each day, Tsangarides would stay on in the studio to "do a rough mix of what we had done. It gave me some indication of how we were progressing. Also Phil would pretty much sing every day, while he figured out the lyrics. I would then compile a master from the guide vocals. I'd play maybe eight different variations of the vocals and he'd indicate which one he liked best."

For the album, Tsangarides insisted on "no mucking around on keeping all the guitar tracks". In other words, if the guitar tracks weren't up to scratch, they were wiped. "Phil might say, 'Try overdubbing that bit and that bit and then let's hear a playback,'" states Tsangarides. "I decided that this wasn't going to be the way to do it. We were going to get the parts in check first and then, be it rhythm guitar, lead guitar, drums or bass, then work from there. The days of keeping loads of shit for little or no reason were done. If I hadn't chosen to work this way I would have been running from one end of the desk to the other trying to accommodate any overdubs which Phil might want to hear on a playback – that was madness. On the other hand, with the vocals, I kept everything."

Thin Lizzy's final song is "Heart Attack", a fast and furious Gorham/Lynott mongrel. It closes a disappointing Side 2. It's unfortunately another one that further pinpoints a lyrical bankruptcy on Lynott's behalf. Though the album contains some highlights there was only so much Tsangarides could do with the material on hand. It's clear Lynott needed time out of both the band and the industry. So little time was left for Sykes to feature more and contribute more to the songwriting, it left the album somewhat lopsided. Had his initiation to the band been prior to the songwriting sessions the album might well have turned out differently. The lack of emotional engagement on the album was the most worrying aspect, given the rich legacy of Lizzy material that seldom had to beg for the listeners' ears and emotions.

"The *Thunder And Lightning* album felt pretty good to make, though I wasn't in the best of shape at the time, and neither was Phil," states Gorham candidly. "It felt like going back to what we wanted to achieve in the first place because things had got a lot softer and easier going at that point. Whether or not we thought we had a hit or not didn't come into it, because we had returned to the hard rock scenario for which we became known in the first place."

Lynott had again tried to enlist Jim Fitzpatrick for the album artwork, though Lynott's pleas to the record label failed to convince them in the value of the investment. "I never did get around to finishing *Thunder And Lightning*," says Fitzpatrick. "I wouldn't even consider doing it unless I got paid a lot of money. The concept for that was one of the best I had come up with and if it's not used for its original purpose there isn't any point in finishing it. I could see in the roughs that it was going to be one of the best. And really that's where it's always at, in the roughs, where the initial concepts come together and the rest is then just developing it. *Thunder And Lightning* was a better rough than those of *Chinatown* and *Black Rose*. *Thunder And Lightning* was the perfect rough."

Fitzpatrick ended up being owed a substantial amount of money for work he completed; ultimately most of the work was never used due to changes in the industry. As Lynott's clout began to falter, so too did the work for Fitzpatrick and his long association with the band.

"It's easy to keep blaming the industry all the time," says Fitzpatrick. "If you deliver for the industry, they're happy, and if you don't they're not. They invested a huge amount of money in Lizzy, they knew they were going to break them through easily enough. Philip was the black Irish man, leader of a white Irish band (kind of), his accent... it was a great story and the Americans loved it. Irish America was, and still is, vast, so it was there for the taking. Philip really played up that angle when he was out there, though it used to frighten the life out of some people' cos they couldn't get their head around him being black and Irish."

The cover sleeve was eventually handled by photographer Bob Elsdale, who remembers the work coming together very quickly. For the group shot, the band travelled to Elsdale's studio having had "just one meeting with Phil on the south side of Kew Bridge," Elsdale recalls. "It was just Phil I talked to, the others turned up at the studio for the band shoot. We talked through his idea and I shot the image without any art direction as I remember it. I remember Phil coming out of my changing room with a bottle of whisky in one hand and the biggest spliff I have ever seen in the other. Literally, it must have been 12" long and probably 20 or so skins and perfectly made. Almost a work of art. He straight away offered it to me first behind my camera, which I smilingly declined. What a charismatic and charming guy! I could have done Phil a better job on it given time, and I would certainly have gone the extra mile for him. However I thought the band shot was great and should have been used on the front."

Thunder And Lightning was released on 4 March 1983 and quickly peaked at No. 4 on the UK album charts. Prior to the release of the album, a press statement was issued which confirmed the band were breaking up once touring commitments were fulfilled.

A UK tour followed hot on the heels of Lizzy's final studio release, and saw them play to mostly sell out audiences. While "Cold Sweat" reached No. 27 on the UK charts, the remaining singles failed to fly. No video promo was made for it though the band did appear on a variety of television shows to assist the promotion of the song and album. The title track, "Thunder And Lightning", was released while the band was on the road. Footage shot at the RDS show on the Irish leg of the farewell tour was cobbled together to create the promotional video for it. The song edged its way to No. 39 on the singles charts.

Engineer Will Reid Dick was called on to work on the RDS shows. The band soundchecked "Are You Ready", "Angel Of Death" and "Still In Love With You", which Reid Dick personally archived. "I remember going over to Dublin to work on the gigs at the RDS," recalls Reid Dick. "I recorded the gigs but it was a bit of a shambles. They were all getting fairly fucked up at that point."

Meanwhile Thin Lizzy's final single in Lynott's lifetime, "The Sun Goes Down", stalled at No. 52, despite a serious amount of re-working the song in the studio with engineer Tim Martin to try to turn it into a single. There are no records of any promotional video being assembled for Lizzy's final single release or any television appearances being made when it was released in July 1983. The band undertook several festival dates in late summer, making their UK farewell at Reading in August 1983. They completed their final dates in Germany the following month. Thin Lizzy disbanded after a final live performance on 4 September 1983. There was, however, one final trick up their sleeve, as they still owed their record company an album.

15

LIFE: LIVE

Lizzy's farewell tour across Britain, Europe and Japan throughout 1983 was recorded with the intention of producing a final live album to see out their contract with Phonogram. The band could have, if they had wanted, tried to see out the contract with another studio album but of course this would have necessitated a tour to promote it and this Lizzymobile needed to come to a complete stop. The record company too had long since lost interest in the band. The unmanageable Lynott in many ways contributed to his own downfall. With Gorham keen to exit the band stage left, there was simply no way forward other than to use the chance of releasing a live album, to close out their recording career.

The majority of *Life: Live* was culled from performances the band played on the British leg of their farewell tour, principally the Hammersmith Odeon in London, the scene of past glories. Combing through the recorded shows was an intense and sometimes overwhelming affair for Lynott who had positioned himself to produce the album. One upshot of the farewell tour announcement was Gary Moore's involvement. The anger felt at Moore's departure mid-tour in 1979 had subsided and he gathered with all the Lizzy guitarists of the past, excepting Snowy White, to make an all-star jam appearance at one of the Hammersmith shows in London. Robbo was there too and later played another show in Glasgow on the tour after segments recorded at Hammersmith were deemed inadequate for release.

Once the European and Japanese dates of the tour were completed by the end of May, Lynott started the initial work in preparing the live album in June. He also pencilled in a couple of weeks in July when the album wasn't completed during this initial period. Work on preparing the live release stopped altogether when Lynott accepted a proposal from Sweden to perform at a series of festivals over a three week period in July and August. Thin Lizzy themselves were still obligated to perform a series of shows that would take them through until 4 September, after which Lynott continued to construct the final Lizzy release.

Lynott's indecision about working on the album in June led to a call from Lizzy's management team to an old friend: Will Reid Dick. He was roped in to rescue the sessions and bring them to a close as soon as possible, with a keen eye on the budget. Reid Dick had lamented the fact that he never ended up producing a Lizzy album, though the question did arise prior to the start-up sessions for *Renegade* in January 1981. "I was in LA doing some work with John (Alcock)," remembers Reid Dick. "Lizzy were in town playing the Forum I think [the date in question was actually the Santa Monica Civic Theatre]. I'd met this rather nice girl and I was staying at her house, and the phone rang about half eleven at night; I was just going to bed, and it was [Big] Charlie on the other end of the line. So he said Phil wanted to see me urgently and I went down to his hotel, but he'd taken some Quaaludes and was fast asleep when I arrived. So I sat with Charlie for a while and then headed home, but on the way I crashed the car which made life a bit tricky. Charlie seemed to do a lot of organising and was maybe the head of the road crew in a certain way."

The production role didn't come to pass but it was certainly a role that Reid Dick would have welcomed. "I would have certainly liked to have worked with Lizzy again, that's for sure. I suppose I did work with them again later on with the *Life: Live* album but it was too far gone by then. Phil was in a dreadful state, so was Scott, and it was a horrible experience from that point of view. I certainly would have liked to work with them again around that period after *Johnny The Fox*."

The initial work on the *Life: Live* album was done at Polygram Studios, near Marble Arch, before later moving to Wessex Studios. Lynott's erratic behaviour continued as Reid Dick was often left twiddling his thumbs. "Well I'd turn up around two or three in the afternoon and Phil would arrive in around nine or ten in the evening, not one of my better experiences."

Reid Dick continues: "Obviously Phil will have his say at the end of the day, so if he isn't there and doesn't like what you might have done, then you're just wasting your time. It got very annoying in the end, because you know, you make an arrangement and after a few days of little or no work being done I'd say, 'c'mon, we're wasting time and money. Let's make an agreement to all meet at the same time'. So, an agreement on three or four in the afternoon to meet up is made, I'd get there and again, nothing would happen until ten, eleven or twelve at night. It got to the point of some mixing: I did some of that on my own, Phil did some. Phil wanted to be involved in the mix. Overall, I felt fairly uninvolved in a way."

In deference to their long standing professional and personal relationship Reid Dick stayed the course. At Wessex, the pair were using two different studios at the facility. Gorham and Sykes made their appearances and much re-recording was done: "On everything on that album", Reid Dick recalls.

Though Robbo appeared at some live gigs on the tour, he never visited the band during the assembling process of the album in the studio. "Well, Phil asked me to do the Hammersmith gig and I was in the middle of recording the Motörhead album (*Another Perfect Day*) and really didn't want to do it, but I did it anyway and my playing was awful," confesses Robbo. "After listening to the tapes from Hammersmith, O'Donnell asked me to come to Glasgow to do another recording and I did. They used the version of 'Emerald' from Glasgow on the album (*Life: Live*). I didn't do any overdubs on that album though."

Unlike *Live And Dangerous*, where the band sourced some of their finest recorded moments and refined them in the studio, the recording sources used for *Life: Live* found the band at various crossroads. Mainly, the tired kind. The band had run their course, Lynott's voice was shot to pieces and, as Reid Dick recalls, more than a few overdubs took place. "There was a lot of re-recording of everything on that album. I think Phil was doing pretty much what happened on *Live And Dangerous*, as far as I can gather. Most of the guitars were done again. Sykes did some work as did Scott. We did it for months, it seemed like. It went on and on and very slowly, because people were never there, and when they were there, they weren't in the right frame of mind for it."

When Lynott left to fulfil the solo dates in late July and into August, Reid Dick continued to work on mixing, but of course nothing could be signed off without Lynott's approval. When he returned from Sweden, the editing suite at Wessex studios was Party Central, as a variety of friends dropped by including Jimmy Bain. The lack of discipline was costing huge quantities of money but Lynott continued on undeterred. Reid Dick hadn't recorded any of the live shows that were being used as the basis for the album. However he was responsible for the slow version of "Don't Believe A Word".

"Phil liked it," says Reid Dick. "He could be a difficult person to please a lot of the time but I remember him being very pleased with that. It was difficult because there are certain restrictions that you face when you're mixing, and I don't know whether he was fully aware of all of them. I'd sort of help him set it up but there was a certain amount of having to fix things so that it would all fit together. He ended up mixing a lot of the album on his own."

It's much to the detriment of the album that he was left to his own devices at this stage, as anyone that listens to it can hear. Stodgy mixes are strewn across the album while Lynott's vocals are painful to listen to. The album standout, "Are You Ready", itself a little uneven in places, spotlights some of the aggression and persuasive romance of the band. One specific indictment is the many key changes to songs that had to be made so as to accommodate Lynott's faltering vocal range.

The swagger so apparent on *Live And Dangerous* was nowhere in sight on *Life: Live*. Audible stumbles blight the album. The Snowy White appearances were sourced from previous tours as he wasn't invited to the Hammersmith Odeon reunion dates. A knackered Reid Dick exited the studio after the final mix and immediately went on holiday. "The whole process had the feeling that it was fairly terminal. I couldn't see where it could go after that. It reminds me of that gig at the RDS in Dublin: Phil didn't even want to go onstage one of the nights. At that point I hadn't seen them for a while. I got on well with Sykes, he wasn't in that dejected state that other members had got into. I remember thinking that this had gone seriously wrong somewhere."

Life: Live was eventually released on 16 October 1983, nearly two months after their final UK performance. It peaked at No. 29 in the album charts and, with no single to promote its release, it came and went quickly, thus concluding the recorded and released legacy of the band under Philip Lynott's captaincy. It was an unfortunate conclusion to a recording career but, as with all Thin Lizzy releases, there are live renditions of songs worth hearing. There always was with Lizzy. Tsangarides didn't participate in the post-production of the album as he was away working in America at the time though he maintains that "Lizzy were a great band, even at their worst."

Lynott was also quick to chuckle with Tsangarides, particularly in light of the commercial success of *Thunder And Lightning*. "Phil used to say after the album was a success, in his own hammy way: 'When the chips are down you can always rely on Tsangarides to pull it out of the bag'." Drummer Brian Downey, though he takes pride in what Thin Lizzy created, also feels a sense of under-achievement in that "I think the legacy should be much more than what it is. I don't think we got it to where we wanted it to be."

In the aftermath of Lizzy's final gigs in Germany, the band parted ways while Lynott considered his next move. On Lynott's choice to continue working instead of taking much-needed time out, Chalkie Davies reflects: "Musicians don't know what else to do very often, other than play music. Once you've built up a routine of touring and everything else, unless you completely, you know, go live in the country or something, it's sort of what they do. You've got to realise, up until Black Sabbath, Led Zeppelin, Deep Purple and Yes, up until then there had been no, what became, heavy metal or rock groups. They wouldn't have known they'd be still playing at 70 years of age. I don't think any of us equated to that, even though, if we'd have looked around, we would have seen Duke Ellington and people like that doing it.

"I don't think we saw the massive longevity that was involved because there hadn't really been enough time for case studies to prove that the records you listen to first – usually something your sister plays, that you don't really notice that you're listening to – has an effect on the songs you like; the stuff you listen to between the ages of 12 and 20 stays, in most cases, for a very long time and people go back to that – they have the memories and everything else for it. Personally, I've also thought that groups should stop making records after a certain period of time. For me, Led Zeppelin did the right thing and The Who did the wrong thing. There's always a reluctance to quit and move on."

16

AS TIME GOES BY

The aftermath of Thin Lizzy brought different blessings for the band members that oversaw its cessation. Scott Gorham initially retreated from the music world and successfully overcame heroin addiction before renewing his musical vows with bands such as Western Front, 21 Guns and a re-imagined incarnation of Thin Lizzy. He later co-founded Black Star Riders who have released two albums to date.

Darren Wharton maintained his music career and after a few false starts in the mid-1980s he eventually launched Dare who continue to record and tour, though Wharton has also occasionally participated in various Lizzy re-union tours.

Both Downey and Sykes stayed by Lynott's side, as did Mark Stanway, to form Grand Slam in the last weeks of 1983. All four recorded the first Grand Slam material at Lombard Studio in Dublin during December of that year but both Downey and Sykes would depart before the band played a single live performance. Lynott remained and recruited a new line up and helmed Grand Slam throughout 1984. Sykes went on to play with Whitesnake and Blue Murder while also participating in a variety of Thin Lizzy reunion shows.

Downey, meanwhile, stayed in Ireland and played intermittently with local blues bands in Dublin, Gary Moore's band and also took to the drum stool for the continuing Thin Lizzy reunion shows.

Lynott was by far the most productive during this post-Lizzy period and recorded regularly throughout 1984 and 1985. He teamed up with Gary Moore in May 1985 with "Out In The Fields", a Top 5 single in the UK charts. This high was quickly followed by the disappointment of not being invited to participate in *Live Aid*.

Since the break up of Grand Slam, Lynott frequently fielded questions about a Thin Lizzy reunion from the music press and though he appeared grateful for the experience it gave him, he shied away from admitting that a reunion was in any way possible. Perhaps the most likely route back for Thin Lizzy, should Lynott have had the inclination, would have been an appearance at *Live Aid* in July 1985. Thin Lizzy however, were not invited to reform and participate, unlike other acts such as The Who.

Chalkie Davies has strong views on this snub: "I'm one of the people that is still very angry that Lizzy wasn't asked to do *Live Aid*. Thin Lizzy should have been part of the bigger purpose of *Live Aid*. The groups that did best that day, U2 and Queen, if Lizzy had played I think you would have added Philip to that list. I think if Lizzy had played, it would have had a much bigger long term effect and I think that Geldof and Ure were wrong not to pick them. I also think that it was probably tough on Philip to accept that."

A little known fact is that Lynott was backstage early in the day at Wembley Stadium. He travelled with Midge Ure to collect a bass guitar that he later auctioned off when he made an appearance on Irish television, having flown back to Ireland in the afternoon. Lynott's appearance drew gasps from fellow panellists in the *RTE* studios, surprised by his physical condition. He even spent time on the phones accepting donations from the public. Lynott was interviewed briefly and confessed, "I'd love to be up there playing but, because I haven't got a band and stuff like that, obviously it's impossible, but I feel jealous when I watch it now." The following night he joined Clann Éadair for a gig at the Royal Standard in Dublin which was used to generate funds for the *Live Aid* cause.

Lynott hid his disappointment at being excluded from the *Live Aid* jamboree relatively well, knowing if he came out to slag off the venture he'd come off the worse for it. Just prior to the staging of the global event, Lynott contacted his old friend Bill Cayley. Cayley was Lynott's guitar tech during the Lizzy days and by now he managed Ezee Hire Studios in London, and Lynott was a familiar face at the studio, having rehearsed Grand Slam there the previous year. At Ezee Hire, Lynott linked up with engineer Maurice Mulligan on numerous occasions throughout the summer and autumn of 1985.

"We never started working until mid-late afternoon, and when we were ready to try some mixes out I'd set up the board while he went up to the White Horse to order the drinks," says Mulligan. "After a couple, we'd return to the studio to finish the mix, which meant he sat at one end of the giant MCI board and I'd pilot the other end and grouping. His end consisted of a couple of vocal channels and his bass guitar on channels 1-4, which meant I had to re-patch everything so he could sit at that end and sneak the levels up and down, and this is where a lot of the mutual respect and friendship came from."

Lynott, in his lighter moments, was never one to waste an opportunity to wind someone up. A couple of days into the first session, Mulligan turned up for work and Bill Cayley called him into his office, complaining that he and his partner were not amused by being woken up in the middle of the night with random calls from Lynott. "It turns out that he [Phil] called Bill to ask where I had come from," recalls Mulligan, "and had a rant about the fact that no-one had ever had the nerve to tell him to turn the bass down! This all came from a comment I'd made during the last mix which went along the lines of 'Don't you think the bass is a bit loud mate?'

"Although he [Phil] agreed at the time, and it was all taken lightly, he decided to wind Bill up with this when he got back home from the Limelight Club [formerly on Shaftesbury Avenue, London] much later. When I got into Bill's office it was all very acrimonious and I was given the usual 'Do you realise who you were talking to?' speech for a few minutes until Bill couldn't hold a straight face any longer: he then went on to explain that this was his way of getting back at me for having his sleep interrupted and that the main reason behind the phone call was that if I was confident enough to do that [telling Lynott that his bass was too loud] I was more than confident and competent to do the rest of the sessions whenever he came into the studio!"

The final months of Lynott's life don't read well and despite many people rallying around him and trying to nudge him in the right direction, too much rot had set in. He'd be clean for a few weeks before again succumbing to the call of the heroin. His unreliability also led to constant disruptions and cancellations to planned recording sessions. Producer Tony Platt was waiting in the wings as he had been doing quite a lot of work with Robbo during this period.

"Towards the end, I was aware of his solo work because by then I was involved with Brian Robertson, and at that stage Brian stayed fairly close to Phil, right up to the end," says Platt. "My wife and I used to stay with Brian and Chrissie Wood for Christmas. We'd done it for a couple of Christmases, and we got there that particular Christmas and nobody was there. We thought, 'Have we got this wrong?' That was when Brian had to go down to the house because Phil was in a real bad way.

"So Brian was one of the last people to be there with Phil. I was sort of aware of those things, and Brian was always trying to get something happening to try to help to focus Phil, and give him something that would stop him from pushing the self-destruct button. So we talked about how that might happen, but nothing ever came to fruition because there was always something that would get in the way of it. I would have loved to have done it, it would have been great but it would have been really difficult. Lizzy was over and done with by then and there was no more mileage in it, so it would have been a different thing entirely."

Lynott's decision to keep working ultimately proved to be his undoing. Unlike his Lizzy compadre, Scott Gorham, who fled the music scene to save his life, Lynott couldn't turn back from the path he had chosen.

Having been taken ill on Christmas Day, Lynott was hospitalized, during which time he developed pneumonia before succumbing on 4 January 1986. His dabbling with heroin, pills and alcohol had turned to addiction many years before. Having pulled through an overdose, by the time he was admitted to hospital he was slipping in and out of consciousness. The measure of drug abuse inflicted upon his body led to multiple organ failure and ultimately a heart attack. He died aged just 36, with illnesses exacerbated by a sustained period of substance abuse, but primarily septicemia.

The final couple of years of his life might read like a raggedy mess, but it's the ballad of his achievements that chimes loudest. Lynott was brought home to Dublin for burial in St. Fintan's Cemetery, Sutton, Co. Dublin a week after his avoidable death.

On the fifth anniversary of Lynott's death, Brian Downey and Scott Gorham were approached about re-working a demo made while Lynott was still a member of Grand Slam. The song was "Dedication", principally written by Laurence Archer, though Lynott did contribute to the lyric. Though the pair were initially reluctant to participate, when it became apparent that the song would be released as it stood this prompted them into action. It was planned to use "Dedication" as the promotional single for a "Best Of" compilation of Lizzy's hits.

There were some initial problems such as Archer gaining credit as co-writer of the song, though that wasn't reflected on the inlet card credits when it was eventually released as a single. In the end, Archer apparently had to sign away the rights to numerous other songs developed by Grand Slam in order to get any money for it.

Once the legalities were ironed out, work proceeded. An engineer named Chris Sheldon was approached by an A&R employee at Phonogram to have him oversee the mixing of what was essentially a demo.

"I had no meetings with the band at all," says Sheldon. "I was asked to do a mix of the demo, but then Scott Gorham got in touch and said he wanted to come down to the studio and replay some of the guitars on the track, which he did. I had no idea what the history of the song was. It was presented to me as a demo that needed finishing off really. I can remember Scott working out the parts in the studio and some of the harmony guitar parts."

The original version handed to Sheldon was copied onto a 24-track tape with the new guitar parts overdubbed onto that. "This is obviously long before digital recording, so the manipulation available was pretty limited," recalls Sheldon. "Obviously we couldn't risk the original being damaged or erased accidentally as the vocal was irreplaceable. I think we may have edited the song a bit to make it more single-y as such."

Downey also replaced the drum parts which he recalled as "pretty straightforward as the song existed nearly as a whole."

The work was done at the now defunct Swan Yard Studios in Islington. Sheldon continues: "The guitars were definitely embellished and possibly completely replaced, I can't remember. I certainly don't remember the bass being touched."

Engineer Simon Vinestock was also approached around the late autumn of 1990 by Russ Conway, who was working in the A&R Department at Phonogram. Vinestock's initial brief was to remix "The Boys Are Back In Town": "I turned him down because I actually believed the original mix was perfect and I didn't want to ruin it," claims Vinestock. "He told me that if I didn't remix it, someone else would, so I accepted the job and mixed it as closely as I could to the original. It was received at the record company with great success and then I was asked to mix 'Dedication', which I did in the same kind of feel as 'The Boys Are Back In Town'".

Vinestock's work was also completed at Swan Yard Studios, though how much of his mix is contained on the released version is unknown. "Dedication" made the charts across Europe, breaching the Top 40 in the UK, peaking at No. 35, while it raced to No. 1 in Ireland in 1991. But that was it, nothing further was done with any of the unpublished Lynott or Lizzy archive after this time, despite the solid sales of both the single and album.

Various "Best Of" compilations have been released in the intervening years, but it wasn't until 2012 when an announcement was made to confirm a massive haul of over 700 songs. Of course, this number is an exaggeration. There was a huge selection of alternative takes of already published songs. There was amongst them unpublished Lizzy live recordings from a variety of concerts through the years. There was also a series of unpublished demos, incomplete songs and finished songs, some of which have been referenced in this book. A certain amount of these alternative takes and demos have since been utilised for the successful re-release of deluxe editions of the Lizzy back catalogue, which at this point in time have been completed, save for their final album *Life: Live*. The source tapes for this album appear to be missing.

Much more is rumoured to be in the planning stages to make the best use of the unreleased live Lizzy material. For a band so renowned for their live performances it would be entirely appropriate that a series of shows spotlighting this strength make their way to the public domain.

There was also the unveiling of the statue of Lynott in August 2005, and a steady stream of visitors continue to make the pilgrimage to Dublin and have their picture taken with the emerald cowboy. A variety of haunts around Dublin also continue to house various Lizzy memorabilia.

Then there is the issue of Lynott's unreleased solo recordings. The tracks being worked on for possible inclusion on his third solo album were largely unfinished. Other projects he was working on, such as a film soundtrack and an album with Clann Éadair, also remain in an unfinished state. Up to 13 tracks were recorded to varying degrees of completion, and the sessions at Lynott's home studio during January 1985 represent some of their final collaborations. "The reason it stretched over that period," remembers Leo Rickard "was that Phil was away a lot of the time, and, when he did get home to Dublin, sometimes he was just too exhausted to work with us in the studio. So we just had to wait for him to have available time to work at it."

During those final sessions with Lynott they all played and recorded the track "The Frieze Breeches". On a relatively unproductive day, and quite late in the evening, they once more found themselves ensconced in the back garden studio.

"The studio was well insulated for sound," Rickard explains. "It was small, so we were crammed in a bit, but it was fun to be there. I can still see Phil with one foot up on a chair with the bass strapped on and operating the recording machine and drum machine all at the same time while we were doing the 'Frieze Breeches' track. It was fun and a nice memory to have. We finished the sessions at 5:30 a.m. and went into the kitchen in the house and ate a whole tub of banana ice cream between the four of us."

That isn't to say that there isn't material that deserves review; there is, though the best possible destination for such unfinished tracks might be a box set of sorts. Again, these avenues are being explored.

A moral question comes into whether or not it is practical to use these unpublished songs. Take Otis Redding's "Sitting On The Dock Of The Bay". By the time Redding died in a plane crash in December 1967 he had recorded the majority of this song. The backing track was completed as was most of the vocal. The segment where the whistle comes in is what was added after his death as he didn't live to sing the final verse. Though it's a very un-Otis-like track in many ways, it's now probably one of his better known songs and the one most commonly heard on radio.

Queen also reconditioned material with the release of *Queen Forever* in 2014. Brian May and Roger Taylor re-recorded parts and weaved the additional recordings around original songs done back in the early to mid-1980s when Freddie Mercury was still alive. Bands do it, but how far can we go and is there a market for such releases when it comes to Thin Lizzy? The answer is apparently yes, given the positive reviews afforded to the Deluxe re-releases of the past few years with all reviewers keen to offer their opinion on the bonus material. This material, after all, is why the existing fan is going to buy the same album, all over again.

Tony Platt discusses the issues that the Lynott estate faces if choices are made to make available any thus far unpublished material: "My attitude towards it, like with the Queen stuff, they're saying these were outtakes, unreleased outtakes, there is a clue in the word 'outtake'. When you don't use stuff because it isn't quite good enough, then it's never going to be quite good enough, just because somebody has died. I just think, if you uncover some material that's been recorded that has not been released and perhaps weren't outtakes, just a collection of a particular artist's thoughts and musings, then I think that's a different thing.

"So when you're talking about unpublished and unreleased material that Phil had done that had nothing to do with Lizzy, I think that's one thing, but if it's just kind of extra takes of the song or whatever it may be, I just don't see the point in doing that. I think it devalues the rest of the body of work. However, if it's properly put together... The other thing is, when you start to try to finish something off. I think if you've got recordings that stand up in their own right and you judge them as to whether or not they're a true representation of the quality of that artist, then I think it's OK to release them, but don't mess with them. I think when you take something and you try to get people in and finish it in the way that you think the artist would have wanted it to be finished, that's just outrageous, because you have no idea where that artist wanted to take it."

The most impressive posthumous Thin Lizzy release that emerged in recent years was the multi-disc *Live At The BBC*, drizzled as it is with their most well-known hits, and complemented hugely by some lesser known and quirky album tracks. The now out of print release is a superb addition to the canon. Two possible additions to this await release in the form of a Lizzy box set and perhaps a Lynott solo box set. An official gathering of the material written and recorded by Grand Slam would be another interesting and worthwhile excursion. Though "The Rocker" image is constantly relied upon to perpetuate the appeal and longevity of Thin Lizzy, a book revealing Lynott's lyrics and ideas, and how these ideas were developed, is long overdue.

The Autumn of 2015 brought further spotlight on Lynott and, by default, Thin Lizzy when actor Rob Mountford debuted his play *Vagabonds – My Phil Lynott Odyssey* at the Edinburgh Fringe Festival. The critical response has been positive and described as "a hilarious, philosophical, rock 'n' roll one-man show". Mountford hopes to be able to tour the show in Ireland and given the response so far, this objective looks like becoming a reality sooner rather than later. It's a prescient indicator of how musicians and their work can survive the permanency of death and become relevant to a generation they never encountered.

Before the lights go down and I sign off, I'd like to leave you with a memory of Maurice Mulligan, one of the last engineers that Philo worked with: "The two of us and Bill Cayley had gone to watch a young band [FM] who also worked out of Ezee. They were supporting some big US outfit which I really can't remember. Before the gig, we quietly popped into a back room at the pub next door but he [Philip] was spotted, and soon enough he became swamped with well-meaning and adoring fans. Given his status, he duly signed and chatted before Bill announced that we should go into the gig – he'd seen this over the years. Once we got in and found a quiet row down the side of the venue all was good until one by one heads started to turn – he was hard to miss after all – and folks started to move in on the poor bugger from the rows in front.

"After a while this all became too much and he made some apologies to me and Bill, then exited quickly through the stage door. What stuck with me really, and unsurprisingly, was the fact that although he obviously relished the adoration and platitudes thrown at him, it was obvious that he had a more personal side which really needed space to spend quietly with friends, and this was one of those. The following day all was back to normal with a simple apology for leaving early – lovely man."

LIST OF INTERVIEWEES

John Alcock, November 2001, March 2010, May 2015
Laurence Archer, August 2012
Louis Austin, April 2014
Jimmy Bain, April 2008
Eric Bell, January 2000, June 2012
Tim Booth, January 2012
Ted Carroll, Spring 2000-2002
Philip Chevron, September 2002
Ian Cooper, 2009
Roger Cooper, March 2015
Chalkie Davies, January 2015
Robbie Dennis, 2002
Lawrie Dipple, May 2011
Brian Downey, July 2009
Andy Duncan, December 2008
Bob Elsdale, April 2015
Patrick Fenning, June 2015
Dave Flett, 2001
Jim Fitzpatrick, March 2012, April 2012
Scott Gorham, 2001
Nigel Grainge, June 2014
Kirby Gregory, June 2014
Dave Grinsted, May 2015
John Helliwell, August 2010
Tim Hinkley, September 2008
Pete Holidai, January 2015
David Jensen, May 2014
David Knopfler, June 2014
Sören Lindberg, April 2015

Chris Ludwinski, June 2014
David Mallet, 2002
Dave Manwering, April 2015
Jeff Marvel, January 2000
Rodney Matthews, April 2012
Jeanette "Jeanie" Melbourne, February 2015
Ken Morris, March 2015
Maurice Mulligan
Michael O'Flanagan, August 2012
Terry O'Neill, May 2015
Graham Parker, November 2001
Tony Platt, January 2015
Andrew Prewett, March 2015
Suzi Quatro, November 2014
Tex Read, January 2012
Will Reid Dick, April 2010, October 2014
Leo Rickard
Brian Robertson, January 2001, June 2012
Frank Rodgers, 2002, April 2014
Jean Roussel, July 2014
Peter Rynston, May 2015
Chris Sheldon, March 2015
John Slater, 2000
Ed Stone, May 2013
Linda Sutton, March 2015
Nick Tauber, June 2015
Brian Tuite, January 2015
Fiachra Trench, June 2011

Chris Tsangarides, 2002, August 2014

Derek Varnals, May 2015, June 2015

Simon Vinestock, March 2015

Darren Wharton, 2000

Snowy White, February 2015

Daire Winston, May 2015

Kit Woolven, May 2015

ABOUT THE AUTHOR

Alan Byrne is from Carrigaline, County Cork, a suburb of a suburb in the big picture. Assuming you're looking at a big picture.

Are You Ready? is the concluding part of a long standing commitment to a trilogy of books he promised in a moment of bluff back in 1998. The first two parts are: *Thin Lizzy (Soldiers of Fortune)* 2004, published by SAF/Firefly Books, and *Philip Lynott, Renegade of Thin Lizzy* 2012, published by Mentor Books.

ALSO AVAILABLE FROM SOUNDCHECK BOOKS

Sail Away: Whitesnake's Amazing Voyage
Martin Popoff
ISBN: 978-0-9575700-8-5

Be Stiff: The Stiff Records Story
Richard Balls
ISBN: 978-0-9575700-6-1

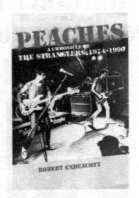

Peaches: A Chronicle Of The Stranglers 1974–1990
Robert Endeacott
ISBN: 978-0-9575700-4-7

Killers: The Origins Of Iron Maiden 1975–1983
Neil Daniels
ISBN: 978-0-9575700-2-3

Beer Drinkers & Hell Raisers
A ZZ Top Guide
Neil Daniels
ISBN: 978-0-9571442-7-9

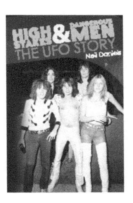

High Stakes & Dangerous Men: The UFO Story
Neil Daniels
ISBN: 978-0-9571442-6-2

Available in paperback from booksellers, online vendors or directly
from *www.soundcheckbooks.co.uk*

Kindle editions available from all Amazon sites